# PRINCIPLES

# of SURVEY ANALYSIS

# PRINCIPLES

# of SURVEY ANALYSIS

## (Formerly titled

## Delinquency

## Research)

TRAVIS HIRSCHI

HANAN C. SELVIN

*Fp*

THE FREE PRESS, *New York*

COLLIER-MACMILLAN LIMITED, *London*

Library of Congress Catalog Card Number: 67–15058

First Free Press Paperback Edition 1973

*printing number*

1  2  3  4  5  6  7  8  9  10

To
*Anna and Rhoda,*

who have their own methods
of coping with delinquency

# Preface to the

# Paperback Edition

This book, which develops several pairs of divergent themes, draws its materials from two sophisticated fields of sociology. The book has had at least two distinct audiences, and it has two authors. It is therefore perhaps inevitable that it should have two names. The book originally appeared under the title *Delinquency Research: An Appraisal of Analytic Methods*. The new title, *Principles of Survey Analysis*, does not reflect changes in the book. Although we have removed several errors and inconsistencies in the tables, and have qualified our discussion of multiple regression, the text is the original.

The two fields of sociology are survey methods and juvenile delinquency. The book, using materials drawn exclusively from delinquency research, remains an attempt to examine the principles of survey analysis. In some cases, we took principles of survey analysis to do research on delinquency and looked for violations. More often, the "examples" were identified first as problems and only later became illustrations of principles. In all cases, we were willing to sacrifice principles and *apparent* generality in favor of close examination of problems actually encountered by researchers analyzing data.

The two audiences for the book have been scholars in the areas of delinquency and criminology and students in courses in research methods. Scholars last longer than students and are not nearly so plentiful. They are also less educable. We have therefore decided to forsake them in favor of a potentially larger audience. In doing so, we reluctantly acknowledge that so many excellent studies of delinquency have appeared since the book was written that it can no longer claim to summarize delinquency research.

Divergent themes noted by readers include the following: A large portion of the book takes tabular analysis for granted; two chapters advance the proposition that linear statistical techniques are "better, faster, cheaper, and more powerful." Even though the entire book concentrates on and attempts to advance the cause of quantitative research, a reviewer has remarked that we "quietly protest the hegemony of statistics." These and other "inconsistencies" in the book reflect change and conflict within the field of sociology and ambivalence on the part of its practitioners.

Such inconsistencies also reflect the fact that the book has two authors, neither of whom has maintained an entirely consistent stance over time. While the book was being written, Hirschi became involved in a large-scale study of delinquency (*Causes of Delinquency*, Berkeley: University of California Press, 1969). His sympathies shifted toward the empirical researcher as opposed to the methodological critic. The book's uneven tolerance for deviations from methodological norms and Chapter 8 are results of this shift. At the same time, Selvin became involved in an intensive study of the logic of survey analysis. His sympathies shifted toward multivariate statistical techniques as opposed to tabular analysis. The book's uneven stance toward tabular analysis and Chapter 10 are results.

We will not attempt to iron out these inconsistent emphases, which, if the book were being written today, would probably be even more pronounced. This too would reflect the situation in sociology as a whole, as well as differences in our own points of view.

If the book were being written today, we would try to respond to suggestions and criticisms offered by Herbert Menzel, Lawrence G. Moseley, and Richard S. Sterne. We have tried, within the limits of a reprinting, to respond to those offered by Arthur S. Goldberger. And we have actually responded to those offered once by Joel Smith and many times by students in our courses. We wish to thank them all.

T.H.

H.C.S.

# Preface to the

# Original Edition

$A$s this book has evolved, it
has come to have three distinct purposes. It is a textbook,
albeit an unusual one, on methods of analysis; a critique of
empirical research on delinquency; and a set of essays on
important topics in methodology. All three purposes involve
one common task: the examination of published analyses of
quantitative data on delinquency. We restrict ourselves to
analysis because of our belief that the quality and ultimate
value of a study depend more on the analysis than on the
design. The best sampling plan and the most skillful interviewing count for naught if the analysis is bad. And, contrary
to what many critics believe, an insightful analysis can often
compensate for weaknesses in the design of a study—for
example, by detecting interviewer bias. Furthermore, the balance between design and analysis in the methodological literature is altogether one-sided. There are many books on
sampling, on interviewing, and on data processing, but there
is no comprehensive, recent treatment of the kinds of analysis considered here. This same emphasis appears in many of
the controversies in delinquency research, which reflect the
view that the quality of the data rather than their "manipulation" is the key to significant progress. By devoting our attention entirely to analysis, we hope to redress the imbalance

in the methodological literature and to suggest some of the things that can be done with the often crude data at the disposal of the student of delinquency.

Our concentration on quantitative techniques derives from the belief that they have greater value than qualitative techniques, both in empirical research and in the teaching of methodology. Quantitative data make it possible to formulate hypotheses more precisely and thus to test them more sharply. And because quantitative data can be analyzed statistically, it is possible to examine complicated theoretical problems, such as the relative importance of many causes of delinquency, far more powerfully than with the verbal analysis of qualitative data. Incidentally, although we do deal with statistical problems at some length in two chapters, most of the book is comprehensible without any formal training in statistics.

The joint focus on methodology and delinquency began with a small grant from the Ford Foundation to do a descriptive study of the statistics of delinquency research. After a false start in this direction, we decided instead to appraise the methodological virtues and defects of the major sociological studies of delinquency published in the 1950s. The title of an early report of some of our work reflected this plan: *The Methodological Adequacy of Delinquency Research.* Since this report, we have both broadened our methodological concerns and dealt more closely with problems of particular importance in delinquency research. Although the methodological points we make have applications in any field of inquiry, we hope that tying them to a particular substantive area will, by demonstrating their relevance to actual research, more than offset the apparent generality obtained by drawing examples from a variety of areas. For that matter, although the studies from which our examples come are not a representative sample of the field of delinquency research, the examples themselves do provide broad coverage of the kinds of problems confronted in the quantitative, causal analysis of delinquency. We hope, therefore, that this book will also serve the student of delinquency by alerting him to some of the special analytical problems of his field.

T.H.
H.C.S.

# Acknowledgments

To the investigators from whose work we have chosen our illustrative examples we owe both gratitude and an apology. We are, of course, grateful to them for allowing us to reprint long excerpts from their work, even though they knew that many of our analyses would be highly critical. Some of them responded to an intemperate early draft of several chapters with criticisms, suggestions, and even with encouragement. Among those especially helpful were Charles J. Browning, Bernard Lander, Karl Schuessler, James F. Short, Jr., Jackson Toby, and William W. Wattenberg. In all cases those who responded to our draft were more concerned to improve our presentation than to defend their own research.

Our gratitude to these investigators is matched by our regret at the false impressions that our use of their work is likely to convey. Because most of our examples involve errors or misconceptions, it is all too easy for the reader to infer that we are condemning the work of a particular investigator or even the entire field of delinquency research. Neither inference is warranted. We have stressed "bad" examples because one such example usually illuminates the methodological point at issue more clearly than a dozen "good" examples. Moreover, frequency of citation is not a guide to our over-all judgment of an investigator. No one can do research without making a mistake now and then; we have ourselves made many of the mistakes discussed in this book, and we undoubtedly will make others in the future. The more an investigator has published, the greater the likelihood of our citing his work frequently. Indeed, frequency of citation is an indication of an investigator's importance in the field of delinquency; wherever possible, we have chosen our examples from studies that are frequently cited by other investigators.

The early draft to which we referred appeared in mimeographed form in 1962 as *The Methodological Adequacy of Delinquency Research*, Publication M6 of the Survey Research Center, University of California, Berkeley. Chapter 8 appeared in *Social Problems*, 13 (Winter, 1966), and is reprinted here in modified form by permission of the Society for the Study of Social Problems.

We wish to thank Charles Y. Glock, Director of the Survey Research Center, and his colleagues for providing each of us over periods of several years: a stimulating, multidisciplinary environment in which methodological disputations were the stuff of everyday life.

# Acknowledgments

Among our friends and former colleagues John Lofland and William Petersen deserve special mention. Their detailed comments on our early draft affected the content, scope, and tone of this version. Herbert Costner, Ian Currie, and Alan B. Wilson reacted vigorously to an early version of Chapter 8. Kenneth Bryson and Karon S. Greenfield read the final manuscript with great care.

Finally, we wish to acknowledge a special debt to Jackson Toby, at whose suggestion we began to think about the methodology of delinquency research, and to the Ford Foundation for its support of our early work.

Although every chapter in this book is a collaborative effort, Hirschi assumes responsibility for all selections from the literature of delinquency.

# Contents

There are behavioral scientists who, in their desperate search for scientific status, give the impression that they don't much care what they do if only they do it right: Substance gives way to form. And here a vicious circle is engendered; when the outcome is seen to be empty, this is taken as pointing all the more to the need for a better methodology. The work of the behavioral scientist might well become methodologically sounder if he did not try so hard to be so scientific!

Abraham Kaplan, *The Conduct of Inquiry*

# part i

# THE

# NATURE

# OF

# METHODOLOGICAL

# CRITICISM

# On
# Approaching
# Methodology

"Methodology" is a scare-word. Among the subjects studied during the education of a sociologist, only statistics arouses more apprehension in advance and more dismay during the course. We think these feelings are unfortunate and unnecessary. They are unfortunate because they keep students from understanding and enjoying what should be a central part of their education; they are unnecessary because they rest on a misunderstanding of the nature of methodology, at least in modern usage. In this brief introductory chapter we want to explain what methodology means to us and to offer some advice on understanding the methodological discussions in this book and on applying their lessons to other sociological reading.

In the fields of logic, education, and statistics, *methodology* has special, technical meanings. All of its sociological uses, however, conform to the dictionary definition of the "science of method." The significance of this definition obviously depends on the root word *method*. There are at least four distinct meanings of *method* in sociology. When Emile Durkheim wrote *The Rules of Sociological Method* in 1895, he was thinking of the content of sociological theory, of the explanations of social phenomena that could legitimately be called sociological. This usage has virtually disappeared; sociologists dealing with these problems today are more likely to use the term *meta-theory*. The most common meaning of *method* today is a set of recipes for the everyday conduct of social research: how to gain rapport with a respondent in an interview, how to construct codes for classifying responses, how to percentage a table. Related to this is the use of *method* to mean statistical techniques, especially in university catalogs of ten or twenty years ago.

To us, these techniques, strategies, and rules of thumb are the tools of the trade, not its intellectual core. This core lies in the relation between data and theory, the ways in which sociologists use empirical observations to formulate, test, and refine statements about the social world. Or, in the words of Lazarsfeld and Rosenberg:

> The term methodology . . . implies that concrete studies are being scrutinized as to the procedures they use, the underlying assumptions they make, the modes of explanation they consider satisfactory.[1]

The task of the methodologist, then, is to explain what the investigator is doing and to determine whether or not these procedures will lead the investigator to the kinds of statements he wants to make. Implicit in this definition is a set of principles or criteria by which the methodologist can judge the adequacy of the procedures. The following chapters include many such principles and criteria—for example, criteria for judging if an observed relation between poor housing and delinquency can reasonably be taken as causal. Two chapters examine the criteria that other methodological critics have used in assessing delinquency research: Chapter 2 considers several broad attacks on the entire field of delinquency, and Chapter 8 takes up other criteria of causality implicit in the attacks of some critics on previous causal statements in delinquency research.

The methodological critic is thus subjected to the same kind of criticism that he applies to empirical investigators. These criteria and principles play a key part in assessing the work of empirical investigators and methodologists alike. Good criteria lead to useful criticism and better research. Bad criteria, such as those discussed in Chapter 8, result in pointless criticism and inhibit needed research. How, then, is one to know which criteria are good, acceptable, or valid, and which are bad, unacceptable, or invalid?

## Methodological Criteria

Some criteria of adequacy rest on logical or mathematical reasoning. For instance, it is easy to show mathematically why a low level of random error of measurement is desirable in studies of the relations between variables: The greater the random error, the more the observed correlations are reduced ("attenuated") below what they would otherwise have been. For problems like this, the methodologist needs only a basic knowledge of mathematics and statistics.[2] Sometimes not even that is necessary. In Chapter 8 we show, without any formal mathematics or statistics, that these "bad" criteria of causality have devastating implications: To accept any one of them is tantamount to denying the possibility of any causal relations.

It is rare to be able to justify one's criteria in this way. Indeed, the validity of most of the criteria in this book is not demonstrable; for example, the three criteria of causality in

Chapter 3 cannot be validated by any kind of logical derivation. They rest, instead, on the consensus of sociologists (and others), a consensus that has grown stronger over the years as these criteria have survived many different critical attacks. In the end, even mathematical derivations rest on such consensus, for all derivations depend eventually on undemonstrable assumptions that people have agreed to accept.

Since all notions of validity rest on consensus among the workers in a field of study, what is acceptable at one time may not be acceptable at another. For over fifty years sociologists were content to infer statements about the difference in suicide rates between Protestants and Catholics from the suicide rates in countries with varying proportions of Protestants and Catholics. Only after the publication of Robinson's classic paper on ecological correlations in 1950 did sociologists come to realize that even the great Durkheim had been guilty of invalid reasoning.[3]

Methodology, then, is not everlasting, revealed truth. It is a living body of ideas that changes with time. There are many methods, and what is right and valid today may be wrong and invalid tomorrow. It would be nihilistic to use this mutability of methodological criteria as an argument for doing away with all methodological judgments. At any given time one has to decide by the standards of that time. True, standards may change so as to redeem a study now considered unacceptable, but this has happened to few studies in the past. Change in the other direction, from acceptable to unacceptable, is the more usual course. This is a fact of life in all empirical sciences: Sooner or later, every generalization perishes. An investigator can only hope that his generalization will live beyond its infancy.

Even when investigators agree on the rules they should follow or the criteria they should meet, they often find it difficult or impossible to do so. For one thing, the criteria may conflict with each other. If one wants to study the relations between child-rearing practices and delinquency, is it better to ask many questions of a small sample or fewer questions of a larger sample? With a limited amount of money, one cannot have both a large sample and many questions.

Sometimes the criteria are so vague as to leave room for a wide range of judgments. In an early draft of Chapter 5 we criticized one investigator for not taking account of a certain variable. In an exchange of correspondence with him, it became clear that there were fundamental differences between him and us on whether or not this variable was really important.

Another reason why a competent investigator may not conform to some criteria of methodological adequacy is that it may be difficult or impossible to meet the conditions for applying the criteria. For example, one criterion of causality requires that the alleged cause occur before the effect. Thus it is possible to ask if inadequate supervision of the child is a cause of delinquency only if the supervision was inadequate before the delinquency began. In some cases, however, the causal order is unclear. Does delinquency cause poor work in school, or does poor work in school cause delinquency? Chapter 4 will treat questions of causal order in more detail. For now, however, it should be clear that methodological rules and criteria are guides to action rather than laws of nature and that it is difficult for even the most competent investigator to conform to all of the criteria he considers valid. All of these points should convey the same message to the student and the methodologist: Before condemning an investigator for violating some criterion or assumption, try to see if he could have avoided the violation and whether or not this might have led him into greater difficulties.

## How to Read This Book

A *methodological riddle:* When it comes to reading the report of an empirical study, what is the difference between a layman, a researcher, and a methodologist? *Answer:* The layman reads the text and skips the tables; the researcher reads the tables and skips the text; and the methodologist does not care very much about either the tables or the text, as long as they agree with each other.

Labored as this riddle may be, it is all too accurate. The layman, however, is not always at fault for skipping the tables; as some of our examples show, it is often difficult to reconcile the tables and the text. Because most of the examples in this book are based on tables, and because part of our task is the methodological analysis of the relations between tables and text, it is essential to understand why tables are difficult to read and what can be done about it. Part of the answer lies in the large amount of information that each number stands for. One cannot skim a table as one skims passages of ordinary text. A single percentage usually stands for an entire sentence; to explain and discuss the figures in a complex table may require several pages. As with any concentrated food, it takes time to digest the figures.

Our first suggestion is to read the tables slowly. This is especially important for the reader who has not had some systematic experience in reading tables. The discussion of tables in Chapter 3 begins simply, so that even the reader who has skipped tables in the past will be able to read the tables in this book (and others as well).[4]

Problems of understanding occur in this book at two levels. There is first the investigator's account of his work. Here, of course, our discussions should be helpful, because we usually begin the analysis of a complicated example by restating the investigator's arguments. Now the reader of this book is also a methodologist, and he should be as much concerned as we are with the extent of agreement between the text and the material analyzed. That is to say, our own discussions are also fair game for the kind of methodological critique that we present here. Because our analysis is necessarily more abstract than the material on which it is based, the reader will do well to proceed even more slowly in reading what we have to say about an example than in reading the example itself.

There is also the opposite danger: that some of the examples (and our analyses of them) will appear too simple. Some investigators are able to express their thoughts so lucidly that the reader finds himself going through the analysis almost as if it were a novel. Perhaps a few of our methodological critiques will read this well also. The danger here lies in misleading the reader about how easy it is to do empirical research or methodology. The difficulties he is sure to find when he tries to do these things himself may prove discouraging. For the record, then, we want to say that any such appearances are misleading. Only in textbooks does a research project move smoothly from hypothesis to conclusion. In real life, research is far less orderly; as in a work of art, what appears natural and simple is usually the product of hard labor.[5] The same consideration applies to our methodological critiques. Some of the shortest and simplest took many hours of hard thought and, occasionally, argument between us. The reader should not be discouraged when he finds that research and methodological analysis are hard work for him too.

A useful technique in learning how to read and construct tables is to work back from the table to the raw (unpercentaged) figures of the original data, as we do several times in the text (at greatest length in Chapter 14), and then combine these figures to yield simpler tables. From the three-variable

9

table of Chapter 14, showing the relations between delinquency, adequacy of supervision, and mother's employment, one can make three two-variable tables—delinquency and supervision, delinquency and mother's employment, and supervision and mother's employment. Constructing, percentaging, and interpreting these three tables will give an insight into three-variable relations that can be had in no other way.

Our final suggestion is to take one's hunches and intuitions seriously. In our own experience, we often began our analysis of an example with the vague feeling that something was wrong, but we were unable at the outset to say just what led to this feeling. As we studied the data from different perspectives, more often than not we found our hunches leading to a useful analysis. One cannot, of course, rely on hunches and such subjective feelings to demonstrate the validity of a methodological argument, but nothing in the canons of methodology prohibits one from taking advantage of hunches to suggest both problems and solutions.

## The Methodologist and the Investigator

Literary critics, historians, and even some sociologists picture social research as a mechanical process of turning people into numbers.[6] As the abstract study of empirical research procedures, methodology is presumably even more guilty of this dehumanization. This naïve view is fostered by the conception of science as a mechanical application of the scientific method. Our discussion of the principles and criteria for research decisions suggests, however, that there is no single scientific method; there are many scientific methods, and the consensus of investigators in each field determines which ones are acceptable at a particular time. In no field that we know of is empirical research a cut-and-dried routine. For social research we can even provide some evidence that there are artistic and subjective components.

In the spring of 1963 an experiment on the analysis of data was conducted at the Survey Research Center of the University of California, Berkeley. The participants were three experienced investigators: Charles Y. Glock, William L. Nicholls, II, and Martin A. Trow. As it happened, all three had done their graduate study at the same university (Columbia), all had worked in close proximity for several years, and all had taught the same course in methodology with one of us (Selvin). If social research is really the mechanical process that its critics claim, then surely there was every reason to expect these three investigators to turn out a standard, assembly-line product.

At the beginning of the experiment, all three investigators received the same instructions. They were to analyze data gathered from a sample of young Italian men to determine the sources of support for capitalism and communism. The experiment was conducted under hothouse conditions: Each investigator had a staff of assistants so that he could order whatever tables he wished and get them back, properly percentaged, in a few minutes (at this time table-running was not yet computerized). As he worked through the analysis, the investigator recorded his comments on a dictating machine. In addition, another experienced researcher sat alongside him as an observer-interviewer. While the investigator scanned each new table, the observer would ask him what he saw in it and what new lines of research it suggested. At the end of a long day each investigator drafted a report on what he already had done and on what further lines he would have followed had there been time.

Perhaps it was only to be expected that all three would arrive at essentially the same conclusions; after all, they were studying the same body of data. What was totally unexpected, and is particularly impressive in view of their similar backgrounds, is that all three followed significantly different plans of analysis. True, a few of the operations were the same for all three investigators and a somewhat larger number for two of the three, but the differences were at least as great as the similarities. And had there been time to allow each investigator to design his own study, the differences would have been far greater.

Differences in judgment, taste, values, and knowledge all affect an analyst's decisions. If the result is not a work of art, it is certainly an individual product—perhaps not as distinctive as a fingerprint, but certainly as distinctive as a thousand independent decisions can make it. It is important for the methodologist to keep this distinctiveness in mind as he studies a piece of research, for it will help him to understand why the investigator has not always done what the methodologist might consider obvious. Or, as Lazarsfeld and Rosenberg put it:

Methodology . . . [has] developed as a bent of mind rather than as a system of organized principles and procedures. The methodologist is a scholar who is above all *analytical* in his approach to his subject matter. He tells other scholars what they have done, or might do, rather than what they should do. He tells them what order of finding has emerged from their research, not what kind of result is or is not preferable.

This kind of analytical approach requires self-awareness on the one hand, and tolerance, on the other. The methodologist knows that the same goal can be reached by alternative roads. . . .[7]

Although we cannot claim to have been analytical, self-aware, and tolerant in all of our discussions, we agree that this is the way a methodological critic should approach his subject. Not all critics, however, have done this. In the next chapter, where we discuss several broad critiques of delinquency research, it will be possible to see how the failure to be analytical, self-aware, and tolerant affects the quality of the methodological criticism.

# Notes

1. Paul F. Lazarsfeld and Morris Rosenberg, eds., *The Language of Social Research*. New York: The Free Press, 1955, p. 4.

2. Although this book requires only simple arithmetic and although only two chapters deal with formal statistics, it would be wrong to infer that methodologists can get along without some minimal level of competence in these fields. Indeed, following Sibley, we believe that all sociologists should have such competence. Courses in statistics are now required almost everywhere for undergraduate and graduate students in sociology, but without mathematics at the level of introductory calculus and matrix algebra (a one-year course in all), this is cookbook statistics. In another generation this much mathematics will be taken by most high-school students; it is a pity that sociology will have to wait that long for all of its students and practitioners to be literate in the language in which more and more of its research is being expressed. See Elbridge Sibley, *The Education of Sociologists in the United States*. New York: Russell Sage Foundation, 1963.

3. William S. Robinson, "Ecological correlations and the behavior of individuals," *American Sociological Review*, 15, 1950, pp. 351–357. See also the further discussion of this point in Chapter 15.

4. An excellent introduction to table reading is in W. Allen Wallis and Harry V. Roberts, *The Nature of Statistics*. New York: The Free Press, 1962, Chapter 9. (This is not a textbook but a fascinating account of what statistics is all about; a prior reading of it will help to make the introductory course in statistics a rewarding intellectual experience.) For a more detailed account of table reading, see Hans Zeisel, *Say It With Figures*. New York: Harper & Row, 1957.

5. Several vivid accounts of the process of research are contained in Phillip E. Hammond, ed., *Sociologists at Work*. New York: Basic Books, 1964.

6. We shall consider some of these attacks in Chapter 2. For a penetrating discussion of the humanists' image of sociology, see Bennett M. Berger, "Sociology and the intellectual: an analysis of a stereotype," *Antioch Review*, 17, 1957, pp. 275–290.

7. Lazarsfeld and Rosenberg, *loc. cit.* (Italics in original)

# Critiques of Delinquency Research

The critic of delinquency research does not have a difficult time justifying his existence. In a matter of hours he can call into question hundreds of studies costing millions of dollars; and he can count on a great deal of social support: Theorists, practitioners, and laymen are virtually unanimous in condemning delinquency research as inconclusive and inconsistent. The would-be critic, however, faces one problem: Almost every aspect of delinquency research, from its metaphysical foundations to the consistency of its operational definition of family size, has already been the object of intense criticism. The usual point of departure for the critics has been a review of the results of delinquency research. Such a review invariably suggests that delinquency research has, to some extent, failed. To the extent that delinquency research has failed, the critic reasons, something must be wrong with its assumptions, methods, or techniques. The task of the critic then is to locate the source of trouble and to recommend ways and means of avoiding it.

At this point the paths of various critics diverge. Some find the difficulty in the philosophical underpinnings of quantitative research,[1] others in the explicit or implicit theories of delinquency that the research assumes,[2] the investigator's training and competence,[3] the procedures of sampling and data collection,[4] the quality of the inferences drawn from the data,[5] and the statistical techniques employed.[6]

The statements of many critics suggest that quantitative research on delinquency has failed altogether—that its results are useless to theory, to practice, and even to future research. Some think that it has failed because it must fail, and, therefore, conclude (quite logically) that it should be abandoned. Others think that it has failed because of the misapplication of basically sound assumptions and methods. Still others, among whom we count ourselves, think that the extent to which delinquency research has failed has been grossly exaggerated, that it is unfair to many studies and to delinquency research as a whole to condemn indiscriminately the results of various investigations as "inconclusive and inconsistent."[7] Partly in order to strike a fairer balance on the state of delinquency research and partly to set the stage for our own critique, we shall here take a closer look at previous critiques and suggest some of the ways they differ from our own.

## Critiques by Opponents of Quantitative Research

Delinquency research has been included, at least by implication, in two recent attacks on quantitative research in general. Pitirim A. Sorokin maintains that "the contemporary stage of the psycho-social sciences can be properly called *the age of quantophrenia and numerology*."[8] And C. Wright Mills argues that what he calls "abstracted empiricism" is helping

16

to insure "that we do not learn too much about man and society."[9]

Sorokin devotes much of his attention to the statistical procedures of quantitative research. Thus he uses studies of crime and delinquency to illustrate the "failure" of correlational techniques:

A multitude of correlational studies investigated the relationship between intelligence and criminality, in some 163,000 cases in all. C. F. Chassell has carefully summed up the results of the bulk of such studies. In the first place, the results of the various studies are contradictory, some exhibiting a positive and others a negative relationship between these variables, some a close and others a very remote relationship. The coefficients of correlation between these variables range from minus .52 to plus .76. . . .[10] About as contradictory and discordant are the coefficients of correlation between delinquency and illiteracy, delinquency and amount of schooling, criminality and school progress, delinquency and educational achievement; intelligence and morality. Thus, after a multitude of painstaking correlational studies, the contradictoriness of their "exact" coefficients of correlation leaves us as ignorant as ever about the real relationship between these variables of criminality-delinquency and intelligence. The hopelessness of the situation is aggravated by the fact that these studies do not give to us an objective basis for deciding which of these discordant coefficients are valid, and which are not.[11]

Although Sorokin sprinkles the word *correlation* liberally throughout this passage in an apparent attempt to establish its guilt by association, he offers no evidence that the correlation coefficient is in any way to blame for the inconsistencies it has helped to reveal. As a matter of fact, in the chapter immediately following his attack on the correlation coefficient, Sorokin presents a detailed (if heavily overdrawn) argument on why a two-variable relation *should* vary from one study to the next—and thus, we suggest, exonerates the correlation coefficient.

Sorokin is equally scornful of the most simple techniques:

Statistical methods cannot predict *even* the states of single units in the predictable mass phenomena. . . . Suppose that statistics show that 72 per cent of paroled criminals with a certain background and certain characteristics make good. This prediction does not, however, insure that J. Brown who has the above background and traits will necessarily make good his parole, or that M. Jones who has a different background and different traits will necessarily violate his parole.[12]

Although present-day statistical prediction is much more elaborate than Sorokin's example, his criticism is invalid on its own grounds. Statistical methods *can* predict the states of single units—they are only unpredictable when nothing is known about the probabilities of the various outcomes or when the probabilities are equal. Neither of these conditions holds in the case of J. Brown. We would be glad to bet on J. Brown's making good on parole. Of course, this prediction does not insure that J. Brown will make good, but this failing is not peculiar to statistical methods of prediction.[13] The case of M. Jones is another matter. Since nothing is known about M. Jones's chances on parole, it is hardly fair to say that knowledge of J. Brown tells us nothing about M. Jones and then to use this as a criticism of statistical prediction techniques.

Sorokin undoubtedly has shown that quantitative research can be misinterpreted.[14] And his own critique demonstrates that, whether the data are quantitative or qualitative, it is easy to get lost in the gap between evidence and conclusions. What he has not done, however, is at least as impressive. He fails to demonstrate the superiority of any other kind of research, and he does not show that the alleged shortcomings of quantitative research stem from its use of one or another statistical technique.

Unlike Sorokin, Mills does not concern himself with the techniques of quantitative research. In fact, Mills does not appear to have any objections to quantitative techniques as such:

The specific methods—as distinct from the philosophy—of empiricism are clearly suitable and convenient for work on many problems, and I do not see how anyone could reasonably object to such use of them.[15]

Like Sorokin, however, Mills argues that while "high skill and acute sensibility" are necessary for both observation and discovery, most quantitative research suffers from being conducted by a "bureaucratically guided set of usually semi-skilled individuals."[16] (Sorokin calls them "the clerks of psychosocial research.")

✳ Even if it is true that invalid research is usually conducted by poorly trained or incompetent people, it does not follow that poorly trained people will necessarily do bad research. For that matter, the use of people with little skill may be seen as one of the happy by-products of the routinization of science:

For it is necessary to insist upon this extraordinary but undeniable fact: experimental science has progressed thanks in great part to the work of men astoundingly mediocre, and even less than mediocre. That is to say, modern science, the root and symbol of our actual civilization, finds a place for the intellectually commonplace man and allows him to work therein with success.[17]

Large numbers of technicians and semi-skilled workers—interviewers, coders, clerks, and programmers—are necessary for most kinds of quantitative research. Their use does present problems, such as cheating by interviewers, but similar problems occur in other kinds of research. Once again, neither the procedures nor the agents of quantitative research are sufficient explanations of its alleged shortcomings.

A more fundamental attack on quantitative delinquency research comes from those, like Irwin Deutscher, who see no point in any study of the relations between variables (thus apparently damning much qualitative research as well):

[Investigators] have dissipated their research energies in a fruitless search for factors, bewildering themselves with the fallacious behavioristic assumption of stimulus-response, in the fruitless quest for "causes." Such a conception of the etiology of deviant behavior has been no more productive than the earlier assumption that people who misbehave are inherently depraved, either as a result of the influence of the devil or the defectiveness of their genetic composition. The older assumption at least had the advantage of not being as wasteful of research funds, intellectual energies, or clinical time. . . . We have been traveling up a dead-end road in our fruitless search for simple cause-and-effect relationships in our quest for factors, traits, and characteristics.[18]

Deutscher's arguments are much like those expressed by Herbert Blumer in his 1956 presidential address to the American Sociological Association, and Deutscher has since gone on to develop these views in his own presidential address to the Society for the Study of Social Problems in 1965.[19] Both of Deutscher's articles will repay careful reading, as will Blumer's; they have many cogent observations on the present state of sociology. In our judgment, however, both men fail in one of their central tasks: to demonstrate that quantitative research of the kind discussed in this book is fruitless and fallacious.

This is not the place to debate the assumptions upon which quantitative research is based. It is the place to recognize, however, that Blumer's and Deutscher's criticisms of quantitative research flow from rejection of these assumptions and not from examination of actual studies. Thus Blumer ignores everything beyond the simplest two-variable relation, and Deutscher uses the disparity between attitudes and behavior as a club to belabor all of quantitative research, without recognizing that quantitative research helped reveal the discrepancy upon which he bases his attack, without recognizing that quantitative procedures need not depend on questionnaire data, and, indeed, without recognizing that quantitative researchers need not and do not assume perfect congruence between words and deeds.

There is, of course, nothing wrong with starting from some philosophical assumptions; indeed, it is impossible to do otherwise. Our dissatisfaction with the kind of global antipositivism represented by Deutscher and Blumer is over its substitution of preconceptions for examination of the data. Convinced beyond possibility of refutation of the invalidity and uselessness of quantitative research, they do not consider how quantitative research might be improved.[20]

The alleged chaos in delinquency research is undoubtedly partly a result of the wide range of assumptions its critics bring to bear on judgments of its adequacy. Thus Michael and Adler, whose methodological criteria are much like our own (and are, if anything, more complex and demanding), occasionally suggest a criterion that allows them to reject criminological research out of hand:

The absurdity of any attempt to draw etiological conclusions from these findings of criminological research, is so patent as not to warrant further discussion. . . . In addition to all the methodological defects which have been enumerated, these investigators have failed to recognize that both human and environmental variables are necessarily involved in the etiology of human behavior. That failure alone would be sufficient to render fallacious any conclusion about the causes of crime.[21]

Along the same lines, Sophia Robison suggests that four sets of factors, the individual, the family, the subculture, and the environment must be considered simultaneously by the delinquency researcher. She also appears to argue that unless one is a psychologist, a sociologist, a psychiatrist, a jurist, and a political scientist, "one cannot arrive at valid generalizations, principles, or laws which have predictive values."[22]

In addition to being impracticable, the notion that the

researcher must take everything into account at once is not justified by inspection of the results of research in either the physical or the social sciences. The strain between complexity and simplicity in science is real enough, but the idea that statements that ignore a great deal are, therefore, false is not supported by logic (otherwise all scientific statements would be false) or by the evidence available.

The only way to know whether or not a relation between, for example, a social factor and delinquency is modified when a psychological variable is taken into account is to consider the appropriate three-variable relation (see Chapter 7). The increasing success of the life sciences in understanding the human body (surely more highly integrated than the social system) suggests that good research is possible without taking everything into account at once.

## Critiques by Other Students of Delinquency

The critiques of delinquency research discussed thus far are based at least in part on assumptions that quantitative researchers cannot share. Since we are able to question the validity of these assumptions, it is relatively easy for us to believe that delinquency research is not as bad as these critics have claimed. Some of the most trenchant attacks come, however, from critics whose assumptions are generally compatible with ours, i.e., they believe in the possibility of valid and useful quantitative research. If, as we claim, the negative picture common to all the critics is overdrawn, we shall have to look closely into the methods by which these sympathetic critics arrive at their negative conclusions.

Take the following observations, which Albert K. Cohen

and James F. Short, Jr. say apply to most studies of the antecedents of official delinquency:

1. The findings are often inconclusive and inconsistent as, for instance, in the numerous studies of the relationship between delinquency and broken homes.

2. They usually define delinquency in very general terms such as residence in a particular institution or commitment for a particular type of legal offense, rather than in terms more specifically and concretely descriptive of the behavior in question. [A footnote mentions some exceptions.]

3. They deal largely with correlations, that is, the observed tendency for delinquency (as defined) to be associated with certain other events and circumstances. They do not, as a rule, deal with these correlations within the context of a general theory of delinquency which would be necessary to *explain the correlations.*[23]

We shall examine all of these points in some detail during the course of this book. For now, however, the crucial point is the first one. Since Cohen and Short did not have space to discuss the evidence for this assertion, we shall turn instead to Barbara Wootton's *Social Science and Social Pathology,* which devotes a great deal of attention to the inconclusiveness and inconsistency of delinquency research.

Wootton examined twenty-one studies, chosen for their "comparative methodological merit." Summarizing their findings on twelve frequently examined relations (e.g., size of family and delinquency), Wootton concludes that they have produced "only the most meagre, and dubiously supported, generalizations."[24]

The twenty-one studies Wootton examines are described by her:

[They] spread over a period of forty years. The subjects investigated cover both sexes and a wide range of ages; and no less variable are the definitions of criminality which are responsible for their inclusion. Some of the studies deal with adult males who

**23**

have served prison sentences; others with adult females in like cases; others again with young men sentenced to Borstal; yet others with children appearing before the juvenile courts, whatever their offence and whatever their sentence, or, alternatively, with those dealt with by these courts in a particular way. Old and young, thieves, sex offenders, persons guilty of crimes of violence, recidivists and first offenders are all represented.[25]

These studies are examined for the evidence they provide on the association of the following twelve factors with criminality or delinquency.

1. The size of the delinquent's family.
2. The presence of other criminals in the family.
3. Club membership.
4. Church attendance.
5. Employment record.
6. Social status.
7. Poverty.
8. Mother's employment outside the home.
9. School truancy.
10. Broken home.
11. Health.
12. Educational attainment.[26]

After a detailed examination of the evidence, Wootton summarizes her findings:

All in all, therefore, this collection of studies, although chosen for its comparative methodological merit, produces only the most meagre, and dubiously supported, generalizations. On the whole, it seems that offenders come from relatively large families. Not infrequently (according to some investigators very frequently) other members of the delinquents' (variously defined) families have also been in trouble with the law. Offenders are unlikely to be regular churchgoers, but the evidence as to whether club membership discourages delinquency is 'wildly contradictory.' If they are of age to be employed, they are likely to be classified as 'poor' rather than as 'good' workers. Most of them come from the lower social classes, but again the evidence as to the extent to which they can be described as exceptionally poor is conflicting; nor is there

24

any clear indication that their delinquency is associated with the employment of their mothers outside the home. Their health is probably no worse than that of other people, but many of them have earned poor reputations at school, though these may well be prejudiced by their teachers' knowledge of their delinquencies. In their schooldays they are quite likely to have truanted from school, and perhaps an unusually large proportion of them come from homes in which at some (frequently unspecified) time both parents were not, for whatever reason, living together; yet even on these points, the findings of some inquiries are negative. And beyond this we cannot go.[27]

Although these are indeed dreary conclusions, we do not think that the dreariness is justified. In fact, we would summarize Wootton's evidence as follows:

1. The larger the family, the more likely the child is to become delinquent.
2. Criminality among other members of the family is fairly strongly related to delinquency.
3. Church attendance is negatively related to delinquency.
4. No good evidence has been collected to suggest that club membership is related to delinquency, either positively or negatively.
5. Poor workers are more likely than good workers to be delinquent.
6. Delinquency is negatively related to social class.
7. Taken as a whole, these studies suggest a relation between poverty and delinquency.
8. Employment of the mother outside the home is not related to delinquency.
9. There is no relation between health and delinquency.
10. The better the child's performance in school, the less likely he is to become delinquent.
11. Truancy and delinquency are highly related.
12. Children from broken homes are at least slightly more likely than children from intact homes to become delinquent.

Even giving full rein to healthy skepticism, these findings allow a great deal to be said about some of the theories underlying them. A theory that poor health is an important cause of delinquency can take little solace from these findings; theories based on the assumption that mother's employment (or the broken home) is a major cause of delinquency fare no better. But the studies Wootton discusses can do more than disconfirm theories; they can provide a realistic beginning for explanations of delinquent conduct—explanations preferable to those based on unreasonable assumptions about the strength of relations between some of these factors and delinquency. These findings are especially noteworthy in being the product of studies carried out in three countries under vastly different conditions, using different definitions of both the independent and dependent variables.

Perhaps we are overstating our argument. How can we see consistency and reasonable conclusiveness where Wootton sees only inconsistency and inconclusiveness? Consider finding number ten, in which we have confidence, but which Wootton questions:

. . . many of them [the delinquents] have earned poor reputations at school, though these may well be prejudiced by their teachers' knowledge of their delinquencies.[28]

One page earlier, this conclusion is only slightly more positive:

It thus appears that there is fairly good agreement on both sides of the Atlantic that those who are found guilty of offences tend to have poor school records. Much of this evidence, however, is based upon the assessments of schoolmasters, which can hardly be regarded as objective, or as reasonably certain to be free of bias.[29]

None of the studies Wootton reviews finds educational attainment positively related to delinquency. All relevant studies (those with a control group) find it negatively related to delinquency. The results are thus consistent. Wootton's main source of uneasiness appears to be the procedures for judging school attainment:

. . . our investigators are not generally explicit on the vital point of whether the assessments quoted were made with, or without, knowledge that the subject was in trouble with the law.[30]

It appears, then, that Wootton grants the consistency of the studies on school attainment and delinquency but is unwilling to grant their conclusiveness—which is perhaps another way of saying "validity." Among other things, the school reports (grades) may measure bias on the part of school officials rather than academic achievement.

When we ask what the investigators could have done to forestall Wootton's uneasiness about the validity of their data, we come to the most important aspect of a critique of delinquency research, which is not its conclusions about how bad it is, but its recommendations for improvement. It is on this point that our approach differs most radically from previous critiques. All too often these critiques have assumed that the facts speak for themselves, that the truth should be obvious in the data. When it is discovered that the facts have not spoken the truth, a slight modification saves this assumption; clean, pure facts speak for themselves:

. . . the most pressing task in the immediate future is not so much to elaborate statistical techniques still further, as to improve the quality of our raw material, and to establish more rigorous standards as to what is, and what is not, admissible.[31]

According to the "pure data" approach, the investigator should be able to collect his data in such a way that the problem of validity never arises:

Yet inaccurate observations remain inaccurate, no matter how sophisticated the statistical processing to which they are subjected: the only effect of such processing is to create a regrettably spurious appearance of accuracy. In those cases, therefore, in which we are not yet able to devise methods of guaranteeing the soundness of our raw data, we should be well advised to resist the temptation to elaborate manipulation.[32]

**27**

One consequence of this assumption is to downgrade the importance of analysis. Good data are enough:

Tons of literature and researches have been devoted to the study of crime causation; yet it is a fact, borne out by painstaking analysis of published reports, that almost invariably the dizzy statistical superstructure involved in such researches has been built up on the wobbly foundation of unverified, inaccurately observed, and incomplete raw materials. Not all the refined statistical technique in the world can transform data not founded on verified fact into truth.[33]

Such statements could hardly come from anyone experienced in manipulating statistical data. Among the first things one learns from such manipulation is that the facts are seldom what they seem: The data contain unsuspected errors and inconsistencies; a set of numbers thought to measure $X$ turns out to bear almost no relation to $X$; conjectures about why variables have certain relations to each other are not supported by analysis. Over-emphasis on the quality of the raw material can thus divert attention from analytic procedures for evaluating and improving the quality of data; it can retard the analysis of less-than-perfect (and therefore unworthy) data; and it can retard the analysis of good, accurate data by suggesting that they will speak for themselves.

Improving the quality of delinquency data is certainly a worthwhile goal, but comments like these overlook its weakness as an explanation of what has happened in the past. Many unfortunate "findings" would doubtless survive a great deal of data scrubbing and polishing, as the following simple example illustrates.

Many studies have found a positive relation between intelligence and delinquency, while other studies have found no relation between these variables.[34] Are such results inconsistent? Consider one of the studies that shows no relation between intelligence and delinquency, the widely cited *New*

*Light on Delinquency and Its Treatment* by Healy and Bronner:

Somewhat to our surprise, since we are still probably a little under the spell of the Aristotelian dictum that good conduct is strongly correlated with good intelligence, the mental age-levels of the two groups prove to be only slightly contrasting. Skillful psychological testing shows that well within the limits of normal mental ability . . . there were 98 of the delinquents and 94 controls. Superior ability was demonstrated by 14 delinquents as compared to 18 controls. No comment on these findings seems necessary; the figures speak for themselves.[35]

Healy and Bronner are correct: Their figures reveal no relation between intelligence and delinquency. A good piece of research, complete with a control group and skillful psychological testing, thus appears to have produced evidence that contradicts the results of previous (and subsequent) research. Unfortunately, however, Healy and Bronner are comparing each delinquent child with his brother or sister nearest in age. Now it is well known that there is a strong relation between the I.Q.'s of siblings. In other words, each time Healy and Bronner located a delinquent with a given I.Q. for their experimental group, they in effect assigned a nondelinquent with an equivalent I.Q. to their control group. With the two groups thus matched on intelligence, is it any wonder that this study shows no relation between intelligence and delinquency?

The very objection that makes this "finding" irrelevant to a discussion of the relation between intelligence and delinquency is sometimes cited as evidence of its unusual importance:

Since it is known that [intelligence] scores vary according to the amount of education and cultural background, a fair comparison can be made only when delinquents and non-delinquents are matched on such factors.

Identity of background is provided in the comparison of delinquent children made by Healy and Bronner with the brother or sister closest in age. Race, ethnic, and general family background were identical. The intelligence quotients of the two groups showed very little difference.[36]

It would be too much to suggest that this kind of methodological analysis could remove all the "inconsistency" in the findings of delinquency research. Nevertheless, much of this inconsistency could be avoided by more careful analyses of data by the original investigator, and more attention by reviewers and critics to the methods by which investigators draw inferences from their data.

In any event, the goal of delinquency research should not be to find *the* relation between variable X and delinquency, but to learn how and *under what conditions* variable X does or does not affect delinquency. We believe that progress toward this goal will come from sound quantitative analysis—whether the data are refined or crude:

... not the least advance in sociology during the last century or so is reflected in the growing recognition that even crude quantitative data can serve the intellectual purpose of enabling the sociologist to reject or to modify his initial hypotheses when they are in fact defective.[37]

# Notes

1. David Matza, *Delinquency and Drift.* New York: Wiley, 1964, pp. 1–27. Matza does not address himself directly to quantitative research, but to *positivism* and its assumption of hard determinism.

2. Delinquency research has been variously accused of being a-theoretical and of having nonsensical theory. Many attacks have focused on multiple-factor theories. See, for example, Albert K. Cohen, "Multiple factor approaches," in Marvin E. Wolfgang, *et al., The Sociology of Crime and Delinquency.* New York: Wiley, 1962, pp. 77–80; Irwin Deutscher, "Some relevant directions for research in juvenile delinquency," in Arnold Rose, ed., *Human Behavior and Social Processes.* Boston: Houghton Mifflin, 1962, pp. 474–476; Louise G. Howton, "Evaluating delinquency research," in Bernard Rosenberg, *et al., Mass Society in Crisis.* New York: Macmillan, 1964, pp. 152–156. If we were to include in this category those who suggest that conceptualization is a key problem, the list would be long indeed. See, for example, Charles J. Browning, "Toward a science of delinquency analysis," *Sociology and Social Research,* 46, 1961, pp. 61–74.

3. This is but one of the many "weaknesses" pointed to in the old, but still impressive *Crime, Law and Social Science* by Jerome Michael and Mortimer J. Adler (New York: Harcourt, 1933). For a reply to Michael and Adler, see Albert K. Cohen, *et al.,* eds., *The Sutherland Papers.* Bloomington: Indiana University Press, 1956, pp. 227–246.

4. Barbara Wootton, *Social Science and Social Pathology.* New York: Macmillan, 1959, pp. 81–135, 301–328.

5. Michael and Adler, *op. cit.,* devote a great deal of attention to the adequacy of data analysis in delinquency research.

6. Pitirim A. Sorokin, *Fads and Foibles in Modern Sociology and Related Sciences.* Chicago: Henry Regnery, 1956.

7. A major problem with sweeping reviews of the results of delinquency research is that they let good and not-so-good studies call each other into question. Although we would not put the matter in these words, we agree with the intent of Sheldon Glueck's comment: ". . . in textbooks on criminology you are likely to find a quotation from some minor piece of superficial so-called 'research' by an inexperienced or obviously prejudiced investigator cheek by jowl with one from a pioneering investigation by original researchers; and both are given equal weight by the textbook writer." Sheldon and Eleanor Glueck, *Ventures in Criminology.* Cambridge: Harvard University Press, 1964, p. 13.

8. Sorokin, *op. cit.,* p. 103.

9. C. Wright Mills, *The Socio-*

31

*logical Imagination.* New York: Oxford University Press, 1959, p. 75.

10. Compare: "[Chassell's] conclusion is that the relation [between morality and intellect] is positive but low, with correlations *usually* between 0.10 and 0.39." Edwin H. Sutherland and Donald R. Cressey, *Principles of Criminology.* 6th ed. Philadelphia: J. B. Lippincott, 1960, p. 119. (Authors' italics)

11. Sorokin, *op. cit.,* pp. 142–143.

12. *Ibid.,* p. 153. (Authors' italics)

13. In arguing that statistical methods cannot perform *even* the most elementary tasks—such as predicting the states of single units—Sorokin suggests the existence of alternative methods that can handle these problems. Unfortunately, he does not say what these procedures are.

14. Why does Sorokin say that 163,000 cases were involved in the studies of the relation between intelligence and delinquency? Does this large number add weight to his argument that correlational studies may produce inconsistent results? If so, what bearing does the total number of cases involved in the various studies have on the range of correlation coefficients obtained? If this is not the purpose of the figure cited, what is its purpose? Is this simply another case of numerology?

15. Mills, *op. cit.,* p. 73.

16. *Ibid.,* p. 70.

17. José Ortega y Gasset, *The Revolt of the Masses.* London: Unwin Books, 1961, pp. 84–85.

18. Deutscher, *op. cit.,* pp. 475, 478.

19. Herbert Blumer, "Sociological analysis and the 'variable,' " *American Sociological Review,* 21, 1956, pp. 683–690; Irwin Deutscher, "Words and deeds: social science and

social policy," *Social Problems,* 13, 1966, pp. 235–254.

20. By coincidence, an early version of our Chapter 8 appears immediately after Deutscher's "Words and deeds" paper in *Social Problems,* 13, 1966, pp. 254–268; this juxtaposition makes it easy to compare the two approaches.

21. Michael and Adler, *op. cit.,* p. 169.

22. Sophia Robison, *Juvenile Delinquency.* New York: Holt, Rinehart and Winston, 1960, Chapter 12, pp. 192, 203–204.

23. Albert K. Cohen and James F. Short, Jr., "Juvenile delinquency," in Robert K. Merton and Robert A. Nisbet, eds., *Contemporary Social Problems.* New York: Harcourt, 1961, p. 111.

24. Wootton, *op. cit.,* p. 134.

25. *Ibid.,* p. 83.

26. *Ibid.,* p. 84.

27. *Ibid.,* pp. 134–135.

28. *Ibid.,* p. 135.

29. *Ibid.,* p. 134.

30. *Ibid.*

31. *Ibid.,* p. 313.

32. *Ibid.*

33. Sheldon Glueck, quoted by Paul W. Tappan, *Juvenile Delinquency.* New York: McGraw-Hill, 1949, p. 55.

34. Recent studies showing an important relation between intelligence and delinquency include: Albert J. Reiss, Jr., and Albert Lewis Rhodes, "The distribution of juvenile delinquency in the social class structure," *American Sociological Review,* 26, 1961, pp. 720–732; Jackson Toby and Marcia L. Toby, *Low School Status as a Predisposing Factor in Subcultural Delinquency,* New Brunswick, New Jersey: Rutgers University, about 1962. (Mimeo)

35. William Healy and Augusta F. Bronner, *New Light on Delin-*

*quency and Its Treatment.* New Haven: Yale University Press, 1936, p. 60.

36. Ruth S. Cavan, *Juvenile Delinquency.* Philadelphia: J. B. Lippincott, 1962, p. 59.

37. Robert K. Merton and Bernard Barber, "Sorokin's formulations in the sociology of science," in Philip J. Allen, ed., *Pitirim A. Sorokin in Review.* Durham: Duke University Press, 1963, p. 357.

# part ii

# CAUSAL

# ANALYSIS

# 3

# Principles

# of

# Causal

# Analysis

To say that an analysis is adequate or inadequate requires some criterion or set of principles against which it can be judged. Since we shall be examining and criticizing many different analyses in the chapters to follow, we present here some of the principles on which we shall base our judgments. We shall also use this discussion to define technical terms and to show the kinds of statistical configurations we have in mind when these terms are used.[1]

## *The Logical Bases of Causal Inference*

We begin by accepting the idea that it is possible and meaningful to discuss such propositions as, Inadequate supervision is a cause of delinquency, and, Assigning street workers to gangs causes a reduction in the rate of serious delinquency.[2] Both of these propositions are of the form A causes B; we

**37**

shall speak of A as the independent variable and B as the dependent variable. The typical question that the empirical investigator faces is how to test such propositions, i.e., how to collect and treat empirical data so as to make reasonable statements about causal hypotheses.

In the empirical social sciences there is general agreement on the criteria for evaluating such statements. Our central task, then, is to apply these criteria to the analysis of empirical data. We shall have very little to say about the sources of hypotheses, the nature of abstract theory, and such broad philosophical problems as inductive inference.[3]

*Criteria of Causality.* In Hyman's account[4] there are three principal requirements that an empirical investigator must meet in order to be able to say that A causes B:

1. A and B are statistically associated.
2. A is causally prior to B.
3. The association between A and B does not disappear when the effects of other variables causally prior to both of the original variables are removed.

We shall consider A a cause of B if all three of these criteria are satisfied; it follows that demonstrating any one of the three to be false is enough to show that A is not a cause of B. For simplicity we shall refer to these three criteria as association, causal order, and lack of spuriousness.

Hyman also advocates another criterion: that one or more intervening variables link the independent and dependent variables. This criterion is psychologically, substantively, and even aesthetically desirable; knowing the process through which A affects B is more rewarding to the investigator than the bare statement that A causes B. Nevertheless, this criterion is not part of the minimum requirements for demonstrating causality. Holding a match to a pile of leaves is a cause of their bursting into flame, even if one cannot describe the intervening chemical reactions.

*Experimentation and observation.* Consider once again the two propositions: Inadequate supervision is a cause of delinquency, and, Assigning street workers to gangs causes a reduction in the rate of serious delinquency. Although these two propositions are formally similar in having an independent and a dependent variable, they differ fundamentally in the kinds of studies that may be used to test them. The investigator of inadequate supervision must take children as he finds them; he cannot decide that this child's mother shall adequately supervise him and that that child's mother shall not. In other words, he cannot manipulate the values of his independent variable. The investigator of juvenile gangs can, however, decide which gangs will receive street workers and which will not. It is this ability to manipulate the values of the independent variable that makes experiments possible.

One additional ingredient is necessary for a genuine experiment.[5] The investigator must use some chance mechanism to determine which gangs get a street worker and which do not. For example, he might toss a coin for each gang, assigning a street worker if the coin falls heads. This randomization allows the experimenter to deal with unwanted or extraneous causal variables and thus to satisfy our third requirement for making a causal inference: that the association between the independent and dependent variables does not result from their having a common cause.

To see why this is so, consider two procedures that the investigator might use instead of randomization in assigning street workers to gangs: 1. allow the gangs to decide for themselves whether or not they will get a worker; or 2. make the decision himself on any basis that he chooses. The objection to the first procedure is clear. If he lets the gangs decide for themselves, the more law-abiding gangs may choose to have workers; any subsequent difference in the rates of serious delinquency may be the result of such differences in the gangs

**39**

themselves rather than the effects of the street workers. The objection to the second procedure is less obvious but equally cogent. Even with the best of intentions the investigator may unknowingly assign street workers to groups that are less predisposed to serious delinquency. No matter what basis of choice is used, any purposive assignment is open to a similar objection.

Randomization, however, meets this objection. If the decision to assign a street worker is made at random, the presence of street workers cannot be associated with any other characteristic of the gangs, such as their predisposition to violence. At least this is what will happen on the average: The number of gangs predisposed to violence among those getting a street worker will be approximately equal to the number predisposed to violence among those not getting a street worker, so that there will usually be a small or zero association between a gang's predisposition to violence and the presence of a street worker.

It is always possible, however, that the process of randomization does not completely remove the association between the extraneous variable and the independent variable. Just as one may get ten heads in ten tosses of an unbiased coin, so randomization may occasionally give more street workers to docile gangs than to violent gangs. With the techniques of statistical inference, it is possible to calculate the probability of such an occurrence. That is, in advance of gathering his data, an experimenter can decide how strong his results must be in order to be reasonably confident that they are not simply the accidental outcomes of randomization.[6]

Although randomization is necessary for a good experiment, it is not sufficient. The field known as the statistical design of experiments is largely devoted to ways of making randomized experiments more powerful and more precise. Here, however, we need pursue this line of thought no further, for there are few areas of research on the causes of delinquency in which one can legitimately experiment. As our proposition about street workers illustrates, experimental research usually deals with the treatment of delinquency rather than its causes. In the far larger number of studies represented by our proposition about supervision the investigator must look to other ways of ensuring that extraneous variables have not produced the observed association between his independent and dependent variables.

Suppose that an investigator has found a relation between inadequate supervision and delinquency. He might then reason:

Inadequately supervised children are likely to come from broken homes, and broken homes are known to be associated with delinquency. Since broken homes are causally prior to both variables of the original relation, could the apparent meaning of the original relation be spurious, i.e., could it have come about through the associations of broken homes with both of the original variables rather than through the effect of inadequate supervision on delinquency?

Unlike the experimenter, the nonexperimental investigator cannot use randomization to remove the association between his extraneous variable and the independent variable. Instead of controlling extraneous variables in the design of the study, he relies on statistical manipulation of the data after they have been gathered.

This statistical analysis can take many forms, including partial correlation, standardization, analysis of variance, and the construction of multivariate tables (cross-classification or cross-tabulation). Although there are reasons to believe that more powerful statistical methods will eventually replace cross-classification as a tool of investigation,[7] most empirical studies of delinquency have relied on tabular analysis. Moreover, tables remain the clearest and simplest way to present the

41

conclusions of an analysis. For these reasons both our examples and our methodological analyses will rely on tables.

## Statistical Configurations in Analysis

Consider once again the proposition: "Inadequate supervision is a cause of delinquency." The first task of the analyst who wants to test this proposition is to see whether or not the two variables, supervision and delinquency, are associated—that is, whether or not there is a difference in the proportion of delinquents between adequately supervised boys and inadequately supervised boys.

In Table 3-1, the proportion delinquent among the suitably supervised boys is 30 percent, while the proportion delinquent among the unsuitably supervised boys is 83 percent, a difference of 53 percentage points.

**Table 3-1—Delinquency by Suitability of Supervision\***

| | SUPERVISION | |
| --- | --- | --- |
| | Suitable | Unsuitable |
| Percent delinquent | 30 | 83 |
| Number of cases | (607) | (382) |

\* This table is adapted from Sheldon and Eleanor Glueck, *Unraveling Juvenile Delinquency.* Cambridge: Harvard University Press, 1950, p. 113.

We are using percentage comparisons to describe the association between two variables; we might have used one or another summary measure of association, such as a correlation coefficient, Yule's $Q$, Cramér's $T$, or the more modern measures developed by Goodman and Kruskal.[8] The numerical measure of the association would have differed according to the coefficient used, but all would have led to the same interpretation: that there is a moderate association between supervision and delinquency.

After measuring the association, the analyst must demonstrate that his independent variable, supervision in our example, is causally prior to his dependent variable, delinquency. There are serious problems in this demonstration, as we shall show in Chapter 4; however, these problems are not tabular or even statistical in the usual sense of that term.[9]

In demonstrating lack of spuriousness, the third criterion of causality, the analyst goes beyond the two-variable table to examine three-variable relations, or even more complicated configurations. It will suffice here to consider only the simplest form, the three-variable table.

**Table 3-2—Delinquency and Suitability of Supervision by Mother's Employment***

| Supervision: | HOUSEWIFE | | REGULARLY EMPLOYED | | OCCASIONALLY EMPLOYED | |
|---|---|---|---|---|---|---|
| | Suitable | Unsuit-able | Suitable | Unsuit-able | Suitable | Unsuit-able |
| Percent delinquent | 31 | 85 | 20 | 77 | 33 | 89 |
| Number of cases | (442) | (149) | (80) | (110) | (85) | (116) |

*Mother's Employment*

* This table is adapted from Sheldon and Eleanor Glueck, "Working mothers and delinquency," *Mental Hygiene*, 41, 1957, p. 331.

Table 3-2 permits reexamination of the relation between the suitability of supervision and delinquency, with mother's employment held constant.[10] In this case, the proposed antecedent variable, mother's employment, does not affect the relation between suitability of supervision and delinquency: The relation is as strong within categories of mother's employment as it is when mother's employment is left free to vary (see Table 3-1). The analyst can thus conclude that the observed relation is not spurious, at least with respect to mother's employment. (Following Lazarsfeld, we shall refer to the disappearance of a relation as *explanation* when the third variable is causally prior to the independent variable and as *interpretation* when the third variable intervenes between the independent and dependent variables.)

This, then, is the basic procedure for demonstrating causality: Starting with an association between a causally prior independent variable and a dependent variable, the analyst considers possible antecedent variables that might account for the observed relation. If he finds such a variable, he declares that the apparent causal relation is spurious, and he moves on to a different independent variable. If he fails to find the original relation spurious, he tentatively concludes that his independent variable is a cause of his dependent variable.

This conclusion must be tentative, for it is always possible that another antecedent variable may do what those already examined have not done. Logically, then, the demonstration of causality is never complete.[11] In practice, however, analysts become increasingly confident of their provisional causal interpretation as they fail to find it spurious.

## Noncausal Analysis

The reader familiar with delinquency research may find this account of causal analysis too austere. Surely there is more to analysis than association, causal order, and lack of spuriousness. We agree wholeheartedly; in the foregoing we have deliberately restricted ourselves to the elements of *causal* analysis, but there is indeed more to research than the demonstration of causality.

*Intervening variables.* One may think of research as a linking together of apparently different things. Thus the theorist frames propositions relating independent variables to dependent variables, and the empirical researcher shows how the indicators of these concepts are related (the two roles meet within a single person in the processes of conceptualization and operationalization). The theorist links concepts verbally; for example, Cohen ties status frustration to gang-delinquency through the mechanism of reaction formation, and Miller joins social class and delinquency through a system of values.[12] Gold advances the following three-variable hypothesis:

. . . the higher the quality of recreational and educational facilities, the more attractive the community will be to its youngsters, and consequently, the less likely they will be delinquent.[13]

In empirical research, there is a range of complexity in the demonstration of links between variables. At one extreme, the researcher, like the theorist, provides a conjectural link; he speculates about the intervening variable, but he does not look at the appropriate three-variable relation. At the other extreme, Blalock and Boudon have shown how to fit relatively complex mathematical models of causal linkages to empirical data.[14] Most analysts work between these two extremes, using three-variable tables to link an independent variable and a dependent variable. The statistical configuration of the three-variable table showing that $C$ links $A$ and $B$ is the same as that of the three-variable table used to show that $D$ makes the relation between $E$ and $F$ spurious. In both cases the original two-variable relation disappears in the three-variable table. The only difference is in the causal order of the independent variable and the additional variable: In demonstrating spuriousness the new variable is causally prior to the independent variable, but in demonstrating a causal link the new variable intervenes between the independent variable and the dependent variable.

Table 3-2, which was previously used to show that the relation between adequacy of supervision and delinquency did not disappear when the effects of an antecedent variable (mother's employment) were removed, can also be used to illustrate the disappearance of the relation between mother's employment and delinquency when the effects of an intervening variable (adequacy of supervision) are removed. In actual practice, of course, one would examine the three-variable relation of Table 3-2 for only one of these purposes, depending on which of the two-variable relations had appeared first, the relation between supervision and delinquency (Table 3-1) or the relation between mother's employment and delinquency.

It is necessary to construct this latter relation in order to show what happens when the effects of supervision are removed. This construction does not require returning to the punched cards. As indicated in Chapter 1, it is possible to construct this table from the data given in Table 3-2, and it is a useful exercise for the reader to do so. We shall outline the procedure here and leave the details to the reader:

1. Multiply the percentage in each column of Table 3-2 by the number of cases at the bottom of the column, to get the numerator of each percentage (e.g., in the first column, 31 percent of 442 is 137, the number of boys who were delinquent, suitably supervised, and sons of housewives).

2. Subtract these numbers from the figures at the bottoms of the columns to get the number in each column who were *not* delinquent (e.g., 442 − 137 = 305 boys who were non-delinquent, suitably supervised, and sons of housewives).

3. Combine figures from appropriate columns to get the number of delinquents whose mothers were housewives, the number of nondelinquents whose mothers were housewives, and so on (e.g., the number of delinquents whose mothers were housewives is the sum of 137 and the corresponding figure of 127 obtained in the same way in the second column of Table 3-2).

4. Compute the percentages for the table showing delinquency by mother's employment.

This undoubtedly seems more complicated than it is. We could easily have given the recomputed table, but we believe the reader will learn more by working it out for himself. A comparison of this recomputed table with Table 3-2 shows how a large association between mother's employment and delinquency essentially disappears when the effects of supervision are removed; in other words, supervision is the link between mother's employment and delinquency.

*Examining conditional relations.* The most common outcome of introducing a third variable into a two-variable relation is neither the persistence of the original relation, as in demonstrating lack of spuriousness, nor the vanishing of the relation, as in demonstrating spuriousness or showing a link between two variables; instead, the analyst finds that the new variable interacts with the original independent variable, so that the effects of the independent variable differ from one value of the new variable to another.

In Table 3-3 the proportion of delinquents rises as the strictness of the discipline exercised by the mother falls. It is almost automatic in such cases to ask whether the effect of discipline is the same for boys as for girls—in other words, to look at the three-variable relation in Table 3-4. In the left-hand half of Table 3-4 there is virtually no relation between discipline and delinquency among the boys, but in the right-hand half there is a larger relation among the girls than was true for the original relation in Table 3-3. This outcome, which Lazarsfeld has called *specification*, may lead the analyst to redefine his problem. Attempts to show how laxity of discipline by the mother produces delinquent behavior would henceforth be restricted to girls.

*Description of variation.* Locating intervening variables

and studying interaction are operations that grow out of causal analysis. Other operations may not involve causation at all. Even before examining the association of delinquency with some independent variable, the analyst may want to show how delinquency is distributed in his sample—say, how many are seriously delinquent, moderately delinquent, and not delinquent at all. He might do this, for example, in order to compare the rates of delinquency in his sample with those in other studies.

**Table 3-3—Delinquency by Strictness of Mother's Discipline***

|  | STRICTNESS OF DISCIPLINE | | |
|---|---|---|---|
|  | Strict | Fairly easy | Very easy |
| Percent delinquent | 25 | 30 | 37 |
| Number of cases | (220) | (332) | (195) |

* This table is adapted from F. Ivan Nye, *Family Relationships and Delinquent Behavior.* New York: Wiley, 1959, p. 82.

A table may have both dependent and independent variables and still serve a descriptive function rather than be part of a causal analysis. Thus an investigator may report arrest rates by sex and then go on to analyze the causes of delinquency in each sex separately, rather than try to show that sex is a cause of delinquency. In short, what determines whether a table serves a descriptive or an analytic purpose is not the nature of the variables included in it but what the analyst does with them.

**Table 3-4—Delinquency and Strictness of Mother's Discipline by Sex***

|  | Boys | | | Girls | | |
|---|---|---|---|---|---|---|
|  | STRICTNESS OF DISCIPLINE | | | | | |
|  | Strict | Fairly easy | Very easy | Strict | Fairly easy | Very easy |
| Percent delinquent | 32 | 32 | 38 | 18 | 27 | 37 |
| Number of cases | (104) | (158) | (97) | (116) | (174) | (98) |

* Source: same as for Table 3-3.

*Determination of meaning.* Finding out what variables mean is an important part of most empirical studies. Answers to questions on sex or age make sense to everyone, but answers to questions on social class or delinquency are something else. What meaning does one attach to empirical data that purport to measure these variables? The methodological problem here is the relation between a theoretical concept and its empirical indicator: how to operationalize a theoretical concept and how to conceptualize an empirical indicator. The statistical problems in these procedures may be fully as complex as those of causal analysis.

Causal analysis, then, is only part of the overall task of the empirical analyst. Depending on his interests and his data, it can become the major part of his work, or it can be reduced to nothing, as in descriptive accounts of life in delinquent gangs. Even in these studies, however, the idea of causal analysis is always implicit in the analyst's thinking, for what, after all, is the purpose of a description that does not lead to greater understanding of causal relations?

# Notes

1. Some of the general treatments of causal analysis that we have found most useful in our own research and teaching include: Herbert H. Hyman, *Survey Design and Analysis*. New York: The Free Press, 1955; Hans Zeisel, *Say It with Figures*. New York: Harper, 1957; W. Allen Wallis and Harry V. Roberts, *The Nature of Statistics*. New York: The Free Press, 1965; C. A. Moser, *Survey Methods in Social Investigation*. New York: Macmillan 1958; Claire Selltiz *et al.*, *Research Methods in Social Relations*. New York: Holt, Rinehart and Winston, 1959; Matilda White Riley, *Sociological Research*. New York: Harcourt, Brace & World, 1963.

2. On the meaning of such propositions, see Robert R. Brown, *Explanation in Social Science*. London: Routledge and Kegan Paul, 1963.

3. Our position is essentially Karl Popper's : that the task of science is to formulate universal propositions; that it is impossible to prove the truth of a universal proposition, but it is possible to disprove or "falsify" it; that the best strategy for a scientist is to formulate each proposition so that it will survive the most stringent tests he can devise; and that, when this proposition fails, he formulates a new proposition that passes all of the previous tests, and thus begins anew the cycle of "conjecture and refutation." Karl R. Popper, *The Logic of Scientific Discovery*. New

York: Basic Books, 1959. See also his *Conjectures and Refutations: The Growth of Scientific Knowledge*. New York: Basic Books, 1963.

4. *Op. cit.*, Chapters 5–7.

5. We are using *experiment* in the sense it has had among statisticians ever since the pioneering work of R. A. Fisher. See his *Design of Experiments*. New York: Hafner, 1953 (first published in 1935).

6. See Chapter 13 for a more extended treatment of statistical inference.

7. See Chapter 10.

8. Leo A. Goodman and William H. Kruskal, "Measures of association for cross classifications," *Journal of the American Statistical Association*, 49, 1954, pp. 732–764. See also Herbert Costner, "Criteria for measures of association," *American Sociological Review*, 30, 1965, pp. 341–353.

9. For a formal treatment of the intuitive notion of causal order, see Hubert M. Blalock, Jr., *Causal Inferences in Nonexperimental Research*. Chapel Hill: University of North Carolina Press, 1964.

10. Although it is almost always logically incorrect to speak of holding a variable constant, the usage is so common as to defy attempts to change it. The danger of this usage is that the analyst may believe the words rather than look at what he is actually doing. To divide boys into

**50**

two groups—say, those under twelve and those twelve or more—is not to hold age constant. A better statement is that age is held more nearly constant. A correct, if cumbersome formulation is: The relation between $X$ and $Y$ is reexamined in groups in which the variation of $X$ is reduced from what it was in the original relation. Since the purpose of such control is to remove the effects of the test factor, i.e., to produce a zero relation between the test factor and the independent variable, the possibility of spuriousness remains to the extent that there is residual variation in the test factor.

11. To avoid awkward constructions we shall often refer in the text to the demonstration of causality, but the reader should bear in mind the limitations of such demonstrations discussed here.

12. Albert K. Cohen, *Delinquent Boys*. New York: The Free Press, 1955. Walter B. Miller, "Lower class culture as a generating milieu of gang delinquency," *Journal of Social Issues*, 14, 1958, pp. 5–19.

13. Martin Gold, *Status Forces in Delinquent Boys*. Ann Arbor: Institute for Social Research, University of Michigan, 1963, p. 39.

14. Blalock, *op. cit.*, and Raymond Boudon, "A method of linear causal analysis: dependence analysis," *American Sociological Review*, 30, 1965, pp. 365–374.

# 4

# Causal

# Order

An investigator takes the first step toward demonstrating causality by showing that the independent and dependent variables are statistically associated. The most common way to do this is to construct a percentaged table, such as Table 4-1. In this table, 39 percent of the delinquents and 67 percent of the nondelinquents attend church regularly, a difference of 28 percentage points. This finding appears important and easy to understand; most religions emphasize proper behavior, and those who go to church should, therefore, behave better.

For this reason, perhaps, the Gluecks let the facts in this table speak for themselves:

As in the case of recreational activities, so in church attendance, no intensive exploration was made of the reasons for the lesser adherence to religious duties on the part of the delinquents. Our concern was only to ascertain the facts in regard to regularity of attendance.[1]

### Table 4-1—Delinquency by Church Attendance*

| Attendance | DELINQUENTS | | NONDELINQUENTS | |
| --- | --- | --- | --- | --- |
| | Number | Percent | Number | Percent |
| Regular | 193 | 39.3 | 334 | 67.1 |
| Occasional | 266 | 54.2 | 143 | 28.7 |
| None | 32 | 6.5 | 21 | 4.2 |
| Totals | 491 | 100.0 | 498 | 100.0 |

* This table is taken from Sheldon and Eleanor Glueck, *Unraveling Juvenile Delinquency.* p. 166.

What are the facts in this case? The Gluecks' table does show that delinquents are less likely than nondelinquents to attend church regularly. Facts, of course, may be meaningful or meaningless, important or trivial. The misleading simplicity of these facts becomes apparent when one asks why delinquents are less likely than nondelinquents to attend church regularly. Does this mean that attendance at religious services somehow protects a boy from becoming delinquent? Or does it mean that after a boy has become delinquent, he is less likely to attend church?

These questions stem from the second criterion for judging the claim that one variable causes another, the criterion of causal order.

A solution to the problem of causal order, at least in principle, is the longitudinal or panel study. In an ideal version of this design, the investigator would select a sample of infants and continually collect data on them until they became adults. The practical difficulties of panel studies are undoubtedly the major reason for their infrequent use in delinquency research. Nevertheless, any less than ideal panel study may fail to solve the problem of causal order. The researcher using this technique may neglect to gather appropriate data; he may fail to analyze his data properly; and he may conceptualize his variables in such a way that solutions to the problem are virtually impossible.

Despite the attacks on cross-sectional studies, they undoubtedly will continue to be a major tool of research in delinquency. The most obvious reason is that, compared to the panel study, they are fast and inexpensive. The longer the term of the panel study, the more the procedures, findings, and theories are those of an earlier period. To attempt to bring the research up to date in any of these areas is to risk losing the distinctive virtues of the panel study. Finally, there are several ways of solving the problem of causal order in cross-sectional studies, at least in part. For all these reasons, we shall devote our attention to the problems of causal order in cross-sectional studies only.

## Collecting and Analyzing the Data

*Collecting data.* In their study of five hundred delinquents and five hundred nondelinquents, the Gluecks fail to distinguish consistently between factors that preceded delinquency and those that may well have resulted from either delinquent acts or institutionalization. They find, for example, that 98.4 percent of the delinquents, as opposed to 7.4 percent of the nondelinquents, had delinquent friends. The Gluecks interpret this as showing that "birds of a feather flock together." Such a tendency, they say,

... is a much more fundamental fact in any analysis of causation than the theory that accidental differential association of non-delinquents with delinquents is the basic cause of crime.[2]

One implication of the "birds of a feather" proverb is that delinquents choose other delinquents as friends. If this is so, companionship follows delinquency and, therefore, cannot be its cause.[3] However, the simple fact of statistical association provides no basis for choosing between "birds of a feather" and differential association. Looking at the same table, Reckless thought he had found support for the hypothesis that companionship is "unquestionably the most telling force in male delinquency and crime."[4] If the differential association hypothesis is given as much support by these findings as is the "birds of a feather" hypothesis, there is an obvious need for additional information in choosing between them.

What kind of information would be required? Some years after the publication of *Unraveling*, the Gluecks explain why they rejected the differential association hypothesis:

It should be emphasized that throughout the work in analyzing the data of *Unraveling*, we insisted on the fundamental importance of *sequence in time*. That is why we ruled out gang membership (frequently emphasized as a cause of delinquency) and other influences which were found to have occurred long after definite proof of antisocial behavior. The onset of persistent misbehavior tendencies was at the early age of seven years or younger among 48 percent of our delinquents, and from eight to ten in an additional 39 percent; thus a total of almost nine-tenths of the entire group showed clear delinquent tendencies before the time when boys generally become members of organized boys' gangs.[5]

Reckless agrees that the kind of data mentioned by the Gluecks would support their rejection of the differential association hypothesis, but he asserts that they do not have such data:

Actually, the Gluecks had no justification for excluding companionship on the basis of their evidence, because they did not show that most of the boys who got into trouble before eight or eleven years of age were lone-wolf offenders and were not with companions at the time.[6]

The Gluecks believe that the delinquents in their sample did not belong to gangs or have delinquent friends until some time after they became delinquents. Data supporting the Gluecks' belief would be a serious blow to the differential association hypothesis. Could the Gluecks have gathered such data? The following excerpt from a case history published by the Gluecks in 1956 shows that they could have (and perhaps even that they did):

Frankie, from his earliest years, has run unbridled in the streets, usually rather far from his home. When only five he began to indulge in destructive play *with a companion somewhat older than himself*, largely breaking windows 'for excitement.' At six he started to truant from school *with another boy.* . . . At other times he and *his special pal* would 'hop' on street cars. . . .

Frankie further recalls that when he was six years old he 'swiped' four wheels from a baby carriage parked near his house. This he did in the company of *another boy who was older than himself and already a confirmed delinquent.*

Frankie soon became adept at stealing toy popguns from the variety stores for the use of *his 'gang,'* . . .

At about the age of six Frankie was introduced *by a somewhat older boy* to sex play with other boys. . . .

In frequent truck-hopping expeditions, *always in the company of another boy,* he would steal chocolates, pickles. . . . This soon extended to 'clipping' sweets from candy shops, a practice in which his gang indulged. . . . It was not long before Frankie . . . *with one of his older companions* began to steal from parked automobiles any objects that appealed to him. *At this time he was barely eight.*[7]

If this case is typical, it suggests that differential association—in fact, indoctrination—could be a crucial variable in the causation of delinquency. Our concern, however, is not to use the case of Frankie against the "birds of a feather" hypothesis, but to show how the Gluecks could have gathered (and perhaps did gather) information relevant to this controversy. If Frankie was able to recall his earliest delinquencies, the presence or absence of friends, and whether they were older or younger, there is reason to think that the other delinquents and even their parents could have provided such data on causal order.

In fact, the parents of the delinquents appear to hold the differential association view. The Gluecks, however, treated the parents' responses as data on themselves rather than as information about the boy.[8]

Another indication of the lesser concern of the parents of the delinquents is found in the reasons which they gave for the misconduct of their boys. Half of them (48.8%) were insistent that the boy's misconduct was the result of the influence of bad companions. . . .[9]

*Analytical Solutions.* Analytical solutions to the problem of causal order become particularly important when delinquency may be a cause as well as an effect. The mere fact of arrest, or adjudication is often thought to produce differences between delinquents and nondelinquents that were not present prior to the official action. As late as 1959 a thoughtful student of the subject could remark:

. . . we still remain obstinately blind to the fact that the one distinctive factor in the offender's experience is the way in which he has been treated by an outraged community; and that this experience, no less than an inherent predisposition to delinquency, may well account for any peculiarities that he does manifest.[10]

One of the first reviews of *Unraveling Juvenile Delinquency* attacks the Gluecks for their failure to consider this problem.

The most elementary caution in criminological research is the recognition that an examination of institutionalized offenders (or delinquents) will provide information about *institutionalized offenders* and *not* about offenders in general. An institutionalized offender is characteristically, in great part, an institution product.[11]

Sheldon Glueck responds vigorously to this criticism:

Our boys spent, on the average, 7.12 months in correctional institutions, 61.8 percent having been there less than six months. . . . By contrast, they had had an average of 10.84 months on probation, over half of them six or more months. . . . The institutions to which they were committed are open industrial schools with a regime of education, athletics, recreation, religious guidance, etc. No lockstep and bars are involved. Surely nobody with even an elementary firsthand knowledge of psychology or the conditioning of delinquent attitudes and behavior could seriously claim that the brief stay in such an institution would crucially overbalance all the other experiences of a young lifetime gained in the home, school, and community! We solemnly assure this critic [Rubin] that our delinquent lads did not have the 'prison pallor,' did not talk out of the corner of the mouth, did not glance apprehensively over the shoulder.[12]

As Glueck points out in this reply to the critics of *Unraveling*,[13] much of their data concerns factors that could not easily have been affected by the institutionalization of the delinquents. However, it is likely that Wootton and Rubin (among others)[14] are unconvinced by this argument, and the Gluecks themselves suggest that some variables could have been affected by institutionalization.[15]

There are several ways that this question could have been answered (and could be answered even now). Rubin suggests comparing institutional and noninstitutional delinquents with nondelinquents.[16] Although this comparison undoubtedly would answer questions about the relative effects of institutionalization, such a comparison is obviously beyond the scope of the data collected by the Gluecks. With the data they did collect, however, the question could be partially answered. The Gluecks have data on the time each delinquent boy had spent in correctional institutions prior to their measurement of his characteristics.[17] If institutionalization has an effect on certain personality or physiological characteristics of delinquents, the strength of this effect should vary with the length of time spent in an institution.[18] They could, therefore, refute or confirm the critics' arguments, at least in part, by a simple analysis of their own data.

Similar problems of causal order may exist in studies of boys who have had no contact with the police. Nye asked a sample of high school students to report the number of times they had committed certain delinquent acts "since beginning grade school."[19] Delinquent acts committed by high school students in the past may have affected their later relations with others, as Nye occasionally indicates. He finds that "respect for the judgment of the adolescent [on the part of the mother] is . . . related to delinquent behavior in both sexes." In this case the ambiguity of the causal order of the variables is apparent, and Nye concludes: "We are reluctant, however, to assign a causal relationship because it is probable that the respect of the parent is affected by delinquent behavior."[20]

Nye's problem of causal order is not limited to those relations in which it is easy to see that delinquency may have been the independent variable. Since the delinquent acts reported by his respondents may have been committed some time prior to their measurement, this problem applies to many of the relations reported. For example, Nye found that boys with favorable attitudes toward their fathers' appearance had committed fewer delinquent acts than those with unfavorable attitudes. Since it is difficult to see how delinquent acts could have affected attitudes toward parental appearance, delinquent behavior must somehow be a consequence of attitudes toward the appearance of the father. In order for this to be true, attitudes toward father's appearance must precede commission of delinquent acts. If a delinquent act took place several years prior to the measurement of the attitude, then the boy must have had his present attitude before he committed the delinquent act.

A counter argument might be that a ten-year-old boy does not notice whether his father's clothing is appropriate to the occasion or whether his nails and hair are clean. Indeed, attitudes toward parental appearance may well change rapidly during the high-school period. Now, if any of these contentions is true, Nye's independent variables would follow his dependent variable in time. If so, they cannot be its cause.[21]

In brief, assertions of a causal relation on the basis of an association between two variables are unconvincing unless the investigator faces the problem of causal order, preferably before collecting his data. If there is doubt on the matter (and there almost always will be doubt), the investigator can include the questions necessary to resolve the doubt. Thus the influence of companions on delinquent behavior can usually be measured more meaningfully by asking questions about past associations, rather than by determining current friendships, as Short has shown.[22] Once the data are collected, awareness of this problem should alert the analyst to possible ambiguity and stimulate a search for evidence.

## Conceptualization and Measurement

Thus far we have treated the problem of causal order as empirical, taking the onset of delinquency as a fact to be determined from such data as police records or the recollections of parents. Actually, of course, the point at which a child becomes a delinquent depends on the definition of delinquency one is using. Unless the conceptual issues surrounding the problem of causal order are settled, it may be difficult to determine which causal sequence is supported by the evidence. This difficulty is especially clear in the debate over the significance of the Gluecks' finding that gang membership and delinquency are strongly related. Consider the definition of delinquency used by the Gluecks:

For the purposes of the present study . . . delinquency refers to repeated acts of a kind which when committed by persons beyond the statutory juvenile court age of sixteen are punishable as crimes (either felonies or misdemeanors)—except for a few instances of persistent stubbornness, truancy, running away, associating with immoral persons, and the like. Children who once or twice during the period of growing up . . . steal a toy in a ten-cent store, sneak into a subway or motion picture theatre, play hooky, and the like and soon outgrow such peccadilloes are not true delinquents even though they have violated the law. Indeed it is now recognized that a certain amount of petty pilfering occurs among many children around the age of six or seven and is to be expected as part of the process of trying their wings.[23]

This appears to be a thoughtful and reasonably precise definition of delinquency; from the standpoint of causal order, however, it is ambiguous. The demonstration of this ambiguity requires some careful following of the Gluecks' reasoning. Consider again their arguments against gang membership as a cause of delinquency:

The *onset* of *persistent* misbehavior tendencies was at the early age of seven years or younger among 48 percent of our delinquents, and from eight to ten in an additional 39 percent; thus a total of almost nine-tenths of the entire group showed clear delinquent tendencies before the time when boys generally become members of organized boys' gangs.[24]

. . . over half of the boys who were delinquent became members of gangs, while only three of the lads who remained nondelinquent joined gangs. . . . However, by and large, they were maladjusted and delinquent children long before they were gang members. Gang membership may have multiplied their antisocial activities; it rarely *originated persistent* delinquency.[25]

Delinquency is defined as "repeated acts" or "persistent misbehavior tendencies"; our question is, then, when do repeated acts or persistent misbehavior tendencies begin? The Gluecks implicitly answer this question by pointing to the first delinquent acts. But are the first delinquent acts the beginning of persistent delinquency? The answer is No, since persistence is not defined by the first delinquent acts, but by acts that occur at a later, somewhat indeterminate point.

To illustrate this argument, suppose that the following data were available on five boys whose histories of delinquency were similar to those of the Gluecks' boys:

**Table 4-2—Identifying the Persistent Delinquent: Delinquent Acts by Age (hypothetical)**

| BOYS | 5 | 6 | 7 | 8 | 9 | 10 | 11 | 12 | 13 | 14 | 15 | 16 | CLASSIFICATION |
|------|---|---|---|---|---|----|----|----|----|----|----|----|----------------|
| A | | x | x | x | | | | | | | | | Nondelinquent |
| B | | x | x | | | | x | | | | | | Nondelinquent |
| C | x | | x | | x | | | | | | | | Nondelinquent |
| D | | x | x | x | x | x | x | x | x | x | x | x | Persistent delinquent |
| E | | | x | x | x | x | | x | x | x | x | x | Persistent delinquent |

x = delinquent act(s)

When did the "delinquents" become delinquent? According to the Gluecks' argument, the "onset" of delinquency for D was at age six and for E at seven. But the crucial difference between A, B, and C, on the one hand, and D and E, on the other, is that D and E continue to commit delinquent acts while A, B, and C do not, a difference that does not appear until some years after the "onset" of D's and E's delinquency. The early delinquent acts of A, B, and C presumably have the same causes as those of D and E. Therefore, it is a necessary consequence of the Gluecks' definition that the important differences between the delinquents and the nondelinquents may appear after the onset of delinquent acts.

The Gluecks' argument against the gang membership hypothesis thus requires a subtle shift in their definition of delinquency. The definition with which they begin—"persistent misbehavior"—is not the definition on the basis of which they reject gang membership as a cause of delinquency.

Although it simplifies the gathering of data on causal order, the Gluecks' second definition introduces many theoretical and practical difficulties. If nothing can affect delinquency after its onset, then delinquency implicitly is being defined as an immutable characteristic of the person. Among other things, this suggests that efforts to cure delinquency are hopeless; it also denies the reality of maturational reform, a fact and a problem of great importance.[26]

In short, then, the theoretical definition of delinquency with which the Gluecks begin their study does not require that all causes of delinquency exist prior to the commission of the first delinquent act. It requires only that causes exist prior to the act in question, whether this act be the first or the twenty-first. And the Gluecks' argument that delinquency precedes gang membership, so reluctantly accepted by Reckless, turns out to be invalid.

In studies that rely on self-reports of delinquent acts to determine who is a delinquent, the problems of causal order are likewise as much conceptual as empirical, although they differ from those of studies using official classifications. The investigator using official records usually treats delinquency as a dichotomous attribute: If a boy has been convicted of a crime, he is a delinquent; if he has not been convicted of a crime, he is not a delinquent. The investigator using self-reported acts usually treats delinquency as an ordinal variable: Boys are rated as more or less delinquent, depending on the number and nature of the acts they report. But how is this rating made? How is the investigator to determine whether stealing candy is more or less delinquent than the combination of being insolent to a teacher and playing hooky?

The most common answer to these questions is to combine the various acts into a Guttman scale.[27] If the items conform reasonably well to the scale criteria, the investigator can take them as measuring a single dimension of delinquency.[28] To illustrate these ideas, consider three delinquent acts:

1. Have you ever taken little things (worth less than $2) that did not belong to you?
2. Have you ever taken things of moderate value (between $2 and $50)?
3. Have you ever taken things of large value (over $50)?

For these items to form a Guttman scale, the results would have to look something like those in Table 4-3.

### Table 4-3—Three Delinquent Acts Forming a Perfect Guttman Scale (hypothetical)

| Have you ever taken | BOYS | | | | | | | | | |
|---|---|---|---|---|---|---|---|---|---|---|
| | 1 | 2 | 3 | 4 | 5 | 6 | 7 | 8 | 9 | 10 |
| Things of large value | x | x | | | | | | | | |
| Things of moderate value | x | x | x | x | | | | | | |
| Things of little value | x | x | x | x | x | x | x | x | | |

x = Yes

In other words, in order for a set of delinquency items to form a Guttman scale, a boy committing one of the more serious delinquent acts must also have committed all of the less serious (or more common) acts below it in the scale. That is, boys who have stolen things of large value must also have stolen things of moderate value and of little value.

This suggests that delinquent acts will form a Guttman scale only if the period of time during which the acts may have been committed is relatively long. If the time is limited to, say, one year, those who have committed the more serious acts may not have committed the less serious ones during the same period, and the acts will not form a Guttman scale. It seems to us, therefore, that a researcher using the Guttman technique to scale delinquency items is virtually forced to place no limit on the period of time during which the acts may have been committed. He must, therefore, rate a boy who has committed five types of delinquent acts as more delinquent than a boy who has committed three types of acts, regardless of when the acts were committed. This may be grossly misleading. Suppose the boy with three delinquent acts committed all of them within the preceding year, while the boy with five delinquent acts committed none in that period. At the time of the study, which boy is more delinquent?

This greater validity of measurement is only one of several advantages to be gained by restricting the time period and thereby abandoning Guttman scaling.[29] If the investigator knows when the delinquent acts took place, the causal order problem becomes tractable in a sense that it can never be when the delinquent acts could have occurred at any time in the past. For those independent variables that represent abrupt changes of state (e.g., parents' divorce, dropping out of school), the problem is solved; for those independent variables whose occurrence cannot be fixed precisely (e.g., attitudes toward parents, perceptions of school), it is more persuasive to argue that they are causes if their effects (delinquency) have occurred in the very recent past. Still another advantage of restricting the time period is that it should be easier for the respondent to recall his more recent delinquencies.[30] It seems to us that for both pragmatic and theoretical reasons the boy with three acts in the preceding year should be considered more delinquent. The statistical associations between many independent variables and delinquency should be stronger when it is defined by acts more recent and more concentrated in time. Even if the associations are not stronger, the chain of inference from independent variables to dependent variables based on recollected acts will be shorter. It makes more sense to try to explain recent acts alone than to combine them with acts scattered through many years, even if the recent acts do not form a Guttman scale.

## Developmental Models and Multivariate Analysis

Many theories of deviant behavior and delinquency suggest a sequence of steps through which the person moves from law-abiding behavior to embezzlement, marihuana use, or delinquency. These theories do not derive from survey data nor have they been systematically tested on such data. That this gap is no accident is suggested in a recent statement by Howard S. Becker, which deserves special notice here, both because he has created important developmental theories from observational studies and because his work is likely to come to the attention of students of delinquency.

Multivariate analysis assumes (even though its users may in fact know better) that all the factors which operate to produce the phenomenon under study operate simultaneously. It seeks to discover which variable or what combination of variables will best 'predict' the behavior one is studying. Thus, a study of juvenile delinquency may attempt to discover whether it is the intelligence quotient, the area in which a child lives, whether or not he comes from a broken home, or a combination of these factors that accounts for his being delinquent.

But, in fact, all causes do not operate at the same time, and we need a model which takes into account the fact that patterns of behavior *develop* in orderly sequence. . . .[31]

Although it is true that the quantitative researcher attempting to account for a behavioral outcome is likely to reach erroneous conclusions about the importance of variables unless he remembers that variables important at one stage may be unimportant at others,[32] multivariate procedures are not limited to the kind of prediction that Becker describes. Multivariate analysis can, indeed, discriminate between variables operating at different points in a developmental sequence. In order to illustrate this argument, we shall hypothetically quantify Becker's study, "Becoming a Marijuana User."[33]

Becker lists three steps that appear to be necessary conditions for the use of marijuana:

No one becomes a user . . . without (1) learning to smoke the drug in a way which will produce real effects; (2) learning to recognize the effects and connect them with drug use (learning, in other words, to get high); and (3) learning to enjoy the sensations he perceives.[34]

If an investigator had quantitative data that allowed him to relate these variables to marijuana use, would he be forced to assume that all three operate simultaneously? Insofar as Becker's theory is correct (that is, insofar as step 2 presupposes 1 and step 3 presupposes steps 1 and 2), it would not only be possible for the researcher to assume a developmental sequence; the quantitative data should actually reflect this sequence. Becker's discussion suggests the following kinds of relations between these variables and marijuana use (within a sample of persons who have smoked marijuana):

|  | (1) Experience effects? | | (2) Recognize effects? | | (3) Enjoy effects? | |
|---|---|---|---|---|---|---|
|  | YES Percent | NO Percent | YES Percent | NO Percent | YES Percent | NO Percent |
| Users | 50 (100) | 0 (100) | 75 (67) | 0 (133) | 95 (53) | 0 (147) |

As is always true in such a developmental sequence, the nearer a variable is to the dependent variable, the stronger its relation to the dependent variable. Furthermore, the independent variables exert their effects on the dependent variable entirely through the intervening variables; they have no direct effect. In other words, the relation of step 1 to marijuana use should be weaker than the relation of step 3, and the relation between step 1 and marijuana use should disappear when step 3 is held constant. Thus, not only should the quantitative data reflect the sequence Becker assumes, they should invalidate the assumption that all three of these variables operate simultaneously to produce the use of marijuana.

To be sure, Becker may be saying something about quantitative data and multivariate analysis that our example ignores: that it is easy to miss such sequences, to assume because a variable is unrelated to the dependent variable when other variables are controlled that it is unimportant as a cause of the dependent variable. We have tried to show that multivariate analysis can handle the kind of theory Becker advocates; we have not argued that multivariate analysis automatically makes assumptions consistent with this kind of theory: It does not. But neither does it force the investigator to assume anything he does not wish to assume. If multivariate analysis is a poor means of generating developmental models, it is, nevertheless, an excellent means of expressing and testing them.

## The "Indefinite Amusement" of the Critic

One could amuse oneself indefinitely by seeing how many of the causal explanations of delinquency, or of the typical aberrations of problem families, or of illegitimacy or of other social deviations can thus be reversed.[35]

Nothing, we suspect, is more infuriating to the researcher than the earnest reversal of what to him are perfectly reasonable assumptions about causal order. Although we have relied somewhat upon this master-key of the critic, our sympathies and, it should be noted, a great deal of evidence are often on the side of the empirical investigator. There are several panel studies of delinquency in which causal order is not a serious problem.[36] The results of these studies are, in our opinion, reasonably congruent with many studies in which causal order is a problem. One implication of this congruence is that the findings of many cross-sectional studies of delinquency would not be appreciably altered by evidence on causal order; another implication is that those studies fortunate enough to avoid the problem can lend support to less fortunate studies.

The point here, of course, is not that the researcher's opinion is as good as the critic's or that too much has been made of the problem of causal order. As at least one of the examples discussed earlier makes clear, conclusions of considerable theoretical importance often depend upon highly debatable assumptions about causal order. Like measurement error, however, causal order is seldom a problem that the investigator can solve completely—and, also like measurement error, it is a problem that should be faced. If it is an error to ignore causal order as a possible source of mistaken inferences, it is equally wrong to let some uncertainties about causal order preclude causal inferences.

# Notes

1. Sheldon and Eleanor Glueck, *Unraveling Juvenile Delinquency.* Cambridge: Harvard University Press, 1950, p. 167.
2. *Ibid.*, p. 164.
3. Like most proverbs, this one is ambiguous. Another possible implication is that the relation between delinquent companions and delinquency is not causal in either direction. At times the Gluecks seem to suggest that some antecedent variable (e.g., "a craving for excitement and adventure") accounts for both delinquency and delinquent companions: "After advancing association with other criminals as a fundamental theory of crime causation, a leading American criminologist [E. H. Sutherland] disposes of the basic problem by saying: 'It is not necessary, at this level of explanation, to explain why a person has the associations he has; this certainly involves a complex of many things.' . . . But this 'complex of many things' may well be the essence of the problem." *Ibid.*, p. 168. Given the magnitude of the relations between delinquency and delinquent companions reported in the Gluecks' study, however, it is unlikely that they could show this relation to be spurious.
4. Walter C. Reckless, *The Crime Problem.* New York: Appleton-Century-Crofts, 1955, p. 77. Reckless may have relied on other data in addition to delinquency of companions.

The Gluecks also present data on gang membership and the age and sex of companions. *Unraveling*, p. 163. In the third edition of his book, published in 1961, Reckless revises the section on the Gluecks' findings and refers to their discussions of causal order published after *Unraveling. Ibid.*, (3rd ed.), pp. 255–258, 311–314.
5. Sheldon Glueck, "Ten years of *Unraveling Juvenile Delinquency*, an examination of criticisms," *The Journal of Criminal Law, Criminology and Police Science*, 51, 1960, p. 296. (Italics in original)
6. Reckless, *op. cit.*, 3rd ed., p. 258.
7. Sheldon and Eleanor Glueck, *Delinquents in the Making.* New York: Harper and Brothers, 1952, pp. 35–36. (All italics except the last added by the authors.)
8. That is, the Gluecks treat the parents' responses as indicators of assumed underlying variables and ignore their face content. Interest shifts from what is said to why it is said.
9. Glueck and Glueck, *Unraveling*, p. 130.
10. Barbara Wootton, *Social Science and Social Pathology.* New York: Macmillan, 1959, p. 306.
11. Sol Rubin, *"Unraveling Juvenile Delinquency.* I. Illusions in a research project using matched pairs," *American Journal of Sociology*, 57, 1951, pp. 108–109.

12. S. Glueck, "Ten years of *Unraveling Juvenile Delinquency*," p. 288.

13. *Ibid.*

14. E.g., Alfred J. Kahn, "Analysis of methodology," in David G. French, *An Approach to Measuring Results in Social Work*. New York: Columbia University Press, 1952, p. 168.

15. "[Physical] defects are found to be present in significantly lower proportion among the delinquents than among the nondelinquents. . . . Also, a lesser number of the delinquents have remediable defects. This can be largely, perhaps entirely, explained by the fact that they have already had the benefit of medical attention in correctional institutions." *Unraveling*, p. 180. Although this is not a serious concession on the Gluecks' part, it does suggest how the direction of association may affect assumptions about causal order.

16. *Op. cit.*, p. 109.

17. *Unraveling*, Table A-10, p. 296.

18. For further discussion of this and other methods of determining causal order, see Herbert H. Hyman, *Survey Design and Analysis*. New York: The Free Press, 1955, pp. 193–226.

19. F. Ivan Nye, *Family Relationships and Delinquent Behavior*. New York: Wiley, 1958, p. 12. Nye's argument that the problem of causal order is not as serious in studies of self-reported delinquency is persuasive: "By studying *delinquent behavior* in a non-institutional population rather than official delinquents, this problem is minimized rather than eliminated because delinquent acts or a 'bad reputation' may, to some extent, affect attitudes toward the child and relationships within and outside the family. These will, however, generally be minor compared with those of an adolescent officially and generally branded 'a delinquent.' Much delinquent behavior is undiscovered and therefore does not directly affect the attitudes of others toward the adolescent." *Ibid.*, p. viii.

20. *Ibid.*, p. 97.

21. Nye discusses attitude toward parental appearance as a variable intervening between socioeconomic status and delinquency. *Ibid.*, p. 112. If this three-variable configuration is assumed, the causal order problem becomes less serious, since socioeconomic status should ordinarily not have changed much in a few years. However, Nye's references to socioeconomic status illustrate a common problem in quantitative research: how to avoid the use of words the data have eliminated from the dictionary. Since socioeconomic status is unrelated to delinquency in Nye's sample, it cannot be used to clarify observed relations between independent variables and delinquency, unless, of course, this clarification is rather complex, as Nye's is not.

22. James F. Short, Jr., "Differential association and delinquency," *Social Problems*, 4, 1957, pp. 233–239.

23. *Unraveling*, p. 13.

24. "Ten years of *Unraveling Juvenile Delinquency*," p. 296. (Authors' italics)

25. *Delinquents in the Making*, p. 89. (Authors' italics)

26. The Gluecks themselves have, of course, contributed greatly to the literature on maturational reform. For a summary and critique of this literature, see Wootton, *op. cit.*, Chapter V. The ability of many sociological theories to handle maturational reform has recently been questioned by David Matza. See his *Delinquency and Drift*. New York: Wiley, 1964,

pp. 21–27. A theory that confronts this problem may be found in Scott Briar and Irving Piliavin, "Delinquency, situational inducements, and commitment to conformity," *Social Problems*, 13, 1965, pp. 35–45.

27. A brief account of Guttman scaling is contained in Matilda White Riley, *Sociological Research, Vol. I: A Case Approach*. New York: Harcourt, Brace & World, 1963, pp. 470–478.

28. Scott was able to divide his pool of items to form two distinct scales, each measuring a different kind of theft. Arnold used a more varied pool of items to construct scales measuring vandalism, theft, and attacks against people. See John Finley Scott, "Two dimensions of delinquent behavior," *American Sociological Review*, 24, 1959, pp. 240–243; and William R. Arnold, "Continuities in research: scaling delinquent behavior," *Social Problems*, 13, 1965, pp. 59–66. The other two studies using Guttman scaling that we have examined are Nye, *op. cit.* (a fuller account is in F. Ivan Nye and James F. Short, Jr., "Scaling delinquent behavior," *American Sociological Review*, 22, 1957, pp. 326–331), and Robert A. Dentler and Lawrence J. Monroe, "Social correlates of early adolescent theft," *American Sociological Review*, 26, 1961, pp. 733–743.

29. Scaling is discussed further in Chapter 12.

30. Restricting the time period during which the delinquent acts may have taken place may control for, or, at least, allow study of, the effects of age. See John P. Clark and Eugene P. Wenniger, "Socio-economic class and area as correlates of illegal behavior among juveniles," *American Sociological Review*, 27, 1962, pp. 826–834, and our discussion of age in Chapter 5.

31. Howard S. Becker, *Outsiders*. New York: The Free Press, 1963, pp. 22–23. Our discussion focuses largely on Becker's statement about multivariate analysis and not on his argument for developmental or sequential models. For discussions of these models, see, for example, William S. Robinson, "The logical structure of analytic induction," *American Sociological Review*, 16, 1951, pp. 812–818; Neil J. Smelser, *Theory of Collective Behavior*. New York: The Free Press, 1963, pp. 12–21. A recent example of a theory constructed explicitly on the model proposed by Becker may be found in a paper by John F. Lofland and Rodney Stark, "Becoming a world saver: a theory of conversion to a deviant perspective," *American Sociological Review*, 30, 1965, pp. 862–875.

32. For example, social origins are important in determining whether a student completes high school and enters college. Therefore, in the general population, social origins will be found to be an important correlate of becoming a college professor. At a later stage of the process, however, say at the completion of graduate school, the decision to enter college teaching may be little affected by social origins.

33. Becker, *Outsiders*, pp. 41–58.

34. *Ibid.*, p. 58.

35. Wootton, *op. cit.*, p. 324.

36. William McCord and Joan McCord, *Origins of Crime*. New York: Columbia University Press, 1959. Jackson Toby and Marcia L. Toby, *Low School Status as a Predisposing Factor in Subcultural Delinquency*. New Brunswick, New Jersey: Rutgers University, about 1962. (Mimeo)

# 5

# Genuine
# and
# Spurious
# Relations

An appreciable association between two variables, A and B, together with evidence that A is causally prior to B, suggests that A is a cause of B. To demonstrate that A is causally related to B, however, it is necessary to establish that the relation between the two variables is not a result of their common relations to other causally prior (antecedent) variables. Consider again the association between church attendance and delinquency, but this time with the hypothetical data of Table 5-1[1], and assume that the analyst has evidence that church attendance is causally prior to delinquency. If he wishes to demonstrate that church attendance and delinquency are causally related, he must show that their relation to each other is not a result of their common relation to some antecedent variable, such as age. Now suppose that age is related to delinquency (older boys are more likely to be delinquents) and to church attendance (older boys are less likely to attend church). These relations with age may produce a relation between church attendance

### Table 5-1—Delinquency by Church Attendance (hypothetical)

| | CHURCH ATTENDANCE | |
|---|---|---|
| | Regular or often percent | Seldom or never percent |
| Delinquent | 44 | 56 |
| Nondelinquent | 56 | 44 |
| | 100 | 100 |
| | (150) | (150) |

and delinquency like that in Table 5-1, even if there is no relation between church attendance and delinquency among boys of the same age. The analyst meets this contingency by examining the relation between church attendance and delinquency within groups of boys homogeneous in age—that is, by "holding age constant."[2] When age accounts for the observed relation between church attendance and delinquency, the table he constructs to examine this relation will look like Table 5-2.

### Table 5-2—Delinquency by Church Attendance and Age (hypothetical)

| | 14 OR YOUNGER | | 15 OR OLDER | |
|---|---|---|---|---|
| Church attendance: | Regular or often percent | Seldom or never percent | Regular or often percent | Seldom or never percent |
| Delinquent | 33 | 34 | 66 | 67 |
| Nondelinquent | 67 | 66 | 34 | 33 |
| | 100 | 100 | 100 | 100 |
| | (100) | (50) | (50) | (100) |

This table illustrates the disappearance of an original relation (Table 5-1) when it is examined within categories of a third variable. In this case the third variable is causally prior to the independent variable, and the analyst will thus conclude that the apparent meaning of the original relation is spurious. The relation between church attendance and delinquency has been explained away as the result of the associations between age and church attendance, on the one hand,

and between age and delinquency on the other; since the original relation disappears in groups formed according to the values of an antecedent variable, it cannot be considered a causal relation.

All too often, however, the delinquency researcher ignores antecedent variables. He picks up a two-variable table, tests it for statistical significance, adds it to the "findings" he has collected, and moves on to the next two-variable table. In so doing, he may present tables that suggest causal relations when he could have demonstrated that no such relation exists.[3]

In a widely cited study, Reiss reports that "delinquents with weak ego controls are significantly younger" than are either "relatively integrated" or "defective superego" delinquents.[4] Because the weak-ego delinquents are younger than the other types of delinquents and because of the known correlates of age, one would expect to find that

1. Fewer of the weak-ego delinquents would have left school.
2. Fewer would be employed, either full-time or part-time.
3. More of them would still be in grade school.
4. More would have parents who are living together.
5. More would come from large families.
6. Fewer would have delinquent siblings.
7. Fewer would belong to a gang.
8. Fewer would have foreign-born parents.

These are, in fact, some of Reiss's findings. The point here is that an antecedent variable known to be related to the dependent variable and almost certainly related to many of the independent variables has been left free to vary. Unless this variable is held relatively constant, one cannot know whether the "social correlates of psychological types of delinquency" that Reiss discovered are causally related to the delinquent types or whether these relations are causally spurious. The observed differences may be simply a result of differences in

age among the three groups. Reiss notes the possible importance of age. Thus he says that the differences in the proportions enrolled in elementary grades "are in part accounted for
by differences in age."[5] Elsewhere Reiss suggests that a variable
other than age may account for an observed difference:

Although delinquents with relatively integrated and defective
super-ego controls attend school in about equal proportions, a
significantly larger proportion of delinquents with defective super-
ego controls are enrolled in primary grades. This difference is not
primarily due to differences in age between the two groups. Rather,
it represents greater educational retardation of the delinquents
with defective super-ego controls.[6]

In fact, however, Reiss's table shows that fewer of those with
defective superego controls are retarded (30.2 percent as
against 32.0 percent "retarded over one year"). The point is
not that there may be a typographical error in the table or
that Reiss may have inadvertently misread his figures. It is
again a question of analytic strategy: Unless relations are
examined within categories of antecedent variables, there is no
way to determine which antecedent variable accounts for an
observed difference, or, in fact, whether the relation is genuine
or spurious.

Problems of causal order may complicate the task of determining the meaning of an observed relation. Thus when
Reiss found that progress in school and residential mobility
both affect delinquency, he should have examined the appropriate three-variable table in order to clarify the causal structure of his variables. Since we do not have the data to construct this table we shall assume, for the sake of illustration,
that the relation between progress in school and delinquency
disappears when it is examined separately for those boys whose
families have moved in the past five years and those whose
families have not moved. Is this a case of explanation or of
interpretation? It is explanation if boys are more likely to fail

in school as a result of having moved, but it is interpretation if a boy's parents decide to move because he is having trouble in school. Dealing with problems like this requires data that Reiss did not have—data, for example like that in Rossi's study of residential mobility.[7] This lack of data, however, is not sufficient reason for failing to examine three-variable relations, for only by looking at such relations will the necessity for additional data become clear.

The effects of antecedent variables that stem from the research procedures themselves, rather than from the nature of the phenomenon being investigated, are called *contamination*.[8] Recognizing possible contamination in his study may have led Reiss to conclude that he could not justify a causal analysis:

> The research is not designed to discover the direction of causation since experimental controls were not introduced in making the psychiatric judgments. It seems . . . reasonable to assume in some instances that the psychiatrist may have isolated the several types by using the social correlates as a basis of judgment. . . .[9]

To the extent that the last statement is true, causal analysis would be meaningless (Reiss would be examining a relation between two measures of the same thing).

Inability to solve one kind of problem, however, should not lead to neglect of other problems that can be solved. Whether or not the psychiatric judgments were in part based on the social correlates, the question of causal order between personality types and their correlates is worth examining. With some of the correlates it would make sense to treat personality type as the independent variable—for example, to assume that it precedes truancy. In other comparisons, personality type is obviously a dependent variable—for example, the nativity of the father precedes the son's personality. The direction of causation is clear in many of the relations Reiss presents; however, even complete inability to determine causal

**77**

order would not have justified his failure to control antecedent variables. The direction of causation in the original relation may be uncertain, but failure to control known antecedent variables makes the fact of causation uncertain.

On the whole, delinquency researchers have been more sensitive to antecedent variables in the design stage of research than in the analysis. Thus several studies report eliminating the effects of age by matching pairs of individuals in the experimental and control groups, and by other means.[10]

Paying attention to some antecedent variables in the design of the study, however, does not lessen the importance of considering others in the analysis. The Gluecks went to some pains to match their delinquents and nondelinquents, individual by individual, in assembling their sample: for every delinquent of a given age, ethnicity, neighborhood, and intelligence, there was a nondelinquent with the same pattern of characteristics.[11] They did not, however, carry this concern into their analysis.

The Gluecks present their data in dozens of two-variable tables, in which delinquents are compared with nondelinquents. Many of these tables show strong relations between the independent variable and delinquency. On some occasions, it is evident that an independent variable shown in one table may be strongly related to an independent variable shown in another table. The question thus arises, Are these variables independent causes of delinquency, or is the relation of one of them to delinquency a spurious result of its relation to the other? This question has more force when the relation between the two independent variables is logically necessary rather than empirical.

The Gluecks find, for example, that the families of delinquents are larger than those of nondelinquents: for delinquents the average number of children per family is 6.85, for nondelinquents, 5.90, a difference reported as significant at the 1 percent level.[12] The Gluecks also find that delinquents are more likely to be middle children (60.0 percent) than are nondelinquents (47.8 percent), as shown in Table 5-3.[13]

**Table 5-3—Rank of Boy Among Brothers and Sisters by Delinquency***

| Rank | DELINQUENTS | | NONDELINQUENTS | | DIFFERENCE |
| | Number | Percent | Number | Percent | Percent |
| --- | --- | --- | --- | --- | --- |
| Only child | 24 | 4.8 | 43 | 8.6 | —3.8 |
| First-born | 78 | 15.6 | 97 | 19.4 | —3.8 |
| Middle | 300 | 60.0 | 239 | 47.8 | 12.2 |
| Youngest | 98 | 19.6 | 121 | 24.2 | —4.6 |
| Total | 500 | 100.0 | 500 | 100.0 | |

* This table is from Sheldon and Eleanor Glueck, *Unraveling Juvenile Delinquency.* Cambridge: Harvard University Press, 1950, p. 120.

Now, suppose that size of family is causally related to delinquency, that as this variable increases, the likelihood that a child will become a delinquent also increases. Suppose further that birth order is not causally related to delinquency, that first-born, middle, and last-born children have equal delinquency propensities. How should these assumed facts show themselves in data like the Gluecks'?

Obviously, family size should be related to delinquency, as it in fact is in the Gluecks' data. At first glance it might appear that the Gluecks' findings invalidate the assumption that birth order is not a cause of delinquency, since this variable is also related to delinquency in their data. But it would be unusual to find a sample in which family size was related to delinquency while birth order was not. The larger the family, the greater must be the proportion of middle children. One-third of the children in a family of three are middle children; one-half of the children in a family of four are middle children. Since, in the Gluecks' data, delinquents do come from larger families than nondelinquents, a larger proportion of delinquents are likely to be middle children (and a smaller proportion are likely to be only, first-born, or last-born children), whether or not birth order is causally related to delinquency. Thus, the Gluecks' findings are perfectly compatible with the assumption that family size is a cause of delinquency while birth order is not.

In fact, the Gluecks' table on the relation between birth order and delinquency can be derived with only minor discrepancies from their table on the relation between number of children and delinquency.

**Table 5-4—Number of Children in Family by Delinquency***

| | DELINQUENTS | | NONDELINQUENTS | | DIFFERENCE |
|---|---|---|---|---|---|
| Children | Number | Percent | Number | Percent | Percent |
| 1 child | 24 | 4.8 | 43 | 8.6 | —3.8 |
| 2 children | 29 | 5.8 | 62 | 12.4 | —6.6 |
| 3 children | 46 | 9.2 | 61 | 12.2 | —3.0 |
| 4 children | 70 | 14.1 | 76 | 15.2 | —1.1 |
| 5 children | 66 | 13.2 | 74 | 14.8 | —1.6 |
| 6 children | 78 | 15.6 | 48 | 9.6 | 6.0 |
| 7 children | 72 | 14.4 | 49 | 9.8 | 4.6 |
| 8 children or more | 114 | 22.9 | 87 | 17.4 | 5.5 |
| Total | 499 | 100.0 | 500 | 100.0 | |

*This table is from Sheldon and Eleanor Glueck, *Unraveling Juvenile Delinquency.* Cambridge: Harvard University Press, 1950, p. 119.

Since 50 percent of the children in two-child families are first-born and 50 percent are youngest children, we assign 14.5 delinquents (50 percent of the 29 in the first column of the second row) and 31 nondelinquents (50 percent of the 62 in the third column of the second row) to these birth-order categories. Doing the same for three-child families (in which one-third are first-born, one-third middle, and one-third youngest), we assign 15.3 delinquents and 20.3 nondelinquents to each birth-order category. Continuing through the table in this manner yields Table 5-5, which should be compared with the Gluecks' table (Table 5-3).

At this point it may help to recapitulate our argument.

**Table 5-5—Relation Between Birth Order and Delinquency
Derived from Relation Between Number of Children
and Delinquency**

|  | DELINQUENTS | | NONDELINQUENTS | | DIFFERENCE |
|---|---|---|---|---|---|
|  | Number | Percent | Number | Percent | Percent |
| Only child | 24 | 4.8 | 43 | 8.6 | —3.8 |
| First-born | 98 | 19.6 | 111 | 22.2 | —2.6 |
| Middle | 280 | 56.0 | 235 | 47.0 | 9.0 |
| Youngest | 98 | 19.6 | 111 | 22.2 | —2.6 |
| Total | 500 | 100.0 | 500 | 100.0 |  |

The Gluecks present a table showing a relation between birth order and delinquency and a table showing a relation between family size and delinquency. The necessary relation between birth order and family size led us to ask what might happen to the relation between birth order and delinquency if family size were held constant. Since we could not examine this relation, we reversed the usual procedure and asked what kind of relation would obtain between birth order and delinquency when family size was free to vary if there were no relation between birth order and delinquency when family size was held constant (*i.e.*, if family size explained away the relation between birth order and delinquency). This produced Table 5-5, which shows a relation between birth order and delinquency very much like the relation reported by the Gluecks. In other words, we have produced "facts" identical to those presented by the Gluecks on the basis of radically different assumptions. Although our "facts" are the same as the Gluecks', our "findings" are not. Birth order may be significantly related to delinquency (at the 1 percent level) in the Gluecks' data, but this relation is almost certainly spurious.[14]

It is unusual to be able to make such a strong case for the spuriousness of the apparent relation between two variables without access to additional data. In our other examples we have had to rely on plausible conjectures about relations we could not examine. The researcher thus has a tremendous advantage over the critic: He can test his conjectures on real data. Unless he does so—that is, unless he speculates about the meaning of his results and submits these speculations to empirical test—the "findings" he presents will serve only as an inadequate if not misleading starting point for the speculations of others.

## The Theoretical Significance of "Spurious" Relations

Demonstrating that the apparent meaning of a two-variable relation is spurious should, in our view, lead the analyst to discard the original relation. Some authors, however, have argued that the demonstration of spuriousness may itself be spurious, that there are situations in which the vanishing of a two-variable relation when an antecedent test factor is taken into account should not turn the analyst's interest away from the original relation.

Two sources of confusion with respect to imputations of spuriousness may be exemplified by the following questions: 1. What if the antecedent variable causes the independent variable and the independent variable causes delinquency? Is it then legitimate to consider the relation between the independent variable and delinquency spurious if it disappears when the antecedent variable is taken into account? 2. What if the antecedent variable does not cause the independent variable but is merely related to it because of bias, contamination, or error? Is it then legitimate to consider the relation between the independent variable and delinquency spurious if it disappears when the antecedent variable is taken into account?

Hyman appears to say that the answer to the first question is No:

Spuriousness applies to situations where a variable other than the apparent explanation was found to have produced the observed effect, providing the other variable is not *an intrinsic part of the developmental sequence* which produced the apparent explanation.

One guide, for example, can be noted: instances where the 'control' factor and the apparent explanation involve *levels of description from two different systems* are likely to be developmental sequences.

. . . one might regard an attitude as a derivative of objective position or status or an objective position in society as leading to psychological processes such as attitude. Thus, the concept of spuriousness would not be appropriate.[15]

Hyman argues, then, that if $A$ causes $B$ and $B$ causes $C$, it is inappropriate to conclude that the relation between $B$ and $C$ is spurious if it disappears when $A$ is held constant. This argument confuses assumption and fact. If, in fact, $A$ causes $B$ and $B$ causes $C$, the relation between $B$ and $C$ will not disappear when $A$ is held constant.[16] Thus the question whether the relation between $B$ and $C$ should be labeled spurious will not arise. If, by assumption, $A$ causes $B$ and $B$ causes $C$, but the relation between $A$ and $C$ does not vanish when $B$ is held constant, the relation between $B$ and $C$ may or may not disappear when $A$ is held constant. If it does disappear, we see no methodological reason why the original relation between $B$ and $C$ should not be labeled spurious.[17]

Some theoretical attacks on the idea of spurious relations appear to be closely tied to the problem of the relative importance of different levels of variables, as in the following excerpt from a review of *The American Soldier* by Gordon W. Allport:

Their caution leads them throughout their exposition to hold constant all available variables so that only a simon-pure relationship between attitude and performance can appear. They call this the conservative way of portraying the relationship. Conservative, it surely is—and to my mind, theoretically questionable. Thus, in the case just cited, they report the relationship between individual attitudes and later combat performance only after holding constant 'background factors' such as age, marital condition, education, AGCT scores. The authors realize that if these factors were not held constant the demonstrated relationship between attitude and performance would be greater. . . . One reason, for example, is that men with higher education have much more favorable attitudes toward combat and also higher combat ratings. By comparing only men of *equal* education they rule out a large part of the potential correspondence.

The reasoning involved in this procedure is, to my mind, false. It says in effect: whenever you are attempting to account for behavior, ascribe as much of the influence as you can to class, status, or ecological determinants—and the remainder you may ascribe to attitude. Here we clearly encounter a sociologistic bias. Let me state the opposite (and to me preferable) interpretation. Nothing ever causes behavior excepting mental sets (including habits, attitudes, motives). To hold education or any other background factor constant is to imply that it alone may directly determine behavior. It is illegitimate to by-pass in this way the personal nexus wherein all background influences must be integrated. Background factors never directly cause behavior; they cause attitudes; and attitudes in turn determine behavior.[18]

Although it appears to deal with important questions of theory, Allport's objection to spuriousness confuses the general question of the relation between sociology and psychology with the particular question of what to do about an observed set of facts. Suppose, for example, that an analyst finds a positive association between a boy's hostility toward his father and the likelihood of his becoming delinquent, and that he then introduces social class as a test factor. Regardless of what happens—whether the original relation persists in each class, disappears, or changes in any other way—the analyst cannot take these results as indicating that attitudes are causes of behavior or that social factors are not. All he can say is that this particular attitude (hostility) is, or is not, a cause of this particular behavior (delinquency).[19] The relation between hostility and delinquency will be causal if the original association persists unchanged, spurious if it disappears.

Suppose, further, that in this example the original association does disappear and the analyst concludes, as we believe he should, that hostility is not a cause of delinquency. Is he thereby also concluding, as Allport suggests, that no attitude is a cause of delinquency? Of course not: Hostility is not a cause of delinquency, but there are undoubtedly other psychological variables that do connect social class and delinquency.

Thus far we have implied that antecedent variables must be temporally as well as causally prior to the independent variable. Yet in many (or perhaps most) cases of possible spuriousness, the question of the temporal order of the test factor and the independent variable is not crucial—as long as the independent variable does not have its effect on the dependent variable by way of the test factor. (In the latter case, the test factor would be considered an intervening variable. This configuration is discussed in Chapter 6.) In several of the examples used in this chapter, we have suggested possible antecedent variables that are not easily seen as causes of the independent variables in the sense that they precede the independent variables in time. One cannot meaningfully conclude that family size is temporally prior to birth order, that age is temporally prior to church attendance, or that psychiatric judgments precede social class. Nevertheless, these variables may be causally prior to the independent variables and are thus legitimately considered possible antecedent variables.

## Age As an Antecedent Variable

Several times in this chapter we have mentioned age as an antecedent variable that investigators of delinquency should take into account, but it is hard to think of age as a causal variable. Can age cause church attendance, or, for that matter, delinquency? A partial answer is suggested by one of the delinquency researchers who read an early draft of this section:

In your own paper, for example, you seem to take chronological age as being a variable. Rigorously speaking, of course, chronological age has no influence per se. What does have an influence is the fact that during a given period of time certain processes may have occurred. What we have here, then, is a time dimension whose significance consists solely in that it affords opportunity for events to have occurred. This being the case, can you really consider age an antecedent condition?[20]

We do, indeed, consider age an antecedent condition—for the reason Wattenberg suggests. Although age in itself[21] may have no influence, it is a measure of time: Our suggestion that age be taken into account amounts to asking that length of exposure to causal variables be taken into account. Unless time is controlled, the researcher does not know whether the differences he observes are the effects of the independent variable or whether they come from a difference in length of exposure to causal variables. For example, suppose an experimental and a control group of pigs are weighed, and then the former is fed a diet supplement. Obviously if the experimental group is weighed thirty days later and the control group twenty days later, differences in weight gained may not be due to differences in the quality of feed. Therefore, if differences in weight gain disappear when time of exposure (i.e., the amount of feed) is held more nearly constant, the experimenter would be justified in considering the apparent effect of the supplement spurious. The same reasoning applies to differences between delinquents and nondelinquents. If at one point in time nondelinquents are younger than delinquents, and are also more likely to attend church, it may be that by the time the nondelinquents have reached the age of the delinquents they will either have quit going to church or have become delinquents, or both. In other words, if age were taken into account, there might be no relation between church attendance and delinquency.

*A Practical Note.* It is important for the reader of a book like this to keep a sense of proportion. Our examples in this chapter may lead him to expect that good investigators look at many antecedent variables. Spuriousness, however, is not the most important problem the analyst faces. Most analysts probably do not test their relations for spuriousness until they have virtually finished their analysis—that is, until they feel ready to take possible counterarguments seriously. The analyst's task, then, is to destroy the plausibility of the potential critic's argument—which he does, in effect, by criticizing his own research and subjecting these criticisms to empirical test.

Testing for spuriousness should be relatively simple. In any field of investigation there are not more than a few plausible counterexplanations of observed results. The investigator familiar with past research can, therefore, include many of the necessary variables in the design of his study and, when he comes to the analysis, can determine whether they account for his results. He need not consider all possible antecedent variables.

# Notes

1. We use hypothetical data instead of the real data of Table 4–1 in order to simplify the following discussion.

2. See the discussion of holding something constant in Note 10, Chapter 3.

3. The "hit and run" technique of looking separately at a series of tables instead of the overall relation between a dependent variable and a set of independent variables is also logically defective. See Chapter 10.

4. Albert J. Reiss, Jr., "Social correlates of psychological types of delinquency," *American Sociological Review*, 17, 1952, pp. 710–718, at p. 713.

5. *Ibid.*

6. *Ibid.*, pp. 712–713

7. Peter H. Rossi, *Why Families Move*. New York: The Free Press, 1956.

8. See Herbert H. Hyman, *Survey Design and Analysis*. New York: The Free Press, 1955, pp. 179–183.

9. Reiss, *op. cit.*, p. 711.

10. Sheldon and Eleanor Glueck, *Unraveling Juvenile Delinquency*. Cambridge: Harvard University Press, 1950, pp. 33–37; Charles J. Browning, "Differential impact of family disorganization on male adolescents," *Social Problems*, 8, 1960, pp. 37–44. F. Ivan Nye (*Family Relationships and Delinquent Behavior*. New York: Wiley, 1958) destroys the relation between age and delinquency in his

sample by requiring more delinquent acts of the older boys before placing them in the "most delinquent" category.

11. Glueck and Glueck, *op. cit.*, pp. 33–39.

12. *Ibid.*, pp. 119–120.

13. *Ibid.*, p. 120.

14. For more recent studies in which the relation between birth order and delinquency is presented without controlling for number of children, see Nye, *op. cit.*, p. 37, and William McCord and Joan McCord, *Origins of Crime*. New York: Columbia University Press, 1959, pp. 117–118. For an excellent example of the value of reworking previously published data, as well as laudable responsiveness to criticism, see William C. Kvaraceus, *The Community and the Delinquent*. New York: World Book Co., 1954, pp. 247, 263.

15. Hyman, *op. cit.*, pp. 256–257.

16. This theorem was first proved by David Gold, "Spuriousness, developmental sequences, and independent causation in non-experimental research," a paper presented at the annual meeting of the American Sociological Association, New York, 1960. More explicitly, it states that if the partial associations between A and C vanish when B is held constant, then the partial associations between B and C will *not* vanish when A is held constant; in Lazars-

feld's terms, if *B* interprets the relation between *A* and *C*, then *A* cannot explain the relation between *B* and *C*.

17. Hubert M. Blalock (*Social Statistics*. New York: McGraw-Hill, 1960, pp. 339–343) says it makes little sense to control *A* if $A \to B \to C$ is assumed and no sense to control *B* if $A \to B \to C$ is assumed. Since the purpose of control is to test such assumptions, this argument too confuses assumption and fact.

18. Gordon W. Allport, Review of *The American Soldier*, *Journal of Abnormal and Social Psychology*, 45, 1950, p. 172, quoted by Hyman, *op. cit.*, pp. 257–258.

19. See Chapter 3 for a more adequate account of what is involved in demonstrating causality or noncausality.

20. William W. Wattenberg, letter, November 6, 1962.

21. In discussions of causality phrases like our *in itself* or Wattenberg's *per se* may conceal important problems; see the section on "measurable variables" in Chapter 8.

# 6

# Links
# in the
# Causal
# Chain

Each introduction of an antecedent variable marks a fork in the analyst's road. If the apparent meaning of the relation between two variables turns out to be spurious, the analyst shifts his attention to other relations. If the relation persists essentially unchanged, he will usually want to clarify its meaning. If the relation between church attendance and delinquency in our example (Table 5-1) is examined for different values of such antecedent variables as age and parents' religion and still persists, this strengthens the belief that there is a genuine causal relation between church attendance and delinquency. But this still would not explain how differences in church attendance from one boy to another lead to differences in delinquency.

The analyst who wants to connect the independent and dependent variables through some sequence of intervening variables must begin by speculating about possible meanings of the relations. For example: Boys who regularly attend religious services learn respect for the law and are, as a result,

less likely to become delinquent. If he has the right intervening variables in his data, he can then examine the appropriate
three-variable relations to see whether the intervening variable
suggested by his speculations does in fact connect the independent and dependent variables.

The new variables used in this process of *interpretation*
differ from those introduced in attempts at *explanation* in
that they are seen as intervening in the causal sequence between church attendance and delinquency rather than as
being antecedent to church attendance. For example, "respect for the law" in the conjectural interpretation above is
treated as an intervening variable: It is a consequence of
church attendance and a cause of nondelinquency. The only
way in which the test for whether an intervening variable interprets the original relation differs from the test for whether an
antecedent variable explains away the relation is in the causal
ordering of the independent variable and the new variable, or
test factor. Statistically, the procedures are identical. In both
cases the original relation between the independent and dependent variables is reexamined in groups classified according
to the values of the test factor. In this example, the analyst
examines the relation between church attendance and delinquency within groups having different levels of respect for the
law. To the extent that the original relation vanishes in these
three-variable tables, the analyst has found a link between the
two original variables. If the original relation disappears when
respect for the law is held constant, one can think of it as
being dissolved into two relations: Church attendance leads
to respect for the law, and respect for the law leads to a low
rate of delinquency.

Although the statistical configurations of successful attempts at explanation and interpretation are the same, the
analyst's purposes in the two cases are different. In the first
he decides whether or not to get rid of the original relation

(i.e., whether its apparent meaning is spurious); in the second he accepts the original relation as causal and attempts to show how the two variables are connected.

As we noted in Chapter 5, attempts at explanation in delinquency research are rare; unfortunately, this is even more true for attempts at interpretation. One reason for the neglect of interpretation is that data on possible intervening variables are often unavailable. For example, Jackson Toby found that girls and preadolescent boys have high rates of delinquency in areas with high rates of family disorganization. He expected to find this relation because:

. . . the well-integrated family gives firm supervision, whereas the disorganized family is unable to do so. Therefore, girls and pre-adolescents from disorganized households are more exposed to criminogenic influences than girls and pre-adolescents from well-integrated households. . . .[1]

According to Toby, there are two links in the chain between family disorganization and delinquency: supervision and exposure to criminogenic influences. A test of Toby's interpretation would require examination of the relation between family disorganization and delinquency with either supervision or exposure to criminogenic influences held more nearly constant.[2] Data on such variables are seldom available for the kind of large area Toby was studying, so he was unable to test his suggested interpretation.

Even when they have the necessary data, analysts often fail to submit their conjectures to an empirical test. For instance, Nye reports:

Parental appearance is seen as affecting indirect control by increasing or decreasing affectional identification with parents. . . . Direct control may be facilitated, also, if good parental appearance results in the adolescent inviting his friends to his home so that more of his recreational time is spent within the range of parental observation.[3]

This passage describes two three-variable relations, which the analyst apparently assumes to have the following sequences: 1. parental appearance → affectional identification → delinquency; and, 2. parental appearance → place of recreation → delinquency. Nye has indicators of both intervening variables, and he reports some of the two-variable relations between them and the other variables.[4] He does not, however, examine either of the appropriate three-variable tables—for example, the relation between parental appearance and delinquency in groups homogeneous on affectional identification. He thus leaves the meaning of his figures unnecessarily in doubt.

Conjectural interpretations are most common in attempts to summarize a series of two-variable tables. Thus the Gluecks found that delinquents differed from nondelinquents in many aspects of family life. Their summary of some of these findings is condensed as follows:

As regards affectional relations between the parents and the boys . . . the delinquents were much more the victims of the indifference or actual hostility of their fathers and mothers, and were, *in turn*, less attached to their parents. . . . [There was] a greater feeling on the part of the delinquent boys that their parents were not concerned about their welfare. Whether as a result of this or of other elements in the family life, the delinquents did not identify with or seek to emulate their fathers nearly as much as did the non-delinquents. How much this, *in turn*, has to do with the more erratic discipline imposed on the delinquent boys by their fathers and the fathers' far greater resort to physical punishment can only be surmised.[5]

The phrase *in turn* appears twice. The first time, the Gluecks are asserting a relation between two of their independent variables, parental hostility and attachment to parents; the second time they are saying that they do not know, and cannot discover, whether or not other independent variables (emulation of the father, father's disciplinary practices) are related to each other. Both assertions could be checked by simple cross-tabulations. More important, the three-variable relations suggested by these two-variable relations could easily be examined. If parental disciplinary behavior affects attitudes that are related to delinquency, then these attitudes intervene between disciplinary practices and delinquency. Here, then, the Gluecks stop with a conjecture when they could easily have gone on to an empirical test.

Does this mean that conjectural interpretations (and conjectural explanations) should be avoided? Of course not: In our opinion, such conjectures are bad only when data are available to substantiate or refute them, and the analyst is satisfied to stop with the conjecture. When the analyst fails to indicate that his conjecture is just that—a hypothesis and not an empirical finding—he is likely to mislead his readers, and his readers' readers, as in the following summary of the above findings from a textbook on juvenile delinquency:

Delinquents were also found to be more often the victims of indifferent or hostile parents, and, *as a consequence*, they were less attached to their parents than were the members of the control group. This emotional deprivation led the delinquents to feel that their parents did not care about their welfare. Accordingly, they made little attempt to emulate or respect their parents.[6]

Students and laymen are often impatient with the shilly-shallying and technicalities in research reports. They want solid facts they can memorize for examinations or translate into action. Nevertheless, the purpose of research is to test hunches, not to provide a setting for their illegitimate transformation into fact.[7] As in the admonition that a driver should act as if every one else on the road were out of his mind, so an author should assume that his readers will do their best to misinterpret what he says. This caution is well expressed in an appraisal of "The Kinsey Report" by three statisticians:

In conclusion, we are convinced that unsubstantiated assertions are not in themselves inappropriate in a scientific study. In any complex field, where many questions remain unresolved, the accumulated insight of an experienced worker may well be worth putting on record although no documentation can be given. . . . The author who values his reputation for objectivity will take pains to warn the reader, even at the risk of repetitiousness, whenever an opinion or an unsubstantiated conclusion is being presented, and will choose his words with the greatest care in his presentation.[8]

Misinterpretation of an author's conjectures is one thing; the ease with which they can be dismissed is another, more serious matter. As Ruth Kornhauser has suggested in a review of delinquency theories, "it is the kind of intervening variable a theory stresses that is crucial" in differentiating one theory from another.[9] In other words, the researcher who discovers a relation between some variable and delinquency and then offers only a conjectural interpretation has done nothing in the way of confirming his own theory and refuting the theories of others. As was true with respect to causal order, two-variable relations offer as much support to one interpretation as to another. Thus the well-known relation between socioeconomic status and official delinquency provides as much evidence for a social control theory as for an opportunity theory:

Boys with low socioeconomic status are not concerned about success. The absence of success-goals reduces the personal cost of engaging in criminal activities. Thus the high rates of crime among lower-class boys.

Boys with low socioeconomic status are frustrated in their attempts to achieve success through legitimate means. They therefore attempt to achieve success through illegitimate means.

The admonition that delinquency researchers should conduct their research within the context of a general theory that will explain the correlations they observe is a good one, but it does not go far enough.[10] Entire sets of zero-order correlations are consistent with more than one conceptual scheme. Unless the researcher attempts to test at least elements of the general theory he is using by examining some of these two-variable relations with the effects of the hypothesized intervening variable removed, his theory will continue to be little more than a way of talking about the results of quantitative research.

Perhaps the most striking case of the use of different kinds of intervening variables is found in a comparison of those who use the attitudes of officials and those who use the attitudes of children to interpret a set of correlations between social characteristics and adjudicated delinquency. One researcher will argue that the major variables intervening between social characteristics and delinquency are attitudes of boys and girls, such as hostility toward parents. Another will prefer to link social characteristics to delinquency through the attitudes of public officials:

Studies dealing with the family status of children incarcerated in institutions show that most of the inmates, especially the girls, come from broken homes. This phenomenon is not unusual since juvenile court judges are traditionally obsessed with the 'broken-home-causes-delinquency' thesis and despair of any other disposition of such cases.[11]

This argument implies that there may be no differences between girls from broken and unbroken homes in the likelihood that they will commit delinquent acts. However, juvenile court judges, believing that girls from broken homes are more likely to become delinquent, more often sentence them to institutions. The relation between broken homes and (institutionalized) delinquency is thus produced by the attitudes of judges. It is possible to interpret many of the relations in research on adjudicated delinquency in the same way—for example, the relations between delinquency and family size, criminality of the father or siblings, affection of father for boy, emotional ties of boy to mother, parental discipline, church attendance, bodily constitution (mesomorphy), and race. Consider mesomorphy, for example: Judges may see in a muscular, broad-shouldered boy more of a threat to the community than they see in his pale and skinny counterpart. If this is so, the differences in the proportions of mesomorphs among delinquent and nondelinquent populations could well stem from this attitude on the part of the judge.[12]

It is not our purpose to advance this particular interpretation of the results of research on adjudicated delinquency. However, if attitudes of officials account for observed relations (or if analysts think they do), the search for intervening variables appears in a new light. Suppose that judges and other officials do react differently to children from broken homes and that this differential reaction accounts for the greater likelihood that a child from a broken home will be institutionalized.[13] Insofar as this is true, the delinquency researcher will not be able to find a personality characteristic of the child that accounts for the relation between broken homes and delinquency. In other words, if attitudes of officials are responsible for associations between social characteristics and delinquency, then most quantitative studies of adjudicated delinquents, lacking data on the attitudes of officials, would be unable to demonstrate this fact.

Although most studies of adjudicated delinquents would not allow a direct test of the "attitudes of officials" hypothesis, they do allow tests of the major alternatives to this hypothesis, such as the attitudes of the delinquents. In this indirect strategy one must first list all of the plausible hypotheses that can account for the observed relation. Next one tests as many of these hypotheses as the data allow. If the relation survives the test, then the investigator gains confidence in his original hypothesis. This, it will be recalled, is the procedure that Durkheim used in disposing of extra-social factors as causes of suicide.[14] It is admittedly a cumbersome procedure, and it has a serious logical flaw; nevertheless, the analyst is surely better off trying such a line of attack than relying on the frail support of a conjectural interpretation. He may not have Durkheim's skill or good fortune, but he usually has better data.

# Notes

1. Jackson Toby, "The differential impact of family disorganization," *American Sociological Review*, 22, 1957, pp. 505–512, at p. 508.

2. If the causal structure is as hypothesized $(A \rightarrow B \rightarrow C \rightarrow D)$, the original two-variable relation of $A$ and $D$ will vanish when either $B$ or $C$ is held constant.

3. F. Ivan Nye, *Family Relationships and Delinquent Behavior*. New York: Wiley, 1958, p. 111.

4. *Ibid.*, pp. 72, 105, 115–116.

5. Sheldon and Eleanor Glueck, *Unraveling Juvenile Delinquency*. Cambridge: Harvard University Press, 1950, p. 133. (Authors' italics)

6. Milton L. Barron, *The Juvenile in Delinquent Society*. New York: Alfred A. Knopf, 1954, pp. 130–131. (Authors' italics)

7. The reader who dislikes our throwing stones at delinquency researchers may derive some comfort from the fact that one of us is not without sin. See David Gold, "Some comments on 'The Empirical Classification of Formal Groups,'" and Hanan C. Selvin and Warren O. Hagstrom, "Reply to Gold," *American Sociological Review*, 29, 1964, pp. 736–739.

8. William G. Cochran, Frederick Mosteller, and John W. Tukey, *Statistical Problems in the Kinsey Report*. Washington: American Statistical Association, 1950, p. 136.

9. Ruth Kornhauser, "Theoretical issues in the sociological study of delinquency," University of California, Berkeley, Center for the Study of Law and Society, April 1963, Mimeo. p. 1.

10. Albert K. Cohen and James F. Short, Jr. in Robert K. Merton and Robert A. Nisbet, eds., *Contemporary Social Problems*. New York: Harcourt, 1961, p. 111.

11. Negley K. Teeters and John Otto Reinemann, *The Challenge of Delinquency*. Englewood Cliffs, N.J.: Prentice-Hall, 1950, p. 153.

12. Other conjectures about the meaning of the finding that mesomorphs are more likely to be delinquent may be found in Cohen and Short, *op. cit.*, p. 93, and Sheldon and Eleanor Glueck, *op. cit.*, Chapter XV, pp. 273–274.

13. For purposes of exposition, we are assuming the ideal-typical case of complete interpretation. In actual practice the intervening variables that completely interpret a relation are likely to be a combination of personality characteristics and the attitudes of officials.

14. Emile Durkheim, *Suicide* (Trans. and ed. by George Simpson and John A. Spaulding). New York: The Free Press, 1950, Part I.

# 7

# Interaction
# of
# Variables

In addition to explanation and interpretation, two other types of outcome may result from the introduction of a third variable into a two-variable relation. The original relation may remain essentially unchanged in the partial tables formed according to the values of the third variable, or it may be stronger for some values and weaker for others. These outcomes are called, respectively, *internal replication* and *interaction*.[1]

Since much delinquency research is action-oriented, identification of the conditions under which a relation holds more or less strongly may have immediate practical value. But a statement of interaction is more than mere description—for example, in directing attention to areas of high and low delinquency. Like explanation and interpretation, it has theoretical or conjectural analogs. For example, Cloward and Ohlin's theory of delinquency suggests that the effects of the absence of legitimate means depend on the availability of illegitimate means.[2] And in Merton's theory of anomie the outcome of pressures toward deviance depends on the value of such variables as internalization of norms.[3]

Interactions are fairly common in the empirical literature on delinquency. Nye ran all of his tables separately for boys and girls, and he found that many relations varied considerably by sex. For example: Among boys, the relation between attitudes toward the father's appearance and delinquent behavior was relatively strong; among girls, the relation was negligible.[4] McCord and McCord find many pronounced interactions, some of them excellent examples of situational intensification.[5] The Gluecks have published two books on the data from *Unraveling* in which interaction is the only outcome they consider.[6]

## Consistent and Inconsistent Partial Relations

Most of these interactions make obvious sense, as in Nye's example, but sometimes the greater complexity of these three-variable relations seems to bemuse the analyst. This is especially likely to happen when the partial relations derive from the design of the study rather than from the analysis.

In order to make this discussion clear, we present first a hypothetical example, in which an analyst examines the two-variable relation between I.Q. and delinquency and finds that the boys with higher I.Q.'s are less likely to be delinquent. Now suppose that, for whatever reason, he divides his sample into two halves by an essentially random process—say, according to whether the boy's serial number in the study is odd or even.

The most likely single outcome of this procedure is internal replication; since the division into two halves is unrelated to either the independent or the dependent variable, the two partial relations should be approximately equal. Precisely equal relations, however, would be very rare, so that the most probable class of outcomes is actually interaction. And once in a while, purely by chance, there will be a strong interaction, perhaps strong enough to be called specification.

Now suppose that the analyst tries to make substantive sense out of this specification. Which of the partial relations should he report? The answer, of course, is that he should not report either. If the partial relations produced by this random division are sufficiently different to be called interaction or specification, then the only proper course for the analyst is to disregard the random division altogether and to discuss the meaning of the original two-variable relation, perhaps by introducing some meaningful, nonrandom variable.[7]

The logic of this hypothetical example will make it easier to understand what happens in a real example, one in which the division of the sample is according to a variable that should have no effect on the observed relation, as in this example from the McCords' *Origins of Crime:*

Information about the boys who received treatment was more detailed than that about control boys. The treated group had been observed for two to eight years, while the control boys had been studied only for one short period in their lives. For our analysis of causative factors, therefore, we concentrated on the 253 boys who had received treatment. We used the control group primarily for confirmation of those relationships which appeared significant.[8]

This decision to perform separate analyses on the treatment and control groups is perfectly reasonable—as is the decision to confirm relations observed in the treatment group by examining the control group. The difficulty arises when the control group results and the treatment group results disagree, as in Table 7-1.

In their main text the McCords restrict their attention to the treatment group, presenting control-group comparisons only in an appendix (we have computed the "Totals" from these two sources). Their conclusions about the effects of a variable are thus based only on relations within the treatment

**Table 7-1—(a) Percent of Boys Convicted of Crimes and Intelligence Quotient by Experimental Group Assignment***

| Intelligence quotient | Treatment group | Control group | TOTALS |
|---|---|---|---|
| Superior (I.Q. over 110) | 26 (23) | 24 (17) | 25 (40) |
| Average (I.Q. 91–110) | 46 (111) | 34 (168) | 39 (279) |
| Dull average (I.Q. 81–90) | 44 (59) | 50 (60) | 47 (119) |
| Sub-normal (I.Q. below 81) | 35 (46) | 25 (8) | 33 (54) |

**(b) Percent of Boys Convicted of Crimes and Neighborhood by Experimental Group Assignment**

| Type of neighborhood | | | |
|---|---|---|---|
| Good | 38 (37) | 26 (47) | 31 (84) |
| Fair | 37 (41) | 33 (49) | 34 (90) |
| Poor | 40 (96) | 44 (32) | 41 (128) |
| Worst | 46 (59) | 49 (122) | 48 (181) |

* This table is adapted from William McCord and Joan McCord, *Origins of Crime.* New York: Columbia University Press, 1959, pp. 66, 71, 203, 204.

group. For example, they comment on the Treatment Group tables in part as follows:

The table indicates that no significant relationship exists between criminal behavior and low intelligence. . . . The conclusion is that low intelligence does not lead a boy into crime. . . .[9]

The pattern revealed, although not statistically significant, hints that neighborhood consistently influences crime causation. . . . Despite our failure to substantiate those theories which place primary emphasis on disorganized neighborhood conditions . . .[10]

Both of these comments would have to be modified in important ways if attention were focused on the control group or on the combined samples. Both relations are, for example, statistically significant within the control group and within the sample as a whole.[11] More importantly, the relations are either stronger or more consistent in the latter groups. Thus, on the basis of the McCords' data, we would not hesitate to say that except for the subnormal, the lower a boy's intelligence, the more likely that he has been convicted of crimes; nor would we agree that their data show that type of neighborhood is unimportant as a cause of crime.[12]

In both *Physique and Delinquency* and *Family Environment and Delinquency*, the Gluecks try to place psychological traits on an assumed "biosocial continuum." That is, they want to find out whether the causes of a particular psychological trait are predominantly constitutional or sociocultural. Their procedure in both books is the same. They examine the relations among their independent variables within the nondelinquent group only:

As in *Physique and Delinquency*, so in this volume, determination of the orientation of traits is derived from an inspection of the 500 nondelinquents who were the subjects of *Unraveling Juvenile Delinquency*; for it is necessary in the disentangling of factor-trait relationships to avoid the involvement of the presence of antisocial behavior with all its complexities.[13]

In other words, if a psychological trait (say, sensitivity) turns out to be related to body type (ectomorphy-mesomorphy-endomorphy) but not to any of a variety of social factors (e.g., lack of family ambition, crowded home), then the trait "is assumed to have an essentially constitutional orientation." The opposite outcome would of course result in the assignment of the psychological trait to the sociocultural end of the biosocial continuum.

We are not concerned here with the Gluecks' goal, but with their procedures, specifically, with their decision to restrict analysis to the nondelinquents. What happens when the results found for the delinquents do not agree with those found for the nondelinquents? Such discrepancies would, of course, remain concealed if analysis were restricted entirely to the nondelinquent group. In both *Physique* and *Family Environment*, however, the Gluecks use an analytic technique that in many cases allows comparison of the results among the nondelinquents with those among the delinquents. The Gluecks use Table 7-2 to show how this technique works.

### Table 7-2—Feeling of Not Being Taken Care of and Body Type by Delinquency*

DELINQUENTS

| | Physique type | TOTAL | No. with trait | No. without trait | Percent with trait |
|---|---|---|---|---|---|
| 1 | Total | 329 | 96 | 233 | 29.2 |
| 2 | Mesomorph | 203 | 74 | 129 | 36.5 |
| 3 | Endomorph | 39 | 7 | 32 | 17.9 |
| 4 | Ectomorph | 43 | 9 | 34 | 20.9 |
| 5 | Balanced | 44 | 6 | 38 | 13.6 |
| | Columns | $a = b + c$ | $b$ | $c$ | $d = b/a$ |

NONDELINQUENTS

| TOTAL | No. with trait | No. without trait | Percent with trait | Differences in percentages between delinquents and nondelinquents |
|---|---|---|---|---|
| 304 | 75 | 229 | 24.7 | 4.5 |
| 96 | 18 | 78 | 18.8 | 17.7 |
| 35 | 11 | 24 | 31.4 | −13.5 |
| 127 | 32 | 95 | 25.2 | −4.3 |
| 46 | 14 | 32 | 30.4 | −16.8 |
| $e = f + g$ | $f$ | $g$ | $h = f/e$ | $i = d - h$ |

* Sheldon and Eleanor Glueck, *Physique and Delinquency*. p. 277. Appendix A, "Explanation of Statistical Method," is by Jane Worcester.

The two most important columns in Table 7-2 are $d$ and $h$. The figures in column $d$ are the proportions of delinquents with each body type who had "a feeling of not being taken care of." Among the delinquents, then, 36.5 percent of the mesomorphs and 17.9 percent of the endomorphs had this feeling, a difference that the Gluecks report as statistically significant. Similarly among the nondelinquents in column $h$,

18.8 percent of the mesomorphs and 31.4 percent of the endomorphs felt that they were not being taken care of; the Gluecks report that none of the differences among the nondelinquents is significant. From this table the Gluecks conclude:

This characteristic [feeling of not being taken care of] does not vary sufficiently among the body types of the nondelinquents to permit of an inference that it inclines toward the constitutional end of the biosocial spectrum.[14]

When the situation is reversed—that is, when there is a relation among the nondelinquents and no relation among the delinquents—the Gluecks reach the opposite conclusion: "that this characteristic is probably oriented in constitution."[15] Like the McCords, the Gluecks find inconsistent results in different parts of their sample. Although the form of these inconsistencies is that of statistical interaction, neither analysis can be meaningfully construed in this way. Both analyses are concerned with the relation between one independent variable and one dependent variable, and there is no more reason to expect this relation to differ in the two subgroups than in the randomly selected subgroups in the example at the beginning of this section.

In the McCords' case, to argue that treatment in the Cambridge-Somerville Youth Study partially removed the effects on delinquency of intelligence and neighborhood would be to assume an efficacy for the treatment that much of their analysis calls into question. In the Gluecks' case, to accept the suggestion that delinquency might affect the relations between physical and psychological traits is to reverse cause and effect.

In sum, where there is good reason to expect the relation between two variables to depend on the values of a third variable, the sample should be divided on the third variable. Sex is perhaps the best example of such a meaningful interacting variable; the causes of delinquency among boys and girls are so different that failing to keep them separate will obscure important relations. Even where there is no reason to expect a particular division of the sample to affect the relations under study, as in the two examples in this section, one might want to analyze one of the subsamples later (perhaps as a partial safeguard against the danger of hunting for relations).[16] If the analyst chooses to do this, he must take both sets of results into account. It is never legitimate to accept the results of one subsample and ignore the results of the others.

## The Analysis of Zero Relations

Judging from the studies we have examined, the usual reaction of the analyst who discovers a small or zero relation is to turn his attention elsewhere, even when there was good reason to have expected a substantial relation.

But the meaning of a zero or near-zero association between two variables is no more obvious than the meaning of a strong association. A strong two-variable association may suggest a causal relation, but a plausible inference of causality requires the introduction of additional variables. Similarly, a weak association suggests a lack of causality, but further analysis may be needed before accepting this suggestion.[17]

At the time it appeared, one of the most startling zero relations in the study of delinquency was Nye's conclusion that there "is no significant difference in delinquent behavior . . . in different socio-economic strata."[18] Nye used father's occupation as an indicator of socioeconomic status and a self-administered questionnaire to measure delinquent behavior. In his analysis Nye employed a variety of statistical techniques:

Delinquent behavior on each item was divided into four categories. . . . The distribution of each delinquent act by socio-economic status was tested separately by the chi-square test. . . . A second test was made in which all delinquent behavior items were dichotomized, and the relationship . . . tested by the use of chi-square. . . . A third test was . . . made. Percentages were computed for the dichotomized delinquency items and significance of differences between proportions were computed. . . . In addition . . . the distribution of delinquency scale types by socio-economic status was tested for significant differences.[19]

Except for changing from separate delinquency items to a scale in the fourth test, Nye's procedures are essentially the same; their agreement adds little to the strength of his analysis. Nevertheless, his purpose in using all of them is clear; he wanted to be absolutely sure that there was no relation between socioeconomic status and reported delinquency.

Nye was aware of the possibility that the relation between socioeconomic status and delinquency may have been appreciably different in subgroups of his sample, for he reexamined the original relation in groups classified according to sex, age, and location (three separate tables). Nye may well have been thinking here of what is the most common explanation of a zero relation: the combining of partial relations of opposite sign and approximately equal magnitude.

An important and successful elaboration of a zero relation along those lines appears in a paper by Glaser and Rice. Although there were good reasons for expecting a positive association between unemployment and crime rates, previous investigators had found either no relation or weak and inconsistent relations. Glaser and Rice investigated this zero relation by holding constant the age of the criminal and the type of crime. They were able to show that "adult crime rates vary directly with unemployment, particularly rates of property offenses by persons 20 to 45 years of age" and that "juvenile crime rates vary inversely with unemployment."[20] Nye's introduction of sex, age, and location may have been based on similar reasoning, but in this case these variables did not succeed in accounting for the zero relation.

A second possible explanation is that Nye's indicator of socioeconomic status, the occupation of his father as reported by the high school student, was weak. In fact, some of Nye's own data suggest this. Several of his independent variables may reasonably be considered correlates of socioeconomic status; these include family stability (broken home), family size (large), father's behavior (goes around the house in his undershirt), and mother's behavior (lets her slip show).[21] Family stability and family size are known to be related to socioeconomic status, and the case for the other two variables is fairly obvious.[22] In Nye's data, all of these variables are "significantly" related to delinquency, and yet father's occupation is not.[23]

Nye should have examined the association between father's occupation and these other indicators of socioeconomic status as possible explanations of his surprising discovery. Large association would have validated his use of father's occupation as an indicator of socioeconomic status, and his finding would have been even more striking. Small association would have cast doubt on the validity of his indicator and would probably have led him to look at his anomalous finding in a different light.

A third possible explanation of Nye's finding is that the relation between father's occupation and delinquency is in the same direction in different subgroups of his sample but that the combining of these subgroups destroyed the relation. Another of Nye's findings suggests how this might have come about. Owning a car, which Nye found positively related to delinquent behavior, is probably also positively related to socioeconomic status. Combining these associations with an assumed negative relation between socioeconomic status and delinquency might produce results like those in Table 7-3.

**Table 7-3—Delinquency and Socioeconomic Status by Car Ownership (hypothetical)**

|                       | Owns Car SOCIOECONOMIC STATUS | | Does Not Own Car SOCIOECONOMIC STATUS | |
|-----------------------|:------:|:------:|:------:|:------:|
|                       | High   | Low    | High   | Low    |
| Percent delinquent    | 40     | 100    | 0      | 20     |
|                       | (500)  | (100)  | (100)  | (500)  |

Socioeconomic status and car ownership are positively related in this table; examination of the totals at the bottom of the table show that five-sixths of the boys with high socioeconomic status own cars, as compared with one-sixth of the boys with low socioeconomic status. And, as Nye found, car ownership and delinquency are positively related; combining the first and second columns shows that 50 percent of car owners are delinquent, as against 17 percent of those who do not own cars, in the third and fourth columns. And, holding car ownership constant, there is a strong negative relation between socioeconomic status and delinquency in both halves of the table. But when the two halves of this table are combined, so that car ownership is left free to vary, as in Table 7-4, the

**Table 7-4—Delinquency by Socioeconomic Status (derived from Table 7-3)**

|                    | SOCIOECONOMIC STATUS | |
|--------------------|:------:|:------:|
|                    | High   | Low    |
| Percent delinquent | 33     | 33     |
|                    | (600)  | (600)  |

relation between socioeconomic status and delinquency disappears.

Of course, none of our three conjectures proves that Nye was wrong, that there is, indeed, a negative relation between socioeconomic status and delinquency in his sample. They merely suggest possible lines of investigation that Nye might have pursued (and, as we noted, he may well have pursued our first suggestion and found it unsuccessful as an explanation of his findings). Just as the investigator who comes across an unexpectedly strong association between an independent variable and delinquency must carry his analysis further to make a plausible case for the causal status of his independent variable, so the investigator who finds an unexpectedly weak relation should continue his analysis before abandoning his belief in the causal status of his independent variable. Most of what we have said in the past four chapters comes down to this: Unless it was predicted, hypothesized, or otherwise expected, no relation, large or small, significant or nonsignificant, ever speaks for itself. The task of the analyst is to make sense out of his data.

# Notes

1. Although, like many sociologists, we have used *conditional relation, interaction,* and *specification* more or less interchangeably, these terms do have distinct meanings. In the simplest, or first order *interaction,* the relation between two variables depends on the values of a third variable; interaction is the statisticians' term and is discussed in all treatments of analysis of variance. As it has been used by Lazarsfeld and Hyman, *specification* is a strong form of interaction, in which at least one partial relation is larger than the original relation or of opposite sign (See Herbert H. Hyman, *Survey Design and Analysis.* New York: *The Free Press,* 1955, Chapter 7). In its proper use, a *conditional relation* is simply a relation between two variables considered only for some particular value of another variable. However, it has often been used synonymously with interaction or specification. Finally, although we have not yet used the term there is *nonadditivity.* In an additive multivariate relation (mathematically, a relation of the form $y = a + b_1 x_1 + b_2 x_2$) the effect of one independent variable on the dependent variable does not depend on the value of the other independent variable; there is no interaction and, of course, no specification. In a nonadditive relation (for example, the multiplicative relation $y = a + b_{12} x_1 x_2$) the effect of one independent variable on the dependent variable depends on the value of the other independent variable. The definitions of all four terms—explanation, interpretation, interaction, and internal replication—can easily be extended to relations involving more than three variables.

2. See Erdman B. Palmore and Phillip E. Hammond, "Interacting factors in juvenile delinquency," *American Sociological Review,* 29, 1964, pp. 848–854, and Richard A. Cloward and Lloyd E. Ohlin, *Delinquency and Opportunity.* New York: The Free Press, 1960, Chapters 4 and 6.

3. Robert K. Merton, *Social Theory and Social Structure,* revised ed. New York: The Free Press, 1957, Chapter 4.

4. F. Ivan Nye, *Family Relationships and Delinquency.* New York: Wiley, 1958, p. 112.

5. The following table is from *Origins of Crime.* New York: Columbia University Press, 1959, p. 86.

*Relation of Home Atmosphere and Type of Neighborhood to Crime Rate*

### PERCENT OF BOYS CONVICTED OF CRIMES

| Home Atmosphere | Good-Fair Neighborhood | Poor-Worst Neighborhood |
| --- | --- | --- |
| Cohesive | 34 (45) | 29 (69) |
| Noncohesive | 39 (41) | 53 (85) |

Note that home atmosphere is strongly related to conviction only in poor neighborhoods and that neighborhood is negatively related to conviction only among those from noncohesive homes. McCord and McCord read this table, in part, as follows: "Although delinquency tends to be concentrated in specific areas, it is the person's home which seems to be the critical factor." An almost equally strong case could be made from these data for the critical importance of neighborhood. The point is that interactions such as this make statements about the relative importance of variables exceedingly hazardous. See James S. Coleman, *Introduction to Mathematical Sociology*. New York: The Free Press, 1964, pp. 224–235.

6. *Family Environment and Delinquency.* Boston: Houghton Mifflin, 1962, and *Physique and Delinquency.* New York: Harper, 1956. By the Gluecks' own standard, most of the tables in *Physique* are internal replications and can thus be summarized by the statement: This relation between a psychological trait and delinquency is unaffected by holding body type constant.

7. In the controversy about the use of significance tests in survey research (see Chapter 13) consistency in the partial relation of such random subdivisions was at one time suggested as a substitute for conventional tests. Whether this use is legitimate or not now appears to depend on whether the analyst had thought of the original two-variable relation before examining the data. For a general discussion of the place of such replications in analysis, see Hanan C. Selvin, "Durkheim's *Suicide:* further thoughts on a methodological classic," in Robert A. Nisbet, *Emile Durkheim.* Englewood Cliffs, N.J.: Prentice-Hall, 1965, pp. 113–136; this essay will also appear in Paul F. Lazarsfeld *et al., The Language of Social Research* (re-vised ed.). New York: The Free Press, forthcoming.

8. McCord and McCord, *op. cit.,* p. 63.

9. *Ibid.,* pp. 65–66.

10. *Ibid.,* pp. 70–71.

11. The McCords report the control group figures as statistically significant; see pp. 203–204. With comparable associations and much larger N's, the two "Total" associations must also be significant (see Chapter 13).

12. With respect to the differences between treatment and control groups, the McCords say: "The pattern of crime in relation to intelligence in the control group . . . *resembles* that found in the treatment group. . . . The differences within the control group were, however, statistically significant. . . . There is one difference in the rate of crime between the control boys and the treatment boys which approaches significance. . . . The relationship between a particular neighborhood and the rate of crime was *more pronounced* among the control boys . . . than among the treatment boys. The difference within the control group is significant. . . . Yet, holding

neighborhood constant, no significant differences in rate of crime appeared *between the treatment group and the control group.*" Pp. 203–204. (Authors' italics) The McCords' emphasis on the similarities between the two relations misses, it seems to us, an important point— that the relations within the control group have crossed the line into statistical significance. By the McCords' own criterion, they have thus crossed into the realm of importance.

13. Glueck and Glueck, *Family Environment and Delinquency*, p. 18.

14. *Physique and Delinquency*, p. 88.

15. For example, *Ibid.*, p. 81.

16. See Chapter 13. The value of reserving such a subsample in advance of looking at the data in order to guard against the acceptance of chance results decreases rapidly after the first hypothesis is tested. Where there are many relations to investigate, it may be better to maximize the precision of the analysis by keeping the sample intact rather than to divide it on irrelevant variables.

17. For a general discussion of the analysis of zero relations, see Hanan C. Selvin, "Durkheim's *Suicide*," *op. cit.*, pp. 119–121. An earlier version of this article (with the same treatment of this topic) appeared in *The American Journal*

*of Sociology*, 63, 1958, pp. 607–619.

18. Nye, *op. cit.*, p. 30. For a thorough discussion of Nye's data on the relation between social status and self-reported delinquency, which concludes, incidentally, that "the findings . . . do not seem to support the contention that data other than official delinquency figures would reveal no social status differences," see Martin Gold, *Status Forces in Delinquent Boys*. Ann Arbor: Institute for Social Research, University of Michigan, 1963, pp. 4–7. Our interest in Nye's finding is mainly methodological, although we note that several studies have replicated his finding of no difference and that those failing to replicate have at best shown small differences between social classes in self-reported delinquency.

19. *Ibid.*, pp. 26–28.

20. Daniel Glaser and Kent Rice, "Crime, age and employment," *American Sociological Review*, 24, 1959, pp. 679–686.

21. *Op. cit.*, pp. 114–115.

22. Nye explains the greater frequency of delinquent acts among those with unfavorable attitudes toward their father's appearance as a consequence of their "greater real or felt loss in status." *Ibid.*, p. 112.

23. Three of the four relations are significant for girls, and two of the four are significant for boys. *Ibid.*, pp. 38, 44, 114–115.

# 8

# False
# Criteria
# of
# Causality*

Smoking per se is not a cause of lung cancer. Evidence for this statement comes from the thousands of people who smoke and yet live normal, healthy lives. Lung cancer is simply unknown to the vast majority of smokers, even among those who smoke two or more packs a day. Whether smoking is a cause of lung cancer, then, depends upon the reaction of the lung tissues to the smoke inhaled. The important thing is not whether a person smokes, but how his lungs react to the smoke inhaled. These facts point to the danger of imputing causal significance to superficial variables. In essence, it is not smoking as such, but the carcinogenic elements in tobacco smoke that are the real causes of lung cancer.[1]

The task of determining whether such variables as broken homes, gang membership, or anomie are causes of delinquency benefits from a comparison with the more familiar problem of deciding whether cigarette smoking causes cancer. In both fields many statistical studies

* An earlier version of this chapter appeared in *Social Problems*, 13, 1966, pp. 254–268.

have shown strong relations between these presumed causes and the observed effects, but the critics of these studies often attack them as "merely statistical." This phrase has two meanings. To some critics it stands for the belief that only with experimental manipulation of the independent variables is a satisfactory causal inference possible. To others it is a brief way of saying that observing a statistical association between two phenomena is only the first step in plausibly inferring causality. Since no one proposes trying to give people cancer or to make them delinquent, the fruitful way toward better causal analyses in these two fields is to concentrate on improving the statistical approach.

As we have pointed out in Chapter 3, all statistical analyses of causal relations in delinquency should satisfy three criteria: association, causal order, and lack of spuriousness. The investigator who tries to meet these criteria does not have an easy time of it. But many investigators make their task even harder by inventing new criteria of causality—or, more often, of noncausality, perhaps because noncausality is easier to demonstrate. To establish causality one must forge a chain of three links (association, causal order, and lack of spuriousness), and the possibility that an antecedent variable not yet considered may account for the observed relation makes the third link inherently weak. To establish noncausality, one has only to break any one of these links.[2]

Despite the greater ease with which noncausality may be demonstrated, many assertions of noncausality in the delinquency literature turn out to be invalid. Some are invalid because the authors misuse statistical tools or misinterpret their findings. But many more are invalid because the authors invoke one or another false criterion of noncausality. Perhaps because assertions of noncausality are so easy to demonstrate, these invalid assertions have received a great deal of attention.

A clear assertion that certain variables long considered causes of delinquency are not really causes comes from a 1960 *Report to the Congress:*

Many factors frequently cited as causes of delinquency are really only concomitants. They are not causes in the sense that if they were removed delinquency would decline. Among these factors are:

> Broken homes.
> Poverty.
> Poor housing.
> Lack of recreational facilities.
> Poor physical health.
> Race.
> Working mothers.[3]

According to this report, all of these variables are statistically associated with delinquency, i.e., they are all concomitants. To prove that they are not causes of delinquency it is necessary either to show that their relations with delinquency are spurious or that they are effects of delinquency rather than causes. Since all of these presumptive causes appear to precede delinquency, the only legitimate way to prove noncausality is to find an antecedent variable that accounts for the observed relations. None of the studies cited in the *Report* does this.[4] Instead, the assertion that broken homes, poverty, lack of recreational facilities, race, and working mothers are not causes of delinquency appears to be based on one or more of the following false criteria.[5]

1. Insofar as a relation between two variables is not perfect, the relation is not causal.
    a. Insofar as a factor is not a necessary condition for delinquency, it is not a cause of delinquency.
    b. Insofar as a factor is not a sufficient condition for delinquency, it is not a cause of delinquency.

2. Insofar as a factor is not characteristic of delinquents, it is not a cause of delinquency.
3. If a relation between an independent variable and delinquency is found for a single value of a situational or contextual factor, then the situational or contextual factor cannot be a cause of delinquency.[6]
4. If a relation is observed between an independent variable and delinquency and if a psychological variable is suggested as intervening between these two variables, then the original relation is not causal.
5. Measurable variables are not causes.
6. If a relation between an independent variable and delinquency is conditional upon the value of other variables, the independent variable is not a cause of delinquency.

In our opinion, all of these criteria of noncausality are illegitimate. If they were systematically applied to any field of research, no relation would survive the test. Some of them, however, have a superficial plausibility, both as stated or implied in the original works and as reformulated here. It will, therefore, be useful to consider in some detail just why these criteria are illegitimate and to see how they appear in delinquency research.

*False criterion 1. Insofar as a relation between two variables is not perfect, the relation is not causal.*

Despite the preponderance of Negro delinquency, one must beware of imputing any causal significance to race per se. There is no *necessary* concomitance between the presence of Negroes and delinquency. In Census Tracts 9-1 and 20-2, with populations of 124 and 75 Negro juveniles, there were no recorded cases of delinquency during the study period. The rates of Negro delinquency also vary as widely as do the white rates indicating large differences in behavior patterns that are not a function or effect of race per se. It is also of interest to note that in at least 10% of the districts with substantial Negro juvenile populations, the Negro delinquency rate is lower than the corresponding white rate.[7]

**117**

There are three facts here: 1. not all Negroes are delinquents; 2. the rates of Negro delinquency vary from place to place; 3. in some circumstances, Negroes are less likely than whites to be delinquent. These facts lead Lander to conclude that race has no causal significance in delinquency.

In each case the reasoning is the same: Each fact is another way of saying that the statistical relation between race and delinquency is not perfect, and this apparently is enough to disqualify race as a cause. To see why this reasoning is invalid one has only to ask for the conditions under which race could be a cause of delinquency if this criterion were accepted. Suppose that the contrary of the first fact above were true, that all Negroes are delinquent. It would then follow necessarily that Negro delinquency rates would not vary from place to place (fact 2) and that the white rate would never be greater than the Negro rate (fact 3). Thus in order for race to have any causal significance, all Negroes must be delinquents (or all whites nondelinquents). In short, race must be perfectly related to delinquency.[8]

Now if an independent variable and a dependent variable are perfectly associated,[9] no other independent variable is needed: that is, perfect association implies single causation, and less-than-perfect association implies multiple causation. Rejecting as causes of delinquency those variables whose association with delinquency is less than perfect thus implies rejecting the principle of multiple causation. Although there is nothing sacred about this principle, at least at the level of empirical research it is more viable than the principle of single causation. All studies show that more than one independent variable is needed to account for delinquency. In this field, as in others, perfect relations are virtually unknown. The researcher who finds a less-than-perfect relation between variable X and delinquency should not conclude that X is not a cause of delinquency, but merely that it is not the only cause.[10]

For example, suppose that tables like the following have been found for variables *A, B, C,* and *D* as well as for X:

**Delinquency by X, Where X Is Neither a Necessary nor a Sufficient Condition for Delinquency, but May Be One of Several Causes**

|  | X | Not X |
|---|---|---|
| Delinquent | 40 | 20 |
| Nondelinquent | 60 | 80 |

The researcher using the perfect relation criterion would have to conclude that none of the causes of delinquency has yet been discovered. Indeed, this criterion would force him to conclude that there are no causes of delinquency except *the* cause. The far-from-perfect relation between variable X and delinquency in the table above leads him to reject variable X as a cause of delinquency. Since variables *A, B, C,* and *D* are also far from perfectly related to delinquency, he must likewise reject them. Since it is unlikely that *the* cause of delinquency will ever be discovered by quantitative research, the researcher who accepts the perfect relation criterion should come to believe that such research is useless: All it can show is that there are no causes of delinquency.

*False criterion 1-a. Insofar as a factor is not a necessary condition for delinquency, it is not a cause of delinquency.*

The not necessary (and of course the not sufficient) argument against causation is a variant of the perfect relation criterion. A factor is a necessary condition for delinquency if it must be present for delinquency to occur, e.g., knowledge of the operation of an automobile is a necessary condition for auto theft (although all individuals charged with auto theft need not know how to drive a car). In the following table the independent variable X is a necessary (but not sufficient)[11] condition for delinquency.

### Delinquency by X, Where X is a Necessary but not Sufficient Condition for Delinquency

|  | X | Not X |
|---|---|---|
| Delinquent | 67 | 0 |
| Nondelinquent | 33 | 100 |

The strongest statement we can find in the work cited by the Children's Bureau in support of the contention that the broken home is not a cause of delinquency is the following:

We can leave this phase of the subject by stating that the phenomenon of the physically broken home as a cause of delinquent behavior is, in itself, not so important as was once believed. In essence, it is not that the home is broken, but rather that the home is inadequate, that really matters.[12]

This statement suggests that the broken home is not a necessary condition for delinquency (delinquents may come from intact but inadequate homes). The variable with which the broken home is compared, inadequacy, has all the attributes of a necessary condition for delinquency: A home that is adequate with respect to the prevention of delinquency will obviously produce no delinquent children. If, as appears to be the case, the relation between inadequacy and delinquency is a matter of definition, the comparison of this relation with the relation between the broken home and delinquency is simply an application of the illegitimate necessary conditions criterion. Compared to a necessary condition, the broken home is not so important. Compared to some (or some other) measure of inadequacy, however, the broken home may be very important. For that matter, once inadequacy is empirically defined, the broken home may turn out to be one of its important causes. Thus the fact that the broken home is not a necessary condition for delinquency does not justify the statement that the broken home is "not [a cause of delinquency] in the sense that if [it] were removed delinquency would decline."[13]

*False criterion 1-b. Insofar as a factor is not a sufficient condition for delinquency, it is not a cause of delinquency.*

A factor is a sufficient condition for delinquency if its presence is invariably followed by delinquency. Examples of sufficient conditions are hard to find in empirical research.[14] The nearest one comes to such conditions in delinquency research is in the use of predictive devices in which several factors taken together are virtually sufficient for delinquency.[15] (The fact that several variables are required even to approach sufficiency is of course one of the strongest arguments in favor of multiple causation.) Since sufficient conditions are rare, this unrealistic standard can be used against almost any imputation of causality.

First, however, let us make our position clear on the question. Poverty per se is not a cause of delinquency or criminal behavior; this statement is evidenced by the courage, fortitude, honesty, and moral stamina of thousands of parents who would rather starve than steal and who inculcate this attitude in their children. Even in the blighted neighborhoods of poverty and wretched housing conditions, crime and delinquency are simply nonexistent among most residents.[16]

Many mothers, and some fathers, who have lost their mates through separation, divorce, or death, are doing a splendid job of rearing their children.[17]

Our point of view is that the structure of the family *itself* does not cause delinquency. For example, the fact that a home is broken does not cause delinquency, but it is more difficult for a single parent to provide material needs, direct controls, and other important elements of family life.[18]

The error here lies in equating *not sufficient* with *not a cause*. Even if every delinquent child were from an impoverished (or broken) home—that is, even if this factor were a necessary condition for delinquency—it would still be possible to show that poverty is not a sufficient condition for delinquency.

In order for the researcher to conclude that poverty is a cause of delinquency, it is not necessary that all or most of those who are poor become delinquent.[19] If it were, causal variables would be virtually impossible to find. From the standpoint of social action, this criterion can be particularly unfortunate. Suppose that poverty were a necessary but not sufficient condition for delinquency, as in the table on page 120. Advocates of the not sufficient criterion would be forced to conclude that, if poverty were removed, delinquency would not decline. As the table clearly shows, however, removal of poverty under these hypothetical conditions would eliminate delinquency.

To take another example, Wootton reports Carr-Saunders as finding that 28 percent of his delinquents and 16 percent of his controls came from broken homes and that this difference held in both London and the provinces. She quotes Carr-Saunders' cautious conclusion:

We can only point out that the broken home may have some influence on delinquency, though since we get control cases coming from broken homes, we cannot assert that there is a direct link between this factor and delinquency.[20]

Carr-Saunders' caution apparently stems from the not-sufficient criterion, for unless the broken home is a sufficient condition for delinquency, there must be control cases (nondelinquents) from broken homes.

In each of these examples the attack on causality rests on the numbers in a single table. Since all of these tables show a nonzero relation, it seems to us that these researchers have misinterpreted the platitude "correlation is not causation." To us, this platitude means that one must go beyond the observed fact of association in order to demonstrate causality. To those who employ one or another variant of the perfect relation criterion, it appears to mean that there is something suspect in any numerical demonstration of association. Instead of being the first evidence for causality, an observed association becomes evidence against causality.

*False criterion 2. Insofar as a factor is not characteristic of delinquents, it is not a cause of delinquency.*

Many correlation studies in delinquency may conquer all these hurdles and still fail to satisfy the vigorous demands of scientific causation. Frequently a group of delinquents is found to differ in a statistically significant way from a nondelinquent control group with which it is compared. Nevertheless, the differentiating trait may not be at all characteristic of the delinquent group. Suppose, for example, that a researcher compares 100 delinquent girls with 100 nondelinquent girls with respect to broken homes. He finds, let us say, that 10 per cent of the nondelinquents come from broken homes, whereas this is true of 30 per cent of the delinquent girls. Although the difference between the two groups is significant, the researcher has not demonstrated that the broken home is characteristic of delinquents. The fact is that 70 per cent of them come from unbroken homes. Again, ecological studies showing a high correlation between residence in interstitial areas and delinquency, as compared with lower rates of delinquency in other areas, overlook the fact that even in the most marked interstitial area nine tenths of the children do not become delinquent.[21]

This argument is superficially plausible. If a factor is not characteristic, then it is apparently not important. But does characteristic mean important? No. Importance refers to the variation accounted for, to the size of the association, while being characteristic refers to only one of the conditional distributions (rows or columns) in the table (in the table on page 119, X is characteristic of delinquents because more than half of the delinquents are X). This is not enough to infer association, any more than the statement that 95 percent of the Negroes in some sample are illiterate can be taken to say anything about the association between race and illiteracy in that sample without a corresponding statement about the whites. In the following table, although Negroes are predominantly (characteristically) illiterate, race has no effect on literacy, for the whites are equally likely to be illiterate.

|  | RACE | |
|  | Negro | White |
|---|---|---|
| Literate | 5 | 5 |
| Illiterate | 95 | 95 |

More generally, even if a trait characterizes a large proportion of delinquents and also characterizes a large proportion of nondelinquents, it may be less important as a cause of delinquency than a trait that characterizes a much smaller proportion of delinquents. The strength of the relation is what matters—that is, the difference between delinquents and nondelinquents in the proportion having the trait (in other words, the difference between the conditional distributions of the dependent variable). In the quotation from Barron at the beginning of this section, would it make any difference for the imputation of causality if the proportions coming from broken homes had been 40 percent for the nondelinquents and 60 percent for the delinquents, instead of 10 percent and 30 percent? Although broken homes would now be characteristic of delinquents, the percentage difference is the same as before. And the percentage difference would still be the same if the figures were 60 percent and 80 percent, but now broken homes would be characteristic of both nondelinquents and delinquents.

The "characteristic" criterion is thus statistically irrelevant to the task of assessing causality. It also appears to be inconsistent with the principle of multiple causation, to which Barron elsewhere subscribes.[22] If delinquency is really traceable to a plurality of causes, then some of these causes may well characterize a minority of delinquents. Furthermore, this inconsistency is empirical as well as logical: In survey data taken from ordinary populations it is rare to find that any group defined by more than three traits includes a majority of the cases.[23]

*False criterion 3. If a relation between an independent variable and delinquency is found for a single value of a situational or contextual factor, that situational or contextual factor cannot be a cause of delinquency.*

No investigation can establish the causal importance of variables that do not vary. This obvious fact should be even more obvious when the design of the study restricts it to single values of certain variables. Thus the researcher who restricts his sample to white Mormon boys cannot use his data to determine the importance of race, religious affiliation, or sex as causes of delinquency. Nevertheless, students of delinquency who discover either from research or logical analysis that an independent variable is related to delinquency in certain situations or contexts often conclude that these situational or contextual variables are not important causes of delinquency. Since personality or perceptual variables are related to delinquency in most kinds of social situations, social variables have suffered most from the application of this criterion:

Let the reader assume that a boy is returning home from school and sees an unexpected group of people at his doorstep, including a policeman, several neighbors, and some strangers. He may suppose that they have gathered to welcome him and congratulate him as the winner of a nationwide contest he entered several months ago. On the other hand, his supposition may be that they have discovered that he was one of several boys who broke some windows in the neighborhood on Halloween. If his interpretation is that they are a welcoming group he will respond one way; but if he feels that they have come to "get" him, his response is likely to be quite different. In either case he may be entirely wrong in his interpretation. *The important point, however, is that the external situation is relatively unimportant.* Rather, what the boy himself thinks of them [it] and how he interprets them [it] is the crucial factor in his response.[24]

125

There are at least three independent variables in this illustration: 1. the external situation—the nature of the group at the doorstep; 2. the boy's past behavior—entering a contest, breaking windows, and the like; 3. the boy's interpretation of the group's purpose. As Barron notes, variable 3 is obviously important in determining the boy's response. It does not follow from this, however, that variables 1 and 2 are unimportant. As a matter of fact, it is easy to see how variable 2, the boy's past behavior, could influence his interpretation of the group's purpose and thus affect his response. If he had not broken any windows in the neighborhood, for example, it is less likely that he would think that the group had come to "get" him, and it is, therefore, less likely that his response would be one of fear. Since Barron does not examine the relation between this situational variable and the response, he cannot make a legitimate statement about its causal importance.

Within the context of this illustration it is impossible to relate variable 1, the nature of the group at the doorstep, to the response. The reason for this is simple: This "variable" does not vary—it is fixed, given, constant. In order to assess the influence of a group at the doorstep (the external situation) on the response, it would be necessary to compare the effects of groups varying in size or composition. Suppose there were no group at the doorstep; presumably the boy would feel neither fear nor joy. Barron restricts his examination of the relation between interpretation and response to a single situation, and on this basis concludes that what appears to be a necessary condition for the response is relatively unimportant.

In our opinion, it is sometimes better to say nothing about the effects of a variable whose range is restricted than to attempt to reach some idea of its importance with inadequate data. The first paragraph of the following statement suggests that its authors are completely aware of this problem. Nevertheless, the concluding paragraphs are misleading:

We recognized that the Cambridge-Somerville area represented a fairly restricted socio-economic region. Although the bitter wave of the depression had passed, it had left in its wake large numbers of unemployed. Ten years after its onset, Cambridge and Somerville still showed the effects of the depression. Even the best neighborhoods in this study were lower middle class. Consequently, our results represent only a section of the class structure.

In our sample, however [therefore], there is not a *highly* significant relation between "delinquency areas," or subcultures, and crime. If we had predicted that every child who lived in the poorer Cambridge-Somerville areas would have committed a crime, we would have been more often wrong than right. Thus, current sociological theory, by itself, cannot explain why the majority of children, even those from the "worst" areas, never became delinquent. . . .

*Social factors*, in our sample, were not strongly related to criminality. The fact that a child's neighborhood did not, by itself, exert an independently important influence may [*should not*] surprise social scientists. Undeniably, a slum neighborhood can mold a child's personality—but apparently only if other factors in his background make him susceptible to the sub-culture that surrounds him.[25]

*False criterion 4. If a relation is observed between an independent variable and delinquency and if a psychological variable is suggested as intervening between these two variables, then the original relation is not causal.*

There appear to be two elements in this causal reasoning. One is the procedure of *conjectural interpretation*.[26] The other is the confusion between *explanation*, in which an antecedent variable explains away an observed relation, and *interpretation*, in which an intervening variable links more tightly the two variables of the original relation. In short, the vanishing of the partial relations is assumed, not demonstrated, and this assumed statistical configuration is misconstrued.

This criterion is often encountered in a subtle form suggestive of social psychological theory:

The appropriate inference from the available data, on the basis of our present understanding of the nature of cause, is that whether poverty, broken homes, or working mothers are factors which cause delinquency depends upon the meaning the situation has for the child.[27]

It now appears that neither of these factors [the broken home and parental discipline] is so important in itself as is the child's reaction to them.[28]

A factor, whether personal or situational, does not become a cause unless and until it first becomes a motive.[29]

The appropriate inference about whether some factor is a cause of delinquency depends on the relation between that factor and delinquency (and possibly on other factors causally prior to both of these). All that can be determined about meanings, motives, or reactions that follow from the factor and precede delinquency can only strengthen the conclusion that the factor is a cause of delinquency, not weaken it.

A different example may make our argument clearer. Given the bombing of Pearl Harbor, the crucial factor in America's response to this situation was its interpretation of the meaning of this event. Is one to conclude, therefore, that the bombing of Pearl Harbor was relatively unimportant as a cause of America's entry into World War II? Intervening variables of this type are no less important than variables further removed from the dependent variable, but to limit analysis to them, to deny the importance of objective conditions, is to distort reality as much as do those who ignore intervening subjective states.[30]

This kind of mistaken causal inference can occur long after the original analysis of the data. A case in point is the inference in the *Report to The Congress*[31] that irregular employment of the mother does not cause delinquency. This inference appears to come from misreading Maccoby's reanalysis of the Gluecks' results.

Maccoby begins by noting: ". . . the association between irregular employment and delinquency suggests at the outset that it may not be the mother's absence from home per se which creates adjustment problems for the children. Rather, the cause may be found in the conditions of the mother's employment or the family characteristics leading a mother to undertake outside employment."[32] She then lists several characteristics of the sporadically working mothers that might account for the greater likelihood of their children becoming delinquent. For example, many had a history of delinquency themselves. In our opinion, such conjectural explanations are legitimate guides to further study but, as Maccoby says, they leave the causal problem unsettled:

It is a moot question, therefore, whether it is the mother's sporadic employment as such which conduced to delinquency in the sons; equally tenable is the interpretation that the emotionally disturbed and antisocial characteristics of the parents produced both a sporadic work pattern on the part of the mother and delinquent tendencies in the son.[33]

Maccoby's final step, and the one of greatest interest here, is to examine simultaneously the effects of mother's employment and mother's supervision on delinquency. From this examination she concludes:

It can be seen that, whether the mother is working or not, the quality of the supervision her child receives is paramount. If the mother remains at home but does not keep track of where her child is and what he is doing, he is far more likely to become a delinquent (within this highly selected sample), than if he is closely watched. Furthermore, if a mother who works does arrange adequate care for the child in her absence, he is no more likely to be delinquent . . . than the adequately supervised child of a mother who does not work. But there is one more lesson to be learned from the data: among the working mothers, a majority did not in fact arrange adequate supervision for their children in their absence.[34]

It is clear, then, that regardless of the mother's employment status, supervision is related to delinquency. According to criterion 3, employment status is therefore not a cause of delinquency. It is also clear that when supervision is held relatively constant, the relation between employment status and delinquency disappears. According to criterion 4, employment status is therefore not a cause of delinquency. This appears to be the reasoning by which the authors of the *Report to The Congress* reject mother's employment as a cause of delinquency. But criterion 3 ignores the association between employment status and delinquency and is thus irrelevant. And criterion 4 treats what is probably best seen as an intervening variable as an antecedent variable and is thus a misconstruction of a legitimate criterion. Actually, the evidence that allows the user of criterion 4 to reach a conclusion of noncausality is, at least psychologically, evidence of causality. The disappearance of the relation between mother's employment and delinquency when supervision is held relatively constant makes the *how* of the original relation clear: Working mothers are less likely to provide adequate supervision for their children, and inadequately supervised children are more likely to become delinquent.

*False criterion 5. Measurable variables are not causes.*

In tract 11-1, and to a lesser extent in tract 11-2, the actual rate [of delinquency] is lower than the predicted rate. We suggest that these deviations [of the actual delinquency rate from the rate predicted from home ownership] point up the danger of imputing a causal significance to an index, per se, despite its statistical significance in a prediction formula. It is fallacious to impute causal significance to home ownership as such. In the present study, the

130

author hypothesizes that the extent of home-ownership is probably highly correlated with, and hence constitutes a measure of community anomie.[35]

As a preventive, "keeping youth busy," whether through compulsory education, drafting for service in the armed forces, providing fun through recreation, or early employment, can, at best, only temporarily postpone behavior that is symptomatic of more deepseated or culturally oriented factors. . . . Merely "keeping idle hands occupied" touches only surface symptoms and overlooks underlying factors known to generate norm-violating behavior patterns.[36]

The criterion of causation that, in effect, denies causal status to measurable variables occurs frequently in delinquency research. In the passages above, home ownership, compulsory education, military service, recreation, and early employment are all called into question as causes of delinquency. In their stead one finds as causes anomie and "deep-seated or culturally oriented factors." The appeal to abstract as opposed to more directly measurable variables appears to be especially persuasive. Broad general concepts embrace such a variety of directly measurable variables that their causal efficacy becomes almost self evident. The broken home, for example, is no match for the inadequate home:

. . . the physically broken home as a cause of delinquent behavior is, in itself, not so important as was once believed. In essence, it is not that the home is broken, but rather that the home is inadequate, that really matters.[37]

The persuasiveness of these arguments against the causal efficacy of measurable variables has two additional sources: 1. their logical form resembles that of the legitimate criterion lack of spuriousness; 2. they are based on the seemingly obvious fact that operational indices (measures) do not cause the variations in other operational indices. Both of the following arguments can thus be brought against any assertion that a measurable variable causes delinquency.

Anomie causes delinquency. Home ownership is a measure of anomie. Anomie is thus the source of variation in both home ownership and delinquency. If the effects of anomie were removed, the observed relation between home ownership and delinquency would disappear. This observed relation is thus causally spurious.

Home ownership is used as an indicator of anomie, just as responses to questionnaire items are used as indicators of such things as authoritarianism, achievement motivation, and religiosity. No one will argue that the responses to items on a questionnaire cause race hatred, long years of self-denial, or attendance at religious services. For the same reason, it is erroneous to think that home ownership causes delinquency.

Both of these arguments beg the question. Conjectural explanations leave the causal problem unsettled. The proposed antecedent variable may or may not actually account for the observed relation.

Our argument assumes that the proposed antecedent variable is directly measurable. In the cases cited here it is not. If the antecedent variable logic is accepted as appropriate in these cases, all relations between measurable variables and delinquency may be said to be causally spurious. If anomie can explain away the relation between one of its indicators and delinquency, it can explain away the relations between all of its indicators and delinquency.[38] No matter how closely a given indicator measures anomie, the indicator is not anomie, and thus not a cause of delinquency. The difficulty with these conjectural explanations is thus not that they may be false, but that they are nonfalsifiable.[39]

The second argument against the causality of measurable variables overlooks the following point: It is one thing to use a measurable variable as an indicator of another, not directly measurable variable; it is something else again to assume that the measurable variable is only an indicator. Not owning one's home may indeed be a useful indicator of anomie; it may, at the same time, be a potent cause of delinquency in its own right.

The user of the "measurable variables are not causes" criterion treats measurable variables as epiphenomena. He strips these variables of all their causal efficacy (and of all their meaning) by treating them merely as indexes, and by using such words as *per se, as such,* and *in itself.*[40] In so doing, he begs rather than answers the important question: Are these measurable variables causes of delinquency?

*False criterion 6. If a relation between an independent variable and delinquency is conditional upon the value of other variables, the independent variable is not a cause of delinquency.*

The rates of Negro delinquency also vary as widely as do the white rates indicating large differences in behavior patterns that are not a function or effect of race per se. It is also of interest to note that in at least 10% of the districts with substantial Negro juvenile populations, the Negro delinquency rate is lower than the corresponding white rate.[41]

The appropriate inference from the available data, on the basis of our present understanding of the nature of cause, is that whether poverty, broken homes, or working mothers are factors which cause delinquency depends upon the meaning the situation has for the child.[42]

Both of these quotations make the same point: The association between an independent variable and delinquency depends on the value of a third variable. The original two-variable relation thus becomes a three-variable conditional relation. In the first quotation, the relation between race and delinquency is shown to depend on some (unspecified) property of census tracts. In the second quotation, each of three variables is said to interact with the meaning of the situation to cause delinquency.

One consequence of showing that certain variables are only conditionally related to delinquency is to invalidate what Albert K. Cohen has aptly named "the assumption of intrinsic pathogenic qualities"—the assumption that the causal efficacy of a variable is, or can be, independent of the value of other causal variables.[43] Invalidating this assumption, which Cohen shows to be widespread in the literature on delinquency, is a step in the right direction. As many of the quotations in this chapter suggest, however, the discovery that a variable has no intrinsic pathogenic qualities has often led to the conclusion that it has no pathogenic qualities at all. The consequences of accepting this conclusion can be shown for delinquency research and theory.

Cloward and Ohlin's theory that delinquency is the product of lack of access to legitimate means and the availability of illegitimate means assumes, as Palmore and Hammond have shown,[44] that each of these states is a necessary condition for the other, i.e., that lack of access to legitimate and access to illegitimate means interact to produce delinquency. Now, if conditional relations are noncausal, neither lack of access to legitimate nor the availability of illegitimate means is a cause of delinquency, and one could manipulate either without affecting the delinquency rate.

Similarly absurd conclusions could be drawn from the results of empirical research in delinquency, since all relations between independent variables and delinquency are at least conceivably conditional (the paucity of empirical generalizations produced by delinquency research as a whole suggests that most of these relations have already been found to be conditional).[45]

Although conditional relations may be conceptually or statistically complicated and, therefore, psychologically unsatisfying, their discovery does not justify the conclusion that the variables involved are not causes of delinquency. In fact, the researcher who would grant causal status only to unconditional relations will end by granting it to none.

Any one of the criteria of causality discussed in this chapter makes it possible to question the causality of most of the relations that have been or could be revealed by quantitative research:

Currently popular "causes" of delinquency range from toilet training to television to the existence of working mothers and the absence of reading skills. Obviously none of these, or any other which might be fashionable at a given moment, is a necessary and sufficient cause of adolescent misbehavior. There were, for example, delinquents before the advent of television and there are today delinquents who do not watch television and certainly many young people who do watch it without behaving abominably as a result. *Any purported "cause" must fail this test of validity.*[46]

Some of these criteria stem from perfectionist interpretations of legitimate criteria, others from misapplication of these legitimate criteria. Still others, especially the argument that a cause must be characteristic of delinquents, appear to result from practical considerations. (It would indeed be valuable to the practitioner if he could point to some easily identifiable trait as the hallmark of the delinquent.) Finally, one of these criteria is based on a mistaken notion of the relation between abstract concepts and measurable variables—a notion that only the former can be the causes of anything.

The implications of these standards of causality for practical efforts to reduce delinquency are devastating. Since nothing that can be pointed to in the practical world is a cause of delinquency (e.g., poverty, broken homes, lack of recreational facilities, working mothers), the practitioner is left with the task of combating a nebulous anomie or an unmeasured inadequacy of the home; or else he must change the adolescent's interpretation of the meaning of events without at the same time changing the events themselves or the context in which they occur.

Mills has suggested that accepting the principle of multiple causation implies denying the possibility of radical change in the social structure.[47] Our analysis suggests that rejecting the principle of multiple causation implies denying the possibility of *any* change in the social structure—because, in this view, nothing causes anything.

# Notes

1. This is a manufactured "quotation"; its source will become obvious shortly.

2. Popper calls this the asymmetry of verifiability and falsifiability. Karl R. Popper, *The Logic of Scientific Discovery*. New York: Basic Books, 1959, pp. 27–48. For a fresh view of the verification-falsification controversy, see Thomas S. Kuhn, *The Structure of Scientific Revolutions*. Chicago: University of Chicago Press, 1962. Kuhn discusses Popper's views on pp. 145–146. Actually, it is harder to establish noncausality than our statement suggests, because of the possibility of spurious independence. This problem is discussed in Chapter 7.

3. U.S. Department of Health, Education, and Welfare, *Report to The Congress on Juvenile Delinquency*, United States Government Printing Office, 1960, p. 21. The conclusion that poor housing is not a cause of delinquency is based on Mildred Hartsough, *The Relation Between Housing and Delinquency*, Federal Emergency Administration of Public Works, Housing Division, 1936. The conclusion that poor physical health is not a cause is based on Edward Piper's "unpublished Children's Bureau manuscript summarizing the findings of numerous investigators on this subject." Since we have not examined these two works, the following conclusions do not apply to them.

4. The works cited are: for broken homes, Negley K. Teeters and John Otto Reinemann, *The Challenge of Delinquency*. Englewood Cliffs, N.J.: Prentice-Hall, 1950, pp. 149–154; for poverty, Bernard Lander, *Towards an Understanding of Juvenile Delinquency*. New York: Columbia University Press, 1954; for recreational facilities, Ethel Shanas and Catherine E. Dunning, *Recreation and Delinquency*. Chicago: Chicago Recreation Commission, 1942; for race, Lander, *op. cit.*; for working mothers, Eleanor E. Maccoby, "Children and working mothers," *Children*, 5, 1958, pp. 83–89.

5. It is not clear in every case that the researcher himself reached the conclusion of noncausality or, if he did, that this conclusion was based on the false criteria discussed. Maccoby's article, for example, contains a conjectural explanation of the relation between mother's employment and delinquency (i.e., without presenting any statistical evidence she suggests that the original relation came about through some antecedent variable), but it appears that the conclusion of noncausality in the *Report* is based on other statements in her work.

6. All of the foregoing criteria are

related to the perfect relation criterion in that they all require variation in delinquency that is unexplained by the noncausal variable. A more general statement of criterion 3 would be: If variable X is related to delinquency when there is no variation in variable T, then variable T is not a cause of delinquency. In order for this criterion to be applicable, there must be some residual variation in delinquency after T has had its effect. Although both forms of this criterion fairly represent the reasoning involved in some claims of noncausality, and although both are false, the less explicit version in the text is superficially more plausible.

7. Bernard Lander, *op. cit.*, p. 32. (Italics in original) An alternative interpretation of the assumptions implicit in this quotation is presented in the discussion of criterion 6.

8. Strictly speaking, in this quotation Lander does not demand that race be perfectly related to delinquency, but only that all Negroes be delinquents (the sufficient condition of criterion 1-b). Precedent for the perfect relation criterion of causality appears in a generally excellent critique of crime and delinquency research by Jerome Michael and Mortimer J. Adler published in 1933: "There is still another way of saying that none of the statistical findings derived from the quantitative data yields answers to etiological questions. The findings themselves show that every factor which can be seen to be in some way associated with criminality is also associated with non-criminality, and also that criminality is found in the absence of every factor with which it is also seen to be associated. In other words, what has been found is merely additional evidence of what we either knew or could have suspected, namely, that

there is a plurality of related factors in this field." *Crime, Law and Social Science.* New York: Harcourt, p. 53.

9. *Perfect association* here means that all of the cases fall into the main diagonal of the table, that (in the 2 × 2 table) the independent variable is both a necessary and a sufficient cause of the dependent variable. Less stringent definitions of perfect association are considered in the following paragraphs. Since Lander deals with ecological correlations, he could reject race as a cause of delinquency even if it were perfectly related to delinquency at the census tract level, since the ecological and the individual correlations are not identical.

10. We are assuming that the causal order and lack of spuriousness criteria are satisfied.

11. To say that X is a necessary condition for delinquency means that all delinquents are X (i.e., that the cell in the upper right of this table is zero); to say that X is a sufficient condition for delinquency implies that all X's are delinquent (i.e., that the cell in the lower left is zero); to say that X is a necessary and sufficient condition for delinquency means that all X's and no other persons are delinquent (i.e., that both cells in the minor diagonal of this table are zero).

12. Teeters and Reinemann, *op. cit.*, p. 154.

13. *Report to The Congress*, p. 21. Two additional illegitimate criteria of causality listed above are implicit in the quotation from Teeters and Reinemann. Inadequacy of the home could be treated as an intervening variable which interprets the relation between the broken home and delinquency (criterion 4) or as a theoretical variable of which the broken home is an indicator (criterion 5).

14. In his *Theory of Collective Behavior* (New York: The Free Press, 1963) Neil J. Smelser suggests sets of necessary conditions for riots, panics, and other forms of collective behavior; in this theory the entire set of necessary conditions for any one form of behavior is a sufficient condition for that form to occur.

15. In the Gluecks' prediction table, those with scores of 400 or more have a 98.1 percent chance of delinquency. However, as Reiss has pointed out, the Gluecks start with a sample that is 50 per cent delinquent. Had they started with a sample in which only 10 percent were delinquent, it would obviously have been more difficult to approach sufficiency. Sheldon Glueck and Eleanor Glueck, *Unraveling Juvenile Delinquency*. Cambridge: Harvard University Press, 1950, pp. 260–262; Albert J. Reiss, Jr., "*Unraveling Juvenile Delinquency*. An appraisal of the research methods," *American Journal of Sociology*, 57, 1951, pp. 115–120.

16. Teeters and Reinemann, *op. cit.*, p. 127.

17. *Ibid.*, p. 154.

18. F. Ivan Nye, *Family Relationships and Delinquent Behavior.* New York: Wiley, 1958, p. 34. (Italics in original)

19. We are, of course, assuming throughout this discussion that the variables in question meet what we consider to be legitimate criteria of causality.

20. Barbara Wootton, *Social Science and Social Pathology.* New York: Macmillan, 1959, p. 118.

21. Milton L. Barron, *The Juvenile in Delinquent Society.* New York: Alfred A. Knopf, 1954, pp. 86–87.

22. *Ibid.*, pp. 81–83.

23. There are two reasons for this: the less-than-perfect association between individual traits and the fact that few traits are simple dichotomies. Of course, it is always possible to take the logical complement of a set of traits describing a minority and thus arrive at a set of traits that does characterize a group, but such artificial combinations have too much internal heterogeneity to be meaningful. What, for example, can one say of the delinquents who share the following set of traits: not Catholic, not middle class, not of average intelligence?

The problem of characteristic traits arises only when the dependent variable is inherently categorical (Democratic; member of a gang, an athletic club, or neither) or is a discrete ordinal variable (performs none, a few, or many delinquent acts). In other words, this criterion arises only in tabular analysis, not where some summary measure is used to describe the association between variables.

24. Barron, *op. cit.*, pp. 87–88. (Authors' italics)

25. William McCord and Joan McCord, *Origins of Crime.* New York: Columbia University Press, 1959, pp. 71 and 167. (Italics in original) A study restricted to known offenders and in which the dependent variable is the seriousness of the first offense concludes: "Delinquency cannot be fruitfully controlled through broad programs to prevent divorce or other breaks in family life. The prevention of these would certainly decrease unhappiness, but it would not help to relieve the problem of delinquency." Richard S. Sterne, *Delinquent Conduct and Broken Homes.* New Haven: College and University Press, 1964, p. 96. Since the range of the dependent variable, delinquency, is seriously reduced in a study restricted to offenders, such conclusions can not follow from the data.

26. Like conjectural explanation, this is an argument, unsupported by statistical data, that the relation between two variables would vanish if the effects of a third variable were removed; here, however, the third variable intervenes causally between the original independent and dependent variables.

27. Sophia Robison, *Juvenile Delinquency*. New York: Holt, Rinehart and Winston, 1961, p. 116.

28. Paul W. Tappan, *Juvenile Delinquency*. New York: McGraw-Hill, 1949, p. 135.

29. Sheldon and Eleanor Glueck, *Family Environment and Delinquency*. Boston: Houghton-Mifflin, 1962, p. 153. This statement is attributed to Bernard Glueck. No specific reference is provided.

30. "Write your own life history, showing the factors *really* operative in your coming to college, contrasted with the external social and cultural factors of your situation." Barron, *op. cit.*, p. 89.

31. *Op. cit.*, p. 21.

32. Eleanor E. Maccoby, "Effects upon children of their mothers' outside employment," in Norman W. Bell and Ezra F. Vogel, eds., *A Modern Introduction to The Family*. New York: The Free Press, 1960, p. 523. In fairness to the Children's Bureau report, it should be mentioned that Maccoby's argument against the causality of the relation between mother's employment and delinquency has a stronger tone in the article cited there (see note 4) than in the version we have used as a source of quotations.

33. *Ibid.*

34. *Ibid.*, p. 524.

35. Lander, *op. cit.*, p. 71.

36. William C. Kvaraceus and Walter B. Miller, *Delinquent Behavior: Culture and the Individual*. Na-tional Education Association, 1959, p. 39.

37. Teeters and Reinemann, *op. cit.*, p. 154.

38. As would be expected, Lander succeeds in disposing of all the variables in his study as causes of delinquency—even those he says at some points are "*fundamentally* related to delinquency."

39. While Lander throws out his measurable independent variables in favor of anomie, Kvaraceus and Miller throw out their measurable dependent variable in favor of "something else." "Series of norm-violating behaviors, which run counter to legal codes and which are engaged in by youngsters, are only symptomatic of something else in the personal make-up of the individual, in his home and family, or in his cultural milieu." *Op. cit.*, p. 34. The result is the same, as the quotations suggest.

40. The appearance of these terms in the literature of delinquency almost invariably signals a logical difficulty.

41. Lander, *op. cit.*, p. 32. This statement is quoted more fully on page 117.

42. Robison, *op. cit.*, p. 116.

43. "Multiple factor approaches," in Marvin E. Wolfgang *et al.*, eds., *The Sociology of Crime and Delinquency*. New York: Wiley, 1962, pp. 78–79.

44. Erdman B. Palmore and Phillip E. Hammond, "Interacting factors in juvenile delinquency," *American Sociological Review*, 29, 1964, pp. 848–854.

45. After reviewing the findings of twenty-one studies as they bear on the relations between twelve commonly used independent variables and delinquency, Barbara Wootton concludes: "All in all, therefore, this collection of studies, although chosen

for its comparative methodological merit, produces only the most meagre, and dubiously supported generalizations." *Op. cit.*, p. 134. Cf. Chapter 2.

46. Irwin Deutscher, "Some relevant directions for research in juvenile delinquency," in Arnold Rose, ed., *Human Behavior and Social Processes*. Boston: Houghton Mifflin, 1962, p. 475. (Authors' italics)

47. C. Wright Mills, "The professional ideology of social pathologists," *American Journal of Sociology*, 44, 1942, pp. 165–180.

*part iii*

# MULTIVARIATE

# ANALYSIS

# 9

# Some Problems of Multivariate Statistical Analysis

The quantitative findings at best measure the correlation of one or more factors with criminality, or recidivism, or some type of criminality. But these indices of correlation, often expressed by the comparison of averages or percentages, neither solve the problem of the relation of the various factors *inter se* nor define the functional dependence of criminality upon a set of related factors.

. . . The method of percentage comparisons is a clumsy method for dealing with a large number of variables, and it tends to give an exaggerated impression of relationships. . . .[1]

As we have shown again and again, the critic often calls the findings of research into question simply by proposing a configuration of relations among variables at least slightly more complex than that examined or reported by the investigator. The investigator himself is, of course, frequently concerned that examination of more complex configurations would force him to alter his interpretation of the configuration he has examined. In the past, limitations of time, money, and sample size usually precluded analysis as complex as that demanded by the critic and desired by the investigator. Now, however, the computer has placed within the reach of most investigators statistical techniques capable of handling large numbers of variables. Only a few years ago, some of these techniques had been applied only to data on such things as weather, crop yield, and prices; illustrations of their use in social statistics texts were often hypothetical and farfetched. It should not be surprising, therefore, that their use on social data has sometimes produced results of questionable methodological and substantive merit.

In this chapter, we want to take a closer look at some of the problems that are particularly significant in multivariate statistical analysis. Our aim is not to present an exhaustive account of any of these techniques, but rather to point out some problems their users have encountered or are likely to encounter. In Chapter 10, we compare one of these techniques, multiple regression, with cross-tabulation as tools of quantitative analysis.

## A Pioneering Study in Multivariate Statistical Analysis

Bernard Lander's *Towards an Understanding of Juvenile Delinquency*[2] has been justly honored as the first work in delinquency to make significant use of multivariate statistical techniques.[3] Since we shall point out some serious methodological errors in this study, it is important to repeat that our purpose in treating an author's mistakes is to help other investigators to avoid such mistakes in their own research and to raise the level of critical awareness among consumers of social research. If the mistakes in Lander's statistical analyses went

146

undetected by editors and reviewers, then there is good reason for looking closely at his work.

Lander relies heavily on partial correlation and factor analysis. His argument for partial correlation is similar to the one we have advanced for partial association—specifically, the introduction of a third variable into a two-variable relation:

Actually despite a high and significant zero order correlation coefficient between delinquency and a specific variable, when other factors are held constant and their influence eliminated, the relationship may prove to be low and not significant. On the other hand, a variable which is only slightly associated with delinquency in the zero order correlation table may prove to be associated in an important fashion after the partial correlations have been computed.[4]

Lander computed correlation coefficients between delinquency rates and seven other properties of Baltimore census tracts. The independent variables, ranked from high to low according to the absolute value of their zero-order correlations with delinquency, are

1. Percentage of Homes Owner-occupied .......... −.80
2. Percentage of Over-crowding .................. +.73
3. Percentage of Non-whites ..................... +.70
4. Percentage of Substandard Housing ............ +.69
5. Median Rentals ............................... −.53
6. Median School Years of Education ............. −.51
7. Percentage of Foreign-born ................... −.16[5]

After inspecting these zero-order correlations, Lander wished to make a "deeper and more fundamental analysis."[6] He computed the partial correlation between each of his independent variables and the delinquency rate. Here is his account of what happens to the variables ranked second and fourth:

In the zero-order correlation table . . . the juvenile delinquency rate is highly correlated with substandard housing and residential over-crowding. In the partial correlation analysis, when the influence of other variables studied is eliminated, instead of positive correlations between these variables and delinquency of $r = +.69$ and $+.73$, we have derived coefficients of partial correlations of .0052 and .0079 as describing the *real* relationship between these variables and delinquency. . . . This indicates that, despite the high correlation coefficients, there is no substantive relationship between these two variables and delinquency when all other factors are held constant and their influence eliminated.[7]

In addition to partial correlation, Lander used factor analysis to answer the question, "How many 'fundamental' or 'underlying' variables must be postulated to account for the intercorrelations among the predicting variables?"[8] The factor analysis revealed that the eight variables (the delinquency rate was included) could be accounted for by two major factors which he named the *anomic* and the *socioeconomic*. The variables that determine the anomic factor are percentage of homes owner-occupied (negatively related), percentage non-white, and the delinquency rate; all of the other variables (with the exception of percentage foreign-born—which stood off by itself) contribute to the socioeconomic factor.

On the basis of his factor analysis, Lander makes the following statements:

The correlation between the *anomic* and the *socio-economic* factors is, as one would expect . . . high (.684). It provides an explanation of the fact that delinquency is so highly correlated with the socio-economic properties of a tract. The association between the factors however is statistical.

The factor analysis indicates that, in Baltimore, areas characterized by instability and *anomie* are frequently the same districts which are also characterized by bad housing, low rentals and overcrowding. But the delinquency is *fundamentally* related only to the anomie and not to the poor socio-economic conditions of the tract.[9]

If Lander's interpretations of his partial correlation and his factor analysis are correct, these are most impressive findings: There is no real relation between substandard housing and delinquency or between overcrowding and delinquency; indeed, there is no real relation between socioeconomic conditions and delinquency. We believe, however, that both of his interpretations are defective because he fails to consider the problem of causal order. As a result, he makes causal statements that his data contradict or, at best, do not support.

The problem of causal order is especially difficult in studies of relations between the properties of aggregates. How, for example, does one determine whether a high rate of substandard housing precedes or follows low median rent? Lander does not ask this question. But unless it is asked, and answered, there is no justification for calling the disappearance of a two-variable relation either explanation or interpretation.

Perhaps the best way to study the logic of Lander's analysis is to follow his own account of it. Thus he cites Durkheim's study of suicide as a case in which the logic of partial correlation was used to advantage:

The analysis [by Durkheim] of the seasonal rates [of suicide] . . . indicates that it is not climate or temperature, as such, which affects the suicide rate but that with the coming of spring and summer, human activities and modes of living change. . . . Thus, it is not weather . . . per se, that [is a] causal factor of suicide. The aforementioned variable [is] . . . also highly correlated with the presence or lack of socially integrating conditions. The rate of suicide thus varies with the degree of social cohesion.[10]

Since Lander uses Durkheim's analysis as a model, it is worth taking a closer look at what Durkheim was trying to do in this passage and to translate Durkheim's account of his aims into more precise language. This relation between the physical and the social displeased Durkheim for theoretical reasons; it violated his principle that social facts can be adequately explained only by other social facts. He therefore searched for a social variable that would account for the relation between length of day and suicide rates. Because no social variable can affect the length of day, Durkheim was clearly looking for an intervening variable to link the variables in his original relation. He found it in the degree of social activity:

Thus everything proves that if daytime is the part of the twenty-four hours most favorable to suicide, it is because it is also the time when social life is at its height. Then we have a reason why the number of suicides increases, the longer the sun remains above the horizon.[11]

Social activity is thus the connection between these two disparate phenomena; it makes the original relation more plausible by showing how it comes about. As we have emphasized, this is much different from explanation, although both types of elaboration are based on the same statistical configuration, the vanishing of the original two-variable relation. In explanation, the new variable is causally prior to the original independent variable; the statistical finding that it accounts for the original relation thus leads to discarding the original relation as causally spurious. In interpretation, the same type of statistical outcome strengthens the original relation. This distinction is of central importance in discussing the logic of Lander's analysis.

In his partial correlation analysis Lander implicitly assumes that all other factors in his study precede substandard housing and overcrowding, and that he has therefore explained away the relations between these two variables and delinquency. The contrary assumption, that these other variables follow substandard housing and overcrowding, leads to the conclusion that all other factors in the study interpret the relations—a markedly different but equally defensible conclusion. The problem is that neither of these conclusions is meaningful, because the seven properties of the census tracts that Lander studies cannot be arranged in any meaningful causal sequence. Although they form a unity, this unity "does not involve a sequence in time, but rather a *configuration* in space."[12] Such a configuration clearly does not imply a causal ordering. Lander's claim that partial correlation has demonstrated the spuriousness of some of the original relations can be rejected without hesitation.

Although, as noted above, Lander at one point makes the implicit assumption that all other factors precede substandard housing and overcrowding, he does not apply this assumption consistently. In computing partial correlation coefficients, his assumed causal ordering shifts from one computation to the next. Thus, although overcrowding was one of the variables taken into account in the partial correlation of delinquency and substandard housing, substandard housing is then taken into account in the partial correlation of delinquency and overcrowding. Since the resulting relations are treated as real or spurious, overcrowding and substandard housing are assumed, at different times, to be antecedent to each other. The same procedure was followed with all other pairs of variables: In the partial correlation of variable $X$ and delinquency, variable $Y$ was treated as antecedent to $X$, but in another computation, $X$ was treated as antecedent to $Y$.

Lander's conclusion, that his partial correlation analysis enabled him to describe "the *real* relationship between these variables and delinquency,"[13] can therefore be rejected on two grounds: 1. There is no simple, meaningful causal ordering among his variables, as he implicitly assumes in his interpretation of the partial correlation analysis. 2. Even if such a causal ordering exists, Lander ignores it in his statistical operations.

There are several procedures that Lander could have used to resolve, at least in part, the ambiguous causal ordering of his variables. First, he might have examined earlier censuses to see how the variables changed over time; quantitative techniques for unraveling causal order in panel data[14] were not available at the time of Lander's study, but even a qualitative examination would have clarified some of his relations. Second, he might have examined newspaper files, records of the building and health departments, and other historical data available in Baltimore. Finally, he might even have interviewed long-time residents to get their recollections of changes in their neighborhoods. In fact, Lander did examine some of these kinds of data,[15] but more to provide a general historical background than to clarify the causal structure of his analysis.[16]

Lander's interpretation of the results of his factor analysis resembles those of his partial correlation analysis. He rejects a correlation of .684 between his anomic and socioeconomic factors as merely statistical. He also argues that "delinquency is *fundamentally* related only to the anomie and not to the poor socio-economic conditions of the tract."[17]

As we read Lander's data, there is no reason to reject socioeconomic conditions as an important determinant of delinquency. Indeed, we reach the opposite conclusion: that socioeconomic conditions are fundamentally related to delinquency even if, as his use of *statistical* and *fundamentally* implies, the relation between socioeconomic conditions and delinquency were to disappear when anomie is held constant. The key element again is the causal ordering of anomie and socioeconomic conditions. We have already suggested some ways in which Lander could have studied causal order empirically. In addition, he could have relied on theoretical arguments. Both Marx and Durkheim, among others, provide theoretical justification for treating socioeconomic conditions as causally prior to anomie. With this causal ordering, the disappearance of the original relation between socioeconomic conditions and delinquency when anomie is held constant, far from ruling out socioeconomic conditions as a cause of delinquency, actually strengthens its causal importance. This is a case of *interpretation*, not of *explanation*. Socioeconomic conditions lead to anomie and anomie, in turn, to delinquency. The key to demonstrating that socioeconomic conditions are a cause of delinquency is precisely the statistical relation that Lander had invoked to get rid of socioeconomic conditions.

## Factor Analysis As a Tool of Causal Inquiry

Factor analysis has probably suffered more from the partisanship of its friends than from the attacks of its enemies:

Factor analysis has the peculiarity, among scientific investigation tools . . . that it can be profitably used with relatively little regard to prior formulation of a hypothesis. Like radar turned upon a fog . . . it necessarily reveals to us whatever organization or structure is present. . . .

Starting with measurements on two or three dozen variables, a factor analyst can thus, without hypothesis formation, arrive at the highly structured answer that there are, say, five factors at work, that their natures are such and such, that they are correlated among themselves in such and such a manner and have certain specific relative magnitudes in respect to their contribution to the variance of a particular variable or of most variables. Of course, it would generally be a richer contribution to understanding if he had first been able to formulate an exact hypothesis to this effect from contributory evidence gathered in other fields or by other methods. . . . But the detailed hypothesis is not essential to the design of the experiment.[18]

What Cattell does not take into account is that factor analysis, unlike such techniques as multiple regression and analysis of variance, treats all variables alike; it makes no distinction between independent and dependent variables. For this reason it should be used only with collections of variables on the same conceptual level—measures of personality, indicators of socioeconomic status, or forms of delinquent behavior.[19] Putting independent and dependent variables into the same factor analysis can only generate confusion:

> . . . Lander located a cluster of indicators that he named the 'anomie' factor. These were the delinquency rate, the per cent of non-whites, and the per cent of homes owner occupied. Lander himself points out the tautological nature of such a finding if we seek a causal solution. . . . He treats all three as indicators of an underlying situation, 'anomie', which he defines as a condition in which social norms do not regulate conduct. Clearly, then, 'anomie' cannot cause delinquency. Delinquency *is* a species of 'anomie.'[20]

The conceptual difficulties become even more acute if one tries to go beyond the simple identification of factors to the computation of factor scores, i.e., to replace the many items that go into a factor analysis by a smaller number of more basic variables. In principle, this is a laudable effort at parsimony: twenty or thirty variables replaced by three or four factors.[21] But what happens when one does this with a factor like Lander's "anomie"? One cannot then go on to study more complex relations than were included in the factor analysis—for example, the joint effects of anomie and socioeconomic conditions on delinquency—because delinquency, the dependent variable, is already part of anomie, one of the independent variables.[22]

Problems of this kind can arise even when the factor analysis includes only independent variables, if they come from different parts of the causal structure. As we have noted in Chapter 5, variables like age often have such strong relations with later independent variables and with delinquency as to make the relations between these independent variables and delinquency spurious. Now consider the effects of such strong relations on a factor analysis involving several of these causes of delinquency. Many of these variables will have stronger relations with age than with each other. These strong relations will thus generate a factor where, without age, there might have been none. Moreover, since age is only one component of this factor, the analyst may overlook its central position and interpret the factor as reflecting the contents of the other items. In short, including a widely correlated antecedent variable like age will generate a spurious factor whose elements have little in common except their relation to the antecedent variable.

*The meaning of factors.* A factor analysis is a confession of ignorance. If one really knows the structure of a complex domain (say, from past research or from experimental manipulation), there is no point in going through a factor analysis again. Factor analysis is primarily useful in getting a crude picture of the major dimensions of variation in a new area of research.[23] These dimensions will then suggest the important independent or dependent variables to include in causal analysis.

There are so many choices of procedure and interpretation open to the factor analyst that two different analysts working on the same body of data may produce different factors (for example, one may think that an orthogonal factor structure fits the data well enough, while another may resort to oblique factors). A *fortiori*, it is even more unusual to get the same factors from different bodies of data, even when these data were gathered on similar populations and with similar instruments. It thus comes as no surprise that Chilton's effort to replicate Lander's study finds that the same variables are related to delinquency but that the factors are different:

My conclusion is that the underlying order or structure of these eight variables for Baltimore in 1940 is basically similar to the structure of these same variables for Detroit and Indianapolis in 1950, and that the factorial results for all three cities are equivocal

155

in respect to the hypothesis that delinquency is closely related to a condition of anomie.

. . . the conclusion [is supported] that some of the same variables are importantly related to juvenile delinquency in all three cities and that these variables cannot be consistently grouped into economic or anomic categories.[24]

In general, there is little point in seeking a precise replication of a methodologically sound factor analysis. If the original sample was large enough to insure stable correlations and if the analyst restricted his interpretations to those factors with strong and clear patterns of loadings, then replications will simply confirm the existence of major dimensions of variation uncovered in the earlier analyses. Since these dimensions (factors) are only means to a more important end—the study of causal relations—and since factor analysis is a poor tool for studying causes, the investigator of ecological data on delinquency should not concern himself with replicating Lander's, Bordua's, or Chilton's factor analyses. Another factor analysis would be worthwhile in such a study only if it included many new variables.[25]

## Some Notes on Multiple Regression

The prospects for the effective use of multiple regression in delinquency research are considerably brighter than for factor analysis. As we have argued above, multiple regression is inherently a more suitable tool for causal analysis, and two recent studies suggest that the promise of multiple regression will be borne out in future research (it is perhaps significant that one of these studies is by an economist and the other by a psychologist). Belton M. Fleisher has investigated the effects of income on delinquency in several different ecological analyses,[26] and Isidor Chein has written an impressive methodological treatise on the use of regression procedures and ecological data to assess the effectiveness of programs to prevent and treat delinquency.[27] In our judgment, both of these investigations are worth careful study by delinquency researchers, especially those who work with ecological data.

This is not to say that these studies are immune to criticism, but rather that they show the power of regression analysis more clearly than any amount of methodological argument. To our surprise, both studies ignore the problem of spuriousness. Fleisher simply looks at the coefficients of his regression equation and reports that some variables are important and others are not. Since Chein has only plans rather than results, one cannot be sure that he will ignore spuriousness; nevertheless, in his unusually detailed and insightful account of the logic of regression analysis there is no mention of causal order or spuriousness.[28]

Fleisher used a stepwise regression procedure, which first computes the regression of delinquency on the single most important independent variable, then adds the next most important variable, and continues in this way until it has included all of the independent variables. It would have been relatively easy for him to follow the history of each variable, noting when it entered the regression equation and what happened to its association with the independent variable as each new variable entered the regression.[29]

A relatively minor error in both studies is to consider the beta-coefficients as measures of the relative importance of variables. This practice is almost universal in regression analysis, but it is, nevertheless, wrong, except in the rare case where the independent variables are essentially uncorrelated with each other. By themselves, the beta-coefficients measure the "direct" contribution of each independent variable to the dependent variable, but they do not take account of the "indirect" contributions that each independent variable makes through its correlations with the other independent variables.[30] The reason for ignoring these indirect contributions in the past has undoubtedly been the extra amount of computational labor required beyond the computation of the regression equation. Now, however, computational labor is no problem; indeed, the stepwise regression programs now in wide use provide a measure of the total (direct and indirect) contributions of each variable without any further calculations. As each new variable enters the regression equation (and, of course, the entire regression equation changes with each new variable), the program computes the multiple correlation coefficient, $R_{0.123}$ . . . . Now the square of the multiple correlation coefficient is the proportion of variation in the dependent variable accounted for by all of the independent variables that have already entered the regression. The increment in $R^2$ produced by a variable when it first enters the regression is thus the desired measure of its direct and indirect contributions to the dependent variable.[31]

Our final comment on these two studies has to do with tests of statistical significance (a topic we shall consider at length in Chapter 13). Fleisher uses such tests throughout, but Chein argues that they are generally inapplicable in this kind of research. Chein's argument rests on the fact that ecological studies are usually based on total populations rather than on samples; with no sample, there can be no sampling error. Similarly, measurement error of the usual kind is hardly a factor in correlations based on aggregate data. A correlation of individual observations is sensitive to shifts in a small number of cases, but where each point of the scatter plot represents hundreds or thousands of cases, such shifts result in imperceptible movements of the points (this is especially true in those of Fleisher's analyses that are based on cities rather than on census tracts; what effect can random error of measurement have on the mean of twenty-five thousand observations?).

Despite these critical remarks, we are impressed with the way in which Fleisher and Chein have used multiple regression in the study of delinquency. Even if tabular analysis were all that it has been thought to be, the greater power and speed of regression analysis would be strong arguments in its favor. If, as we shall try to show in Chapter 10, tabular analysis does not have the virtues claimed for it, then the future course of quantitative research may well be considerably different from what it has been.

# Notes

1. Jerome Michael and Mortimer J. Adler, *Crime, Law and Social Science*, New York: Harcourt, 1933, pp. 52–53, 154.

2. New York: Columbia University Press, 1954.

3. Ernest Greenwood, "New directions in delinquency research: a commentary on a study by Bernard Lander," *Social Service Review*, 30, 1956, pp. 147–157. Lloyd E. Ohlin, Review of *Towards an Understanding of Juvenile Delinquency* by Bernard Lander, *American Sociological Review*, 19, 1955, pp. 616–617.

4. Lander, *op. cit.*, p. 40.

5. *Ibid*, p. 36.

6. *Ibid.*, p. 34.

7. *Ibid.*, p. 46. (Italics in original)

8. *Ibid.*, p. 51.

9. *Ibid.*, p. 59 (Italics in original)

10. *Ibid.*, pp. 42–43.

11. Emile Durkheim, *Suicide* (trans. by John A. Spaulding and George Simpson). New York: The Free Press, 1951, p. 119.

12. Herbert H. Hyman, *Survey Design and Analysis*. New York: The Free Press, 1955, p. 260. (Italics in original)

13. Lander, *op. cit.*, p. 46. (Italics in original)

14. Donald C. Pelz and Frank M. Andrews, "Detecting causal priorities in panel study data," *American Sociological Review*, 29, 1964, pp. 836–848.

15. Lander, *op. cit.*, pp. 91–95.

16. The integration of qualitative and quantitative analyses is more of a cliché than a rule of action in research. All too often, the qualitative data appear only as background, or as quotations to enliven a set of tables. The kind of systematic interweaving of qualitative and quantitative data suggested here could go far to improve future ecological studies of delinquency.

17. Percentage foreign-born, a special case, is ignored in this discussion.

18. Raymond B. Cattell, *Factor Analysis*. New York: Harper, 1952, p. 21.

19. Cf. the discussion of scaling in Chapter 12.

20. David J. Bordua, "Juvenile delinquency and 'anomie': an attempt at replication," *Social Problems*, 6, 1958–59, pp. 230–238. (Italics in original)

21. Harry H. Harman, *Modern Factor Analysis*. Chicago: University of Chicago Press, 1960, p. 337.

22. For another example of the kind of nonsense that can come from mixing independent and dependent variables in the same factor analysis, see Hanan C. Selvin, *The Effects of Leadership*. New York: The Free Press, 1960, p. 250. A factor of "socio-sexual behavior" consisted largely of "being married" and "having sexual intercourse." Fortunately,

this factor analysis had little to do with the rest of the study.

23. See, for example, Selvin, *Ibid.*, Chapter 2.

24. Roland J. Chilton, "Continuities in delinquency area research: a comparison of studies for Baltimore, Detroit, and Indianapolis," *American Sociological Review*, 29, 1964, pp. 71–83; these quotations are from pp. 79–80. Chilton also finds some computational errors in Lander's analysis, but they do not account for the differences between the two factor analyses; furthermore, Chilton himself obtained different factors by using different (but acceptable) procedures (pp. 76–77).

25. Chilton did another factor analysis with nineteen variables, but, as with his more exact replication of Lander's analysis, he did not even try to name the factors, i.e., to discern the meaning of the dimensions of variation uncovered by his factor analysis. It seems to us that this robs Chilton's factors of any value. If Lander's sin is overconceptualization of his factor analysis, Chilton's is the failure to conceptualize at all.

26. Belton M. Fleisher, "The effect of income on delinquency," *American Economic Review*, 56, 1966, pp. 118–137.

27. Isidor Chein, *Some Epidemiological Vectors of Delinquency and Its Control: Outline of a Project.* New York: Research Center for Human Relations, New York University, no date, mimeo.

28. Since Chein has data on several time periods, he will be able to use the Pelz-Andrews procedure for detecting causal order.

29. Richard N. Rosett, an econometrician at the University of Rochester, has suggested to us that Fleisher might have handled his causal analysis more fruitfully as a set of simultaneous equations. Note that the two sociologists who have written most creatively on the logic of causal analysis were both strongly influenced by their studies of econometrics. See Hubert M. Blalock, Jr. *Causal Inferences in Nonexperimental Research.* Chapel Hill: University of North Carolina Press, 1964; and Raymond Boudon, "A method of linear causal analysis: dependence analysis," *American Sociological Review*, 30, 1965, pp. 365–374.

30. Harman, *op. cit.*, pp. 338–348.

31. It is hard to make statements of this sort about multiple regression that are more than half true, because the causal structure that the investigator imposes on the data affects the meaning of his statistics. Thus, for example, the increment in $R^2$ produced by a variable when it first enters the regression is *not* the "desired" measure of its direct and indirect contributions to the dependent variable when variables entering subsequently are considered antecedent to the variable in question. Since this chapter was written, statistical techniques that explicitly take into account or demand complex causal structures have been widely adopted and developed within sociology. These techniques, such as path analysis, avoid many of the problems that stem from the use of what are essentially predictive techniques by the practitioners of an irrepressibly theoretical science. (Arthur S. Goldberger kindly pointed out several errors in our original discussion of multiple regression.)

# 10

# The Shortcomings of Tabular Analysis[1]

The development of punched-card machines in the first third of this century made modern survey research economically possible. Simple causal analysis had relied on tables ever since the eighteenth century, but the new technology made it possible to use tables (hundreds of them, if necessary) to explore complex relations among many variables, as well as to present the relations among a few variables. Now the large electronic computer has brought another new technology, and its impact promises to be as revolutionary for research in the behavioral sciences as the microscope was in biology.

The major impact of the computer on the kind of quantitative analysis discussed in this book will be the replacement of percentaged contingency tables as devices of exploration and causal analysis by one or another member of the family of linear statistical techniques—multiple regression, discriminant analysis, canonical analysis, factor analysis, and analysis of variance.[2] The results of this change will be better, cheaper, faster, and more powerful analyses than can be done with tables, and some new kinds of analysis that cannot be done with tables at all.

These are strong claims, and they run counter to most conventional practices and teaching of research methods. In his introduction to Samuel A. Stouffer's posthumous collection of essays, Paul F. Lazarsfeld praises Stouffer for having clearly formulated as early as the 1930's the difference between contingency tables and partial correlation:

Stouffer doubted whether [correlation techniques] would be appropriate in their conventional form to the new type of material sociologists began to work with, a doubt that the experience of the last thirty years has more than justified. His criticism is especially directed against the use of partial correlation:

'We may find that within groups I and II, a partial correlation between juvenile delinquency and the percentage of foreign born and Negroes is high, holding the other factors constant; while within groups III and IV the partial correlation may be low. This difference may be very important; yet it would be averaged out if all the data were analyzed in a single correlation scheme. . . .'

Here we find clearly formulated the difference between [contingency tables] and partial correlation. This distinction was seen only much later by others; it has finally become the cornerstone of what is now usually called 'survey analysis'.[3]

In order to assess the relative merits of tabular analysis and linear statistical analysis we shall consider each set of procedures in some detail, concentrating on the logic of the procedures rather than on their application to delinquency research. To keep the discussion as simple as possible, we shall compare tabular analysis mainly with multiple regression, the best-known form of linear statistical analysis and the most useful in survey research.

## Four Defects of Tabular Analysis

1. *Interminable analysis.* When does a tabular analyst decide to stop his analysis? More often than not, when he runs out of cases, time, interest, or money. The one criterion that he cannot invoke is that his analysis is complete, that he has explained enough of what there is to explain. He may judge any one table by its degree of association, but what is he to do about the large set of tables that form the core of his analysis? Even in the simplest case, where there is a single, quantitative dependent variable, he is unable to measure the proportion of the variation in this variable that is explained by the entire set of independent variables taken together.[4] In this most basic of all analytic tasks, the measurement of association between the independent variables and the dependent variable, the tabular analyst never knows whether he has explained too little, enough, or, indeed, whether his overlapping sets of independent variables may have explained the same variation more than once!

The situation is altogether different in multiple regression. The square of the multiple correlation coefficient, $R^2_{0.12 \ldots n}$, tells him how much of the variation in the dependent variable has been explained by the $n$ variables that he has included in his regression equation. Furthermore, as explained in Chapter 9, in the stepwise versions possible with large computers, the increment to $R^2$ produced by each additional variable provides him with a measure that tabular analysis can only approximate (and with an unknown degree of error). Finally, it is easier to judge the parsimony of a regression analysis than of a tabular analysis. Other things being equal, an $R^2$ of 0.70 based on six independent variables is more parsimonious than the same $R^2$ based on ten variables.

2. *Wastefully large samples.* Tabular analysis requires sam-

ples of hundreds or thousands of cases. Simply gathering and processing these data costs a great deal of money. At today's prices a sample of one thousand interviews of moderate length would require at least $30,000. Tabular analysis needs such large samples because the measurement of association is based on comparisons of percentages computed within rows or columns. Since the stability of such comparisons depends on the smallest number of cases in the rows or columns compared, large samples are mandatory.[5]

It is possible to be more precise about the role of sample size in the measurement of association. Consider a table of three rows and three columns. In order to measure association by percentage comparisons the investigator must estimate the frequencies in four cells in this table (this is what is meant by saying that such a table has four degrees of freedom.)[6] He then uses the nine percentages to make a more-or-less qualitative assessment of the overall association between the two variables. In short, he asks the data to provide precise information on four parameters, which he then uses to give an imprecise estimate of one parameter!

If all he wants is to measure association, it is obviously simpler, more precise, and more economical to compute a single measure of association directly. Speaking approximately (because the exact answer depends on the degree of departure from independence), the analyst gets the same degree of statistical stability with one-fourth as many cases when he measures the association in a $3 \times 3$ table with a single summary measure rather than with percentage comparisons—and he gets a precise figure rather than a qualitative assessment.

3. *Ambiguous causal inferences.* Some ambiguity is inherent in causal analysis; as we noted in Chapter 5, it is always possible that an antecedent factor not yet considered will make the observed relation spurious. Tabular analysis, however, piles an additional and unnecessary ambiguity on top of

this. Whenever the analyst wants to examine the joint effects of more than two or three independent variables, he is likely to run out of cases (i.e., find some row or column totals too small for stable computation of percentages). For example, after examining the three-variable table showing the joint effects of $X_1$ and $X_2$ on Y, there may be too few cases to construct the four-variable table that includes $X_3$. In this familiar situation the simplest way to determine the effects of $X_3$ is to drop one of the earlier variables—say, $X_2$—and examine the joint effects of $X_1$ and $X_3$ on Y. Now some of the variation in Y had already been accounted for by $X_2$; dropping $X_2$ and examining the joint effects of $X_1$ and $X_3$ on Y thus amounts to throwing away the proportion of variance explained by $X_2$ and bringing in a new combination of variables to explain again what had, in part, already been explained. The tabular analyst not only has no way of knowing how much he has explained of what there is to explain; he frequently—and necessarily—explains the same variations several times over.

Running out of cases has even more serious consequences for the analyst's causal imputations. Since most of the independent variables in any study are associated with each other, removing a variable that had an effect on the dependent variable does not remove its effects. On the contrary, it is still present in the variables that are retained. In the above example, what appears to be the effect of $X_1$ and $X_3$ is also the effect of $X_2$—to some unknown and unknowable extent. In tabular analysis, then, as long as the number of independent variables included in a table is smaller than the number known to be related to the dependent variable, the meaning of any relation is inherently ambiguous. If poverty, race, education, and overcrowding are all individually related to delinquency, or even if pairs or triples of these variables are studied together, the meaning of any one of these tables must always remain in doubt as long as it is impossible to examine the joint effects of all four independent variables. What appears to be the effect of education and overcrowding is also the effect of race and poverty—and of any other independent variables associated with these four.

Linear statistical procedures put all this in a new light. Because they rely largely on relations between pairs of variables to build up the more complex relations, there is almost no limit to the number of independent variables that can be examined at one time. Regression programs that examine the combined effects of fifty or more independent variables in a minute or two are widely available. To be sure, regression analysis brings new problems, which we shall examine in the next section; nevertheless, the greater clarity of its causal imputations is incontestable. A sample of two hundred cases is large enough to compute a regression equation of fifty variables, but a sample of two thousand cases may not be large enough to examine the joint effects of five variables in a percentaged table.

4. *Inefficient search procedures.* At the beginning of an analysis a period of weeks or months goes into what are called search procedures. If questioned about what he is doing, the analyst is likely to reply that he is trying to "get the feel of the data" or to "find out which variables work." There is, of course, much more to this search period than examining the relations between the dependent variable and each of the independent variables. Again, it is the intercorrelation of the independent variables that challenges the analyst. Unraveling these tangled causal relations by tabular analysis is a slow job, even for the experienced analyst. Knowledge of previous research, insight, and a zealous research assistant may shorten the job, but it is basically more of an art than a set of routines.

Searching a multivariate domain is like making a map. With relatively simple tools—a surveyor's transit for measuring angles and a steel tape for measuring distances—one could make a detailed map of, say, the state of Colorado. Given enough time, one could locate every tree and every mud puddle to within a few feet. But is all this detail necessary if one is concerned, most of all, to locate Denver, the Colorado River, and the Rocky Mountains? For locating such gross features aerial photography is quicker and cheaper. Using percentaged tables to find the major features of the analytic landscape is like using the transit and the steel tape to make a crude map; all that extra detail is unnecessary, and it is pointless to pay for what one does not need.

Linear statistical procedures, programmed for large computers, are the aerial photographs of survey analysis. With a continuous or an ordinal dependent variable, stepwise multiple regression searches out the most important independent variables. With a polytomous (categorical) dependent variable, there is stepwise discriminant analysis. If the task is to sort a large number of items that are all on the same conceptual level into different dimensions, then factor analysis is quick and efficient. With such procedures one can map the analytic landscape more effectively in a few days than one can do with tables in several months.

## Objections and Defenses

These are serious charges; when presented in lectures at various centers of research, they have been vigorously challenged. No doubt the defenders of tabular analysis are partly in the familiar historical position of those who see their expert competence threatened by a technological innovation. But then accumulated experience and their knowledge of methodological principles make it necessary to take their objections seriously, to see if the attacks on tabular analysis will stand up to searching criticism and if the claims made for the linear statistical procedures are warranted.

One of the most common objections to these arguments is their emphasis on association. Granted the primary place of association in causal analysis, the tabular analysts argue that they want to know many other things about their data— is there curvilinearity, monotonicity, interaction, homoscedasticity, and so on? All of these properties can be determined from careful examination of tables, and none of them appears in a simple measure of association.

This argument is correct as far as it goes. There are times when it is important to know about one or more of these properties (but seldom, if ever, all of them). For each of these properties there is an appropriate measure that can be computed from the data as needed. Alternatively, one can modify some of the linear models to take into account such deviations as curvilinearity and interaction.[7] A sample large enough to permit answering all of these questions (which is usual in tabular analysis) is unnecessarily large if one wants answers to only one or two.

When an experienced tabular analyst says that looking at tables allows him to "get the feel of the data," he may be referring to two different situations. Looking at a single table does allow him to spot anomalous relations—for example, those that bend where they should be straight or those that show violent interactions. As we have suggested, this kind of "feeling for the data" can come as well from coefficients designed to measure such anomalies as from qualitative inspection of tables. A second kind of feeling for the data comes in examining a large set of tables. Rummaging through a pile of tables suggests patterns of association, provides hints that several variables may be manifestations of some more basic factor, and suggests dependent variables that are highly predictable from the independent variables. As these vague operations are formalized, it turns out that each of them can be performed by one or another of the family of linear statistical procedures. To take one more example, finding the most predictable dependent variable is one of the outcomes of *canonical analysis*.

A word of warning about canonical analysis may spare the interested reader some of the trouble we have had in trying to interpret our own results. In principle, canonical analysis transforms ordinary intercorrelated variables into new independent and dependent *canonical variables* (linear combinations, or weighted sums, of the original variables). These canonical variables have the following properties:

1. The canonical independent variables are uncorrelated with each other.
2. The canonical dependent variables are uncorrelated with each other.
3. The first canonical independent variable has the maximum possible correlation with the first canonical dependent variable (i.e., no other combination of weights would yield a higher correlation), and similarly for each succeeding pair of canonical variables.

In practice, however, it is often impossible to make sense out of any pair of canonical variables beyond the first; the reason seems to be the stringent demands that the model makes on the data.[8] Note, however, that the weights for the first canonical dependent variable tell the relative predictability of each of the original dependent variables, just as the weights for the first canonical independent variable measure the relative power of the original independent variables as predictors (they are, in fact, beta-coefficients). There is no way to get such measures of relative predictability in tabular analysis, which cannot handle more than one dependent variable at a time.

The tabular analyst has no monopoly on insight and feeling for the data. Indeed, the depth of one's insight depends on what there is to see. These powerful statistical procedures generate new material for the analyst to look at, material that is invisible to the tabular analyst. A factor matrix offers at least as much opportunity for displaying insight as a set of tables—and probably less opportunity for mistakes about patterns of association.

Finally, there is the claim that tables are a more flexible tool than these multivariate statistical procedures. One can do almost anything with tables, but each of these statistical procedures has a relatively specific function. We agree; far from seeing flexibility as a virtue, however, we see it as a defect. The flexibility of tabular analysis reminds us of those Swiss jackknives that contain a bottle opener, a screwdriver, a cork-screw, an awl, and assorted cutting blades. They are indeed flexible tools, but, if one wants to drive a screw, an ordinary screwdriver does a better job. And if one wants to study survey data carefully, special tools do a better job than the all-purpose table.[9]

## The Future of Tables

Will tables disappear entirely from reports of quantitative analysis, to be replaced by $R^2$, betas, and other arcane measures? We hope not. Although tables are inferior to linear statistical procedures in exploring complex relations and in helping to establish causal relations, they are unexcelled for presenting the final results of a long and complicated analysis. Once the three or four most important variables have been identified and their causal status made plausible, then showing their joint distribution in a multivariate table allows the analyst to describe their patterns of interaction in much greater detail than with the more elaborate statistical techniques. Furthermore, and this is perhaps the strongest reason for keeping tables as devices of presentation, both the lay reader and the professional social scientist will find them easier to understand.

# Notes

1. An earlier version of this chapter appeared in Hanan C. Selvin, *The Logic of Survey Analysis*. Berkeley: Survey Research Center, University of California, 1964. (Mimeo) This study was supported by a grant from the National Science Foundation.

2. For a discussion of these procedures and computer programs designed for them, see William W. Cooley and Paul R. Lohnes, *Multivariate Procedures for the Behavioral Sciences*. New York: Wiley, 1962.

3. *Social Research to Test Ideas*. New York: The Free Press, 1962, p. xvi.

4. The problem of using tables to measure the combined effects of several independent attributes (categorical variables) was first considered in G. Udny Yule, "On the association of attributes in statistics, with illustrations from the material of the Childhood Society, etc." *Philosophical Transactions of the Royal Society*, 194, 1899, pp. 257–319, at p. 280. More recently, Goodman and Kruskal have suggested for this purpose a modification of their "lambda" measure of association; neither procedure, however, is useful for more than two or three variables, and the "lambda" measure is unsatisfactory on other grounds. See Leo A. Goodman and William H. Kruskal, "Measures of association in cross-classification," *Journal of the American Statistical Association*, 49; 1954, pp. 732–764.

5. The situation is exacerbated by an unthinking reliance on proportionally allocated probability samples, i.e., samples in which each member of the population has the same chance of appearing in the sample. A disproportionally allocated (unequally weighted) sample may cause some complications for the analyst (see Chapter 14), but it is often the only sensible procedure when one wants to study categories of people who comprise a small part of the population—for example, people who change their preferences during an election. See Peter H. Rossi, "Four landmarks in voting research," in Eugene Burdick and Arthur J. Brodbeck, *American Voting Behavior*. New York: The Free Press, 1959, pp. 5–54.

6. With the marginal frequencies given (i.e., known from other tabulations and not necessarily derived especially for this table) and the proper choice of four internal cell frequencies, the remaining five frequencies can be found by subtraction.

7. There is a thorough discussion of such procedures in Isidor Chein, *Some Epidemiological Vectors of Delinquency and Its Control: Outline of a Project*. New York: Research Center for Human Relations, New York University, no date. (Mimeo)

Many computer programs for multiple regression include "transgeneration" options that make it easy to modify the basic linear and additive models.

8. In factor analysis it is often difficult to find one meaningful set of orthogonal factors; in canonical analysis there are two orthogonal sets, the corresponding members of which must be maximally correlated with each other. For a further discussion of the virtues of canonical analysis,

see Jeanne R. Gullahorn, *Multivariate Approaches in Survey Data and Processing: Comparison of Factor, Cluster, and Guttman Analyses and of Multiple Regression and Canonical Correlation Methods*. East Lansing: Michigan State University, 1966. (Mimeo)

9. For another example of analysis that can be done with linear statistical procedures but not with tables, see the discussion of the profile fallacy in Chapter 15.

*part iv*

# CONCEPTUALIZATION

# AND

# INFERENCE

# 11

# Concepts,
# Indicators,
# and
# Indices

A scientific theory might therefore be likened to a complex spatial network: Its terms are represented by the knots, while the threads connecting the latter correspond, in part, to the definitions and, in part, to the fundamental and derivative hypotheses included in the theory. The whole system floats, as it were, above the plane of observation and is anchored to it by rules of interpretation. These might be viewed as strings which are not part of the network but link certain points of the latter with specific places in the plane of observation. By virtue of these interpretive connections, the network can function as a scientific theory: From certain observational data, we may ascend, via an interpretive string, to some point in the theoretical network, thence proceed, via definitions and hypotheses, to other points, from which another interpretive string permits a descent to the plane of observation.[1]

The field of delinquency is marked by the absence of interpretive connections linking theory to research and research to theory. Although there has been no lack of research and no lack of theory, the two have rarely been put together in such a way that a theory was systematically tested or a body of data rigorously interpreted.

From the standpoint of the theorist, one reason for this gap in the field of delinquency is the wide acceptance by delinquency researchers of the eclectic, multiple factor approach. This approach assumes that there are many causes of delinquency:

Crime is assignable to no single universal source, not yet to two or three; it springs from a wide variety, and usually a multiplicity, of alternative and converging influences.[2]

Dissatisfaction with this supposed axiom of the plurality of causes is almost as old as sociology itself.

Thus, it is commonly said that crime may be produced by several different causes and that the same is true with suicide, punishment, etc. If we practice experimental reasoning in this spirit, we shall assemble in vain a considerable number of facts, for we shall never be able to obtain precise laws or determinate relations of causality. We shall be able only to assign vaguely a badly defined consequence to a confused and indefinite group of antecedents.[3]

If experience in the field of delinquency is any guide, Durkheim's prediction could not have been more accurate. In many cases it appears that the greater the number of studies, the less is known about the causes of delinquency. Almost all reviews of the field conclude that the results of research are "inconclusive and inconsistent."[4] Yet this sad condition should not lead, as Durkheim assumed it did, to rejecting the principle of multiple causation. Although the belief in multiple causation is "responsible" for the inconsistency and inconclusiveness of delinquency research (and indirectly for the delinquency researcher's attitude toward theory), none of this calls into question the validity of the principle.

In a sharp critique of the multiple factor approach, Albert K. Cohen indicts its users for confusing explanation by means of a single factor with explanation by means of a single theory[5] which may include several factors. The obvious inability of a single factor to explain all of the delinquency in a single study has thus resulted in the rejection of theory.[6]

Cohen describes another assumption of the users of this approach—which he calls the "assumption of intrinsic pathogenic qualities":

More specifically, this assumption implies (1) that the inherent pathogenic (or beneficent) tendency of each factor in the actor's milieu is independent of the other factors which accompany it and (2) that these tendencies are independent of the actor's personality or the meanings of the factors to the actor.[7]

Users of the multiple factor approach thus tend to reject both theory and analysis.[8] They reject theory because of the illegitimate equation of multiple factors with multiple theories or, on occasion, with *the* multiple factor theory, which, as Cohen points out, "is an abdication of the quest for a theory."[9] They reject analysis because the assumption of intrinsic pathogenic qualities (insofar as it implies that the effects of other things are always equal) denies its necessity.

The delinquency researcher's attitude toward theory and analysis does not follow logically from his acceptance of the principle of multiple causation. In contrast to the theorist, the delinquency researcher is impressed by the principle of multiple causation—and justifiably so: At the level of abstraction at which he works, the evidence in its favor is overwhelming. The lower the level of abstraction, the greater the number of variables, and, therefore, the more multivariable any explanation of delinquency and the less tenable the assumption that other things are equal. Therefore, a relation between unconceptualized variables (e.g., broken homes and incarceration) will seldom be successfully replicated, since the myriad of other things that can vary from one study to the next will vary. If the broken home is only one of many factors affecting delinquency, then the relation between broken homes and delinquency must vary over time and space, not only in magnitude, but also, occasionally, in direction. Thus, it is no accident that the results of delinquency research have been inconclusive and inconsistent.

How can this inconsistency and inconclusiveness be removed? By making use of the two sets of procedures that advocates of the multiple factor approach reject: theory and analysis. The principle of multiple causation is not antithetical to theory or analysis. On the contrary, acceptance of this principle makes theory and analysis that much more essential. As Nowak says:

The lower the theoretical generality of a given statement, the more it is usually multivariable, and the greater is the possibility that, formulated as a statement with wide historical application or as a universal thesis, it will be false.[10]

One way to prolong the life of hypotheses, then, is to make them more abstract. However, evidence in favor of this proposition is sometimes used to criticize delinquency research, as in Wootten's tart comment:

. . . the theories which last longest are those which deal in relatively vague categories such as 'bad parents'. More concrete, measurable factors which can more easily be put to the test are seen to lose their significance as soon as they are subjected to really vigorous scrutiny.[11]

(1.) Without defending such variables as the "badness of parents," it is nevertheless true that the more abstract the formulation, the smaller will be the number of variables and, therefore, the greater the likelihood that a proposition will survive an empirical test.

(2.) Another way to prolong the life of hypotheses is to insure that other things are in fact equal by controlling extraneous variables through the techniques discussed earlier. The importance of these analytical techniques increases with the number of variables the researcher confronts.

Now, if researchers have erred in thinking that multiple causation makes an overall theory of delinquency untenable, theorists have erred in thinking that the idea of a single theory makes multiple causation untenable. The researcher who finds that there are "more than 170 distinct conditions . . . conducive to childish misconduct"[12] is mistaken if he concludes that this number cannot be reduced by theoretical abstraction. The theorist who concludes that his two or three theoretical variables cannot be expanded to hundreds of distinct measures is also mistaken. It is, therefore, ironic that theorists should criticize the results of quantitative delinquency research as "inconclusive and inconsistent."[13] Inconclusiveness and inconsistency are properties, not of facts, but of explanations. It is the task of the theorist to abstract from the apparently inconsistent and inconclusive results of delinquency research a consistent explanation of juvenile delinquency. If, at the level of relations between concrete variables, it were reasonable to expect the results of research to be consistent, all inconsistency could be attributed to research error and the search for *the* relation between these variables could justifiably continue. Meanwhile, the theorist could justifiably continue to ignore the results of past (inconclusive and inconsistent) research. Since it is not reasonable to expect the results of a-theoretical research to be either consistent or conclusive, neither the researcher's quest nor the theorist's disdain is justified.

Both delinquency researchers and theorists, then, throw the baby out with the bath: Researchers have thrown theory out along with single-factor explanations; theorists have thrown the results of research out along with multiple-factor explanations. Thus researchers have had little theory, and theorists have paid little attention to the findings of research, although neither theory nor research has scientific import unless they are related to each other.[14]

The gap between theory and research in delinquency is most evident when one attempts to discuss the questions raised under the heading, concepts and indicators. Concepts belong to the domain of the theorist, indicators to the domain of the researcher. However, the theorist needs indicators to test his theory, and the researcher needs concepts to interpret his data.

The researcher starting with a theory possesses a set of concepts that are related to each other by propositions or hypotheses. For example, the concepts *strain, opportunity,* and *delinquency* might be related to each other in the following manner:

A juvenile who wants something may get it by legal or illegal means. If legal means are available, he will use them. If they are not available, he will be forced to resort to illegal means. Thus delinquent behavior is a function of desire and of access to legal means. In our society, everyone desires the same things: Therefore, there is no relation between desire and opportunity or between desire and delinquency (more precisely, in the particular system to which the theory is being applied, desire [strain] is taken to be a constant). Delinquency thus varies inversely with opportunity to obtain desired goods by legal means.[15]

The first step the researcher must take is to interpret the theory by devising operational definitions or indicators of the concepts employed. For example, he may take father's income as an indicator of opportunity to obtain valued goods by legal means, and police arrests as an indicator of delinquency. The researcher can now state a theoretically derived, testable hypothesis: As his father's income increases, the likelihood that a boy will come to the attention of the police decreases. The table showing the relation between income and contact with the police is a test of this hypothesis. If the relation is not in the direction predicted by the hypothesis, or if there is no relation between the indicators, the theory is said to be falsified.

This test is, of course, far from conclusive, since a relation between father's income and contacts with the police is consistent with almost all theories of delinquency. In recent years, many investigators have tested specific hypotheses derived from one or another theory of delinquency. Often, in fact, they have used one body of data to test a few hypotheses from each of several theories.[16] As would be the case here, the results are usually taken to be inconclusive, whether they appear to confirm or to falsify the theory in question. This inconclusiveness may be interpreted as indicative of a general, expectable lag in research.[17] In our opinion, it also indicates a free-floating quality of delinquency theory: that it is relatively unaffected by the results of research. This is not to say that delinquency theory is too abstract, but rather that it is high time for researchers to become more aggressive in spelling out the implications of their findings for current theories.

This simple theory, its interpretation,[18] and its observational test will serve to illustrate the concept-indicator problems faced by the student of delinquency. These problems will be discussed under the following headings: 1. theoretical concepts; 2. operational definitions; 3. concept-indicator relations; and 4. indicator-indicator relations.

### Theoretical Concepts (What Is Delinquency?)

Almost all delinquency texts begin by asking the question, What is delinquency? They usually present many definitions. Thus there may be a lay definition, a legal definition, a psychological definition, and a variety of sociological definitions.

A glance at the literature of delinquency reveals that a great deal has been written about whether delinquency should be defined as an attribute or a variable, as a homogeneous or a multidimensional concept, whether delinquent acts or the assumption of a delinquent role should be the criterion of delinquency, and so on. On the one hand, students of adjudicated delinquency are accused of studying nonrepresentative, biased samples; on the other hand, students of deviant behavior are accused of studying juveniles who are not really delinquents.

Although delinquency is not explicitly defined in our illustrative theory, it is possible to abstract a definition of delinquency from the theory: Delinquency is that behavior of a juvenile which involves the attempt to obtain desired goods by illegitimate means. It may be objected that this definition is nothing but a restatement of the theory and that so defining delinquency makes the theory tautological. There is nothing wrong with this. In fact, it has been argued that "pure theory is always tautological."[19] But if theory is tautological—that is, if the "logical interrelations between concepts are all derivable from the definitions of the concepts"[20]—what is to be gained by asking what delinquency is, unless the object is to explain delinquency? The answer is that there is little to be gained from definitions unrelated to a theoretical or research concern. In this sense, we agree with Popper:

I use the name *methodological essentialism* to characterize the view . . . that it is the task of pure knowledge or 'science' to discover and to describe the true nature of things, i.e., their hidden reality or essence. . . . This view can be better understood when contrasted with its opposite, *methodological nominalism.* Instead of aiming at finding out what a thing really is, and at defining its true nature, methodological nominalism aims at describing how a thing behaves in various circumstances, and especially, whether there are any regularities in its behavior. . . . The methodological nominalist will never think that a question like . . .'*What is* an atom?' is an important question for physics. . . .[21]

In short, in the proper context, definitions are important. How one defines delinquency determines in large part how one will explain delinquency. The researcher or theorist does not characterize delinquency as behavior that is "non-utilitarian, malicious and negativistic" if his purpose is to advance an "illicit means" or a "culture conflict" theory of delinquent conduct.[22] Either of these theories might be able to account for nonutilitarian delinquency, but at least on the surface the definition suggests that something other than a "means-end" or "differing values" perspective is required.[23] In this sense, then, it is impossible meaningfully to answer the question, What is delinquency? without at the same time answering the question, How should delinquency be explained?

## Operational Definitions (What Is Delinquency?)

In the illustrative theory and its test there are two definitions of delinquency: One definition is implicit in the theory itself, the other is explicit in the test of the theory, i.e., delinquents are those who come to the attention of the police. In answering the question, What is delinquency? most of the efforts of delinquency researchers have been at this second level, the level of the operational definition.

The studies we have discussed use a variety of operational definitions of delinquency. Thus there is Nye's study of delinquent (deviant) behavior, the Gluecks' study of serious offenders, Lander's study of children brought before the juvenile court, and Wattenberg and Balistrieri's study of auto thieves. That these are only a few of many possible operational definitions of delinquency is evident from the following table.

**Table 11-1—Delinquency Data for Ten Fifteen-Year-Old Boys (hypothetical)**

| Cases | 6 | 7 | 8 | 9 | 10 | 11 | 12 | 13 | 14 | 15 | Adjudicated? | Are you a delinquent? |
|---|---|---|---|---|---|---|---|---|---|---|---|---|
| A | x | X | x | X | X | x |   |   |   |   | No | No |
| B |   |   |   | x | x | x | X | X |   |   | No | Yes |
| C | x |   |   |   |   |   |   | X | [X] | X | Yes | Yes |
| D | x |   | x |   | x |   | x |   |   | x | No | No |
| E |   |   |   | X | X | [X] |   |   |   |   | Yes | Yes |
| F |   |   | x |   |   |   |   |   |   |   | No | No |
| G |   | X |   | X |   |   | X | x | x | x | No | Yes |
| H | X | X | X | X | X | X | X | [X] | X | [X] | Yes | Yes |
| I | X | X | X | X | x | x |   |   |   |   | No | No |
| J |   |   |   |   |   |   |   |   |   | [X] | Yes | No |

X—serious delinquent act(s)
[X]—adjudged delinquent
x—minor delinquent act(s)

It is apparent that several statistically related but conceptually distinct dimensions of delinquency are represented by these data: e.g., adjudicated versus nonadjudicated, self-perception as delinquent versus self-perception as nondelinquent; total number of delinquent acts; total number of serious delinquent acts; weighted sum of delinquent acts; persistence, i.e., number of years in which delinquent acts occurred; and the frequency of delinquent acts. Certainly, if additional information (say, the nature of the delinquent acts or the disposition of those handled by the police or courts) were available, additional operational definitions of delinquency would be possible.

Given the many possible operational definitions of delinquency, how does the researcher choose among them? Attempts to determine how delinquency should be operationally defined fall into three categories: 1. Conceptual or empirical examination of the relations among several measures of delinquency; 2. Research involving the relations between delinquency and independent variables; 3. Research designed to test a theory of delinquency (this most important source of

186

operational definitions is not discussed separately but is treated in the section on "concepts and indicators"). The answer to the question, How should delinquency be defined operationally? depends on which of these approaches is followed.

*Relations among the measures of delinquency.* The diversity of acts defined as criminal or delinquent has repeatedly led to the view that they cannot meaningfully be lumped together:

It is vain to seek the causes of crime as such, of crime anywhere and everywhere. Crime is a legal category. The only thing that is alike in all crimes is that they are alike violations of the law.[24]

Sociologically quite distinct forms of behavior by youngsters, for example, come to be designated by the generic term, 'juvenile delinquency.' This often carries with it the assumption that the wide diversity of behavior or the individuals engaging in one or another form of this behavior are of theoretically like kind. Yet, it is questionable that the behavior of the youngster who has purloined some baseball equipment is significantly similar to that of the youngster who periodically assaults members of an out-group.[25]

On logical grounds, statements such as these are difficult to justify. They are equivalent in form to the statement: The only thing all apples have in common is that they are all apples. Furthermore, the history of science is in large part the history of perceiving similarities in phenomena thought to be radically different.[26] All that would be necessary to show that purloining baseball equipment and assaulting a member of an out-group are not sociologically distinct forms of behavior would be a theory which explains them both.

The following is an extreme example of the point of view that it is illegitimate to treat delinquency as a homogeneous phenomenon:

It seems, therefore, time that we recognized that delinquency . . . is not a rational field of discourse. It takes all sorts to make the criminal world. . . . The inherent absurdity of treating . . . delinquents . . . even of a given sex and age group, as sufficiently homogeneous for rational study has been repeatedly demonstrated. It is now over twenty years since Robison made short work of the experience of the New York courts as an index of delinquency in that city. . . . To the Establishment-minded the mere fact of conviction for law-breaking . . . is of such magnitude as to dwarf into insignificance any consideration of what is broken or when or how —the common factor of 'delinquency' . . . being supposed to swamp all individual differences.[27]

The advocate of the multiple-factor approach looks at the vast number of independent variables affecting delinquency and denies the possibility of conceptualization. The advocate of the delinquency-is-a-heterogeneous-phenomenon approach looks at the diversity of the dependent variable and reaches the same conclusion. In both cases, the assumption of a one-to-one correspondence between concepts and indicators replaces the one-to-many or many-to-one correspondence between concepts and indicators assumed by those testing a theory and by those interpreting a set of data.

Efforts have been made to demonstrate the existence of statistically independent dimensions among the measures of delinquent behavior:

The question of whether youthful criminal behavior, or any form of deviant behavior, is unidimensional or multidimensional is an important one. For if several dimensions emerge from a class of actions previously regarded as homogeneous, more regular correlation between these new classifications and antecedent conditions may obtain, from which more accurate predictions can then be made. The categories of deviant behavior usually derive from considerations other than empirical analysis and prediction.[28]

Scott thus suggests that the homogeneity of delinquent acts is an empirical question. He obtained two Guttman scales from a collection of delinquent behavior items asked of a sample of one hundred undergraduate men. These two scales

188

(conceptualized as acts affecting anonymous persons or impersonal property and as acts affecting interpersonal relations) had a correlation of .16.

The test of correlation, then, shows that the two scales constitute two dimensions as the value of the correlation approaches zero; they constitute one dimension, and are components of a larger scale, as the value of the correlation approaches plus or minus one.[29]

Scott's test for multidimensionality is obviously more stringent than those based on what may be deviant cases. For example, in almost any large sample of boys it would be easy enough to find a boy who had committed only one delinquent act—which happened to be very serious. From this one case it could be established that the relation between frequency and seriousness of delinquent acts is not perfect, an argument in favor of the multidimensional approach.[30] If this less stringent criterion is used, the question of dimensionality can be answered a priori: There are as many "dimensions" of delinquency as there are distinct operational definitions of the concept (see Table 11-1). Scott's results suggest that the question of multidimensionality using the restrictive definition (that the separate dimensions be uncorrelated) can also be answered in favor of the multidimensionalist position.

It may appear, then, that the victory of the multidimensionalists is inevitable, that it is illegitimate to treat delinquency as a homogeneous phenomenon. This conclusion is not warranted. How delinquency should be measured cannot be determined solely from analysis of the correlations between the measures of delinquency, any more than how delinquency should be defined can be determined from a comparison of definitions. If a theory does not recognize distinct dimensions of delinquency (e.g., vandalism versus theft), then the correlation between the measures of these dimensions may be of little interest to the theorist.

Delinquency researchers disagree on what kind of relation among operational definitions of delinquency indicates that one theory can explain them all. Consider Scott's finding that his two delinquency scales are virtually unrelated to each other. Does this suggest that two explanations of delinquent conduct are required? Scott concludes that it does:

Perhaps the basic notion provided by these two scales is that delinquent acts affecting anonymous persons or impersonal property occur together in a distinctive pattern which should not be confused with one made up of acts that introduce conflict and injury into interpersonal relations. This in turn suggests differences in the antecedent conditions that give rise to each type of delinquency. Data are not available in this study on the conditions antecedent to the delinquent behavior itself. But the speculation that 'normal' socialization to deviant subcultures is antecedent to 'impersonal' delinquency and that 'abnormal' socialization in disorganized family situations is antecedent to 'personal' delinquency may be warranted.[31]

Scott argues, then, that a zero relation between two measures of delinquency requires two measures to account for them. Now compare this with the following argument:

The question of the empirical interrelations between types of offenses is of interest for sociological as well as etiological reasons. Scott suggests that 'differences in the antecedent conditions that give rise to each type of delinquency' may be understood by this approach. And the work of [Cohen and Short] and [Cloward and Ohlin] should be cited as recent theoretical contributions that hypothesize *specialization* around types of offenses in the development of delinquent subcultures.[32]

In the case of delinquent specialization, the relation between measures of delinquency would not resemble that found by Scott, as Table 11-2 illustrates. Cloward and Ohlin's conclusion, however, is much the same as Scott's: "These are distinctive subcultural adaptations; an explanation of one may not constitute an explanation of the other."[33] It appears, then,

### Table 11-2—Two Analyses of the Dimensionality of Delinquent Behavior (hypothetical)

| | | Scott's Impersonal Delinquency by Personal Delinquency | | | Cloward and Ohlin's "Conflict Pattern" by "Retreatist Pattern" | | |
|---|---|---|---|---|---|---|---|
| | | PERSONAL DELINQUENCY | | | RETREATIST PATTERN | | |
| | | High percent | Low percent | | | High percent | Low percent |
| | High | 50 | 50 | | High | 0 | 100 |
| Impersonal Delinquency | | | | Conflict Pattern | | | |
| | Low | 50 | 50 | | Low | 100 | 0 |

that both zero relations and negative relations between measures of delinquency may suggest the need for more than one theory. If auto thieves are no more likely to shoplift than anyone else, auto theft and shoplifting may require separate explanations; if auto thieves never shoplift, and vice versa, auto theft and shoplifting may again require separate explanations. One possibility remains: positive relations between measures of delinquency.

In the total and matched samples, theft correlated significantly with each of six different types of misconduct. Taken casually, this appears to cast doubt on the value of scaling by type of offense. . . . [However], the forecasting efficiency in predicting vandalism [e.g.,] from knowledge of theft is . . . virtually zero, in spite of over-all association. . . . The next step in this project is creation of Guttman scales for the four most common types of juvenile offenses, truancy, vandalism, injury to persons, and theft. . . .[34]

Although in this case the positive association between measures of delinquency is small and is neutralized by a measure of predictability,[35] it is not difficult to imagine a case of high, nonneutralizable positive association in which it could be argued that two theories are required. If, for example, drug users steal to maintain their habit, there will be a positive association between drug use and theft. In this case, although one theory may account for drug use and, consequently, account for the theft which accompanies it, it may fail to account for theft that is not preceded by the use of drugs.

Research on the relations among the measures of delinquency thus resembles attempts to define delinquency independently of a theory; it also resembles efforts to demonstrate logically that delinquency is not a unidimensional phenomenon. All three approaches are valuable, but they are also severely limited. At some point, the student of delinquency must face the problem of explaining the variation in the measures of delinquency he has isolated. At this point, a different set of criteria emerge for answering the question, How should delinquency be measured?

*Relations between measures of delinquency and independent variables.* The choice of a measure of delinquency may not be as crucial to the results of a study as researchers, theorists, and critics usually take it to be. This argument has been stated by Paul F. Lazarsfeld as the "doctrine of the interchangeability of indices": "Experience has shown that, given a large universe of items, it makes little difference which sample of items is selected to form the classificatory instrument."[36] Lazarsfeld is not saying that all or most children who are classified as delinquent by one measure will be similarly classified by another measure. As the discussion of Table 11-1 shows, the choice of measure may make a great deal of difference. He is saying that these different measures, even if imperfectly related to each other, may have the same relation to an outside variable. If two measures of delinquency are only moderately related to each other (e.g., $r = .5$), and if each is moderately related to socioeconomic status (e.g., $r = .5$ in both cases), then it does not matter which is used in a theoretically oriented study as an indicator of delinquency, even though many of those classified as delinquent by one measure may be classified as nondelinquent by the other. In an action-oriented study, however, such errors of classification may make a great deal of difference to some of the boys and their mothers.[37]

## Concepts and Indicators

The investigator asking the mother of a delinquent whether her son should finish high school and attend college may use her response as a measure of many things—commitment to middle-class values, awareness of current occupational requirements, "achievement motivation," or awareness of her boy's abilities. Alternatively, the researcher asking a variety of questions may use all of them as measures of the same thing. It is thus possible to use one measure as an indicator of a variety of concepts and to use several measures as indicators of the same concept. This one-to-many, many-to-one feature of indicator-concept relations lies at the root of many controversies, occupies much of the space in methodological discussions, is the downfall of those who think that facts speak for themselves, and is a source of opportunity par excellence for the ingenious investigator.[38]

Despite the great importance of the procedures for moving from concepts to indicators and from indicators to concepts, precise rules for bridging this gap do not exist. There is no purely logical method of linking concepts and indicators; there is no logical way to determine whether an indicator is really measuring the theoretically defined concept.[39] In fact, the nearest methodologists have come to codifying these procedures is to pose the questions: Does the interpretation make sense? and, Does it work?

If a measure makes sense as an indicator of a concept, it may be said to have *logical validity*. If a measure discriminates between individuals known to differ on some other measure,

**193**

it is said to have *pragmatic validity*. The extent to which the relations between measures agree with theoretical predictions is called *construct validity*.[40] Since a measure valid by one of these standards may be invalid by another, and since a measure may be used as an indicator of many different concepts, it is misleading to speak of the validity of a measure without specifying the criterion.

Delinquency researchers usually ignore the problem of validity. Delinquency research has been largely a-theoretical; without theory there is nothing with which the results can be compared, and the question of construct validity cannot arise. Moreover, because they work with relatively concrete variables, there is often little inferential distance between their measures and concepts, so that logical validity is not an issue. Finally, since they tend to present only those variables that discriminate between delinquents and nondelinquents, their measures necessarily have pragmatic validity.

As a case in point, take the following numbers reported in *Unraveling Juvenile Delinquency*.

### Table 11-3—Delinquents' Companions[41]

|  | DELINQUENTS | |
|  | Number | Percent |
| --- | --- | --- |
| Delinquents | 492 | 98.5 |
| Nondelinquents | 8 | 1.6 |
| Total | 500 | 100.0 |
|  |  |  |
| Predominantly older | 223 | 44.6 |
| Predominantly same age | 169 | 33.8 |
| Predominantly younger | 22 | 4.4 |
| Varied ages | 86 | 17.2 |
| Total | 500 | 100.0 |

The Gluecks draw the following inference from the two parts of this table: "The delinquents . . . not only chummed largely with other delinquents but gravitated toward older boys."[42] As it stands, this statement simply reports the facts

194

in the tables. However, since it is impossible for delinquents, as a group, to have delinquent companions who are predominantly older than themselves, the meaning of these facts is far from clear.

There are, to be sure, several possible explanations of the discrepancy between the Gluecks' results and what must be true for the population of delinquents as a whole: 1. For some reason, the Gluecks just happened to select more delinquents with older delinquent friends than with younger delinquent friends. 2. The Gluecks' use of a necessarily "age-bounded" sample means that some older delinquents with younger friends will be excluded from the sample; the sample will therefore be weighted toward having older friends.[43] 3. As always, errors of response, recording, and tabulation may account for the results. Thus, it is possible (if unlikely) that repeated measurement on the Gluecks' sample would have produced an age-distribution of companions more like that of an actual population. 4. There may have been a tendency for delinquent boys (and their parents) to perceive their friends as older than themselves whether or not they were older. 5. The delinquents may have lied.

May one, therefore, conclude that the Gluecks' measurements of these variables are invalid? In order to answer this question, it is necessary to ask what the Gluecks wish to learn from their data. If their intention is simply to describe their sample, there is no reason to question the validity of their measures. Their sample may simply not represent any actual population of delinquents; this would make their findings logically possible and thus presumptively valid (explanations 1 and 2 above). However, the Gluecks apparently wish to make statements valid for a population beyond their sample. In a real population of delinquents the statement, Delinquents tend to have delinquent companions who are predominantly older than themselves, is self-contradictory and thus patently invalid.

This example illustrates several points about validity: 1. Measures valid by one standard may be invalid by others. The Gluecks' measures in this case appear to have both logical and pragmatic validity (they discriminate between delinquents and nondelinquents). The criterion of validity we applied to their findings is one of agreement with theoretical expectations, i.e., construct validity. Given that almost all (98.4 percent) of the companions of delinquents were themselves delinquents, it follows that for every delinquent A who has an older delinquent friend B there is a delinquent B who has a younger delinquent friend A. Thus one would expect the number of older delinquent friends to be equal to the number of younger delinquent friends. When the Gluecks' data did not confirm this expectation, the validity of their measure was called into question.[44]

2. Whether a measure is considered valid depends on its use. The researcher who does not go beyond his data cannot have invalid measures. However, every study that goes beyond such statements as, "Responses to the question, How old are you? are related to responses to the question, How many times have you been in trouble with police?" uses concepts and must, therefore, face the question of validity. The statement, As age increases, contacts with the police increase, is not identical to the statement, The older a boy says he is, the more contacts with the police he is likely to report. The former is a statement about a relation between concepts, however low their level may be. The latter is simply a statement about a relation between two measures of something. What this something is cannot always be taken as self-evident. For example, a farfetched but not impossible interpretation of the meaning of the last statement might be: Boys who exaggerate

their age also exaggerate the number of contacts they have had with the police.

3. As in our use of the delinquency of companions to question the validity of the Gluecks' findings on age of companions, it is almost always possible for the researcher to find measures that are useful in assessing the validity of other measures. For example, Nye reports taking the following steps to assure the validity of his measure of delinquency:

Five of the seven items are . . . law violations. It would appear that the scale has some claim to face validity. . . . Even more important than the behavior involved in the scale items as such is its ability to predict the more serious and frequent delinquent behavior characteristic of institutionalized adolescents. The scale can, therefore, be said to adequately distinguish between groups 'known to be different.'[45]

Nye's scale thus makes sense and appears to work, i.e., it performs the job for which it was intended. Furthermore, many of Nye's tables showing relations between his delinquency scale and independent variables agree with his social control theory. These, too, are evidence for the validity of the delinquency scale.

One table, however, does not agree with our expectations, the table showing the relations between father's occupation and reported delinquency. One of our points of attack on this finding was to question the validity of Nye's measure of socioeconomic status.[46] In support of our argument we noted that other measures of socioeconomic status were related to delinquency. Nye's efforts to establish the validity of his delinquency scale and our efforts to establish the *invalidity* of his measure of socioeconomic status thus involve the same procedure: comparison of measures of what is presumably the same thing. As was true for demonstrations of causality, the persuasiveness of claims of validity must depend on the analysis of data.

# Notes

1. Carl G. Hempel, *Fundamentals of Concept Formation in Empirical Science*. Chicago: University of Chicago Press, 1952, p. 36.

2. Cyril Burt, *The Young Delinquent*. London: University of London Press, 1938, pp. 599–600. Quoted by Negley K. Teeters and John O. Reinemann, *The Challenge of Delinquency*. Englewood Cliffs, N.J.: Prentice-Hall, 1950, p. 214.

3. Emile Durkheim, *The Rules of Sociological Method*. New York: The Free Press, 1950, p. 128. As will be shown, it is no accident that Durkheim the theorist is arguing against John Stuart Mill the empiricist.

4. E.g., Barbara Wootton, *Social Science and Social Pathology*. New York: Macmillan, 1959, pp. 34–135; Albert K. Cohen and James F. Short, Jr., "Juvenile delinquency," in Robert K. Merton and Robert A. Nisbet, eds., *Contemporary Social Problems*. New York: Harcourt, 1961, p. 111; Pitirim A. Sorokin, *Fads and Foibles in Modern Sociology*, Chicago: Henry Regnery, 1956, pp. 142–143. These works are discussed in Chapter 2.

5. Albert K. Cohen, "Multiple factor approaches," in Marvin E. Wolfgang *et al.*, eds., *The Sociology of Crime and Delinquency*. New York: Wiley, 1962, pp. 77–80.

6. For a recent attack on "sanctimonious theory" see Sheldon Glueck, "Ten years of *Unraveling Juvenile Delinquency*," *Journal of Criminal Law, Criminology and Police Science*, 51, 1960, pp. 283–308.

7. Cohen, *op. cit.*, p. 78.

8. Cohen points out that the "assumption of intrinsic pathogenic qualities" implies more than that other variables are always constant. To paraphrase, it implies that the relation between a concept and an indicator is everywhere the same. *Ibid.*

9. *Ibid.*, p. 78.

10. Stefan Nowak, "General laws and historical generalizations in the social sciences," *Polish Sociological Bulletin*, No. 1–2, June-December, 1961, p. 30.

11. Wootton, *op. cit.*, pp. 301–302.

12. Cyril Burt, *op. cit.*, quoted by Cohen, *op. cit.*, p. 77.

13. Durkheim, *op. cit.*; Cohen and Short, *op. cit.*; Sorokin, *op. cit.* This complaint usually implies that there is something wrong with research that produces findings inconsistent with other research. As we point out in Chapter 2, this complaint is usually followed by suggestions that researchers be more careful in defining and measuring their variables, and so on. As we have tried to show, such research improvements could, and probably would, leave much inconsistency and inconclusiveness untouched.

14. A good general discussion of the relation between theory and research may be found in Robert K. Merton, *Social Theory and Social*

*Structure*. New York: The Free Press, 1957, Chapters 2–3. In one sense the radical separation of theory and research for purposes of discussion is quite misleading. Theorists are fond of pointing out that even radical empiricists use implicit or preconscious theories. By the same token, it might be said that theorists usually work with some idea of the facts they are attempting to explain.

15. Although the relation between this "theory" and Robert K. Merton's theory of "anomie" is not coincidental, this version is not intended to represent Merton's theory fairly. See Merton, *op. cit.*, Chapters 4–5.

16. See, for example, Albert J. Reiss, Jr., and Albert Lewis Rhodes, "The distribution of juvenile delinquency in the social class structure," *American Sociological Review*, 26, 1961, pp. 720–732.

17. Robert K. Merton, "Anomie, anomia, and social interaction: contexts of deviant behavior," in Marshal B. Clinard, ed., *Anomie and Deviant Behavior*. New York: The Free Press, 1964, pp. 239–242.

18. The procedure for linking a theory to observational data is called by a variety of names, e.g., epistemic correlations, coordinating definitions, rules of interpretation, and rules of correspondence. See Ernest Nagel, *The Structure of Science: Problems in the Logic of Scientific Explanation*. New York: Harcourt, 1961, pp. 93–105. This problem will be discussed again as *validity*.

19. Kingsley Davis, "Malthus and the theory of population," in Paul F. Lazarsfeld and Morris Rosenberg, eds., *The Language of Social Research*. New York: The Free Press, 1955, p. 546.

20. *Ibid.*

21. Karl R. Popper, *The Open Society and Its Enemies*. Princeton: Princeton University Press, 1950, pp. 34–35. For a similar view see Werner S. Landecker, "Types of integration and their measurement," in Lazarsfeld and Rosenberg, *op. cit.*, p. 19.

22. Albert K. Cohen, *Delinquent Boys*. New York: The Free Press, 1955, pp. 24–36.

23. Robert K. Merton, *op. cit.*, pp. 177–181.

24. Robert M. MacIver, *Social Causation*. New York: Ginn and Company, 1942, p. 88.

25. Merton, *op. cit.*, p. 177.

26. Durkheim, *op. cit.*, suggests that science tends to see unity in independent variables, and diversity in dependent variables; he thus agrees with those who argue that delinquency should be treated as a heterogeneous phenomenon.

27. Wootton, *op. cit.*, p. 306. Wootton is referring to Sophia Robison, *Can Delinquency Be Measured?* New York: Columbia University Press, 1936.

28. John Finley Scott, "Two dimensions of delinquent behavior," *American Sociological Review*, 24, 1959, p. 240. Cf. Robert A. Dentler and Lawrence J. Monroe, "Social correlates of early adolescent theft," *American Sociological Review*, 26, 1961, pp. 742–743.

29. Scott, *op. cit.*, p. 242.

30. In the field of social stratification, those who adopt a multidimensionalist position argue that studies of social class should recognize a variety of dimensions, such as wealth, prestige, and power. For evidence that these are indeed separate dimensions, they cite examples of impoverished aristocrats or the new rich, persons high on one dimension and low on another. These may be called deviant cases because even the multidimensionalists agree that in general

the several dimensions are highly related to each other.

31. Scott, *op. cit.*, pp. 242–243.

32. Dentler and Monroe, *op. cit.*, p. 743. (Italics in original) The references are to Albert K. Cohen and James F. Short, Jr., "Research in delinquent subcultures," *Journal of Social Issues*, 14, 1958, pp. 20–37, and to Richard A. Cloward and Lloyd E. Ohlin, *Delinquency and Opportunity*. New York: The Free Press, 1960.

33. Cloward and Ohlin, *ibid.*, p. 32.

34. Dentler and Monroe, *op. cit.*, pp. 742–743.

35. We do not agree with the use of a measure of association based on the predictability of responses in this situation. These measures may have practical value, but their analytic value is limited by their dependence on marginal distributions.

36. Paul F. Lazarsfeld, "Problems in methodology," in Robert K. Merton *et al.*, *Sociology Today*. New York: Basic Books, 1959, p. 60.

37. The doctrine of the interchangeability of indices should be interpreted for what it is, an empirical generalization; it certainly has exceptions.

38. See Lazarsfeld in Merton *et al.*, *op. cit.*, pp. 47–67.

39. An excellent brief discussion of the link between concepts and indicators is in Hubert M. Blalock, Jr., *Social Statistics*. New York: McGraw-Hill, 1960, pp. 9–11. See also Lazarsfeld and Rosenberg, *op. cit.*, pp. 15–108.

40. Claire Selltiz *et al.*, *Research Methods in Social Relations*. New York: Holt, Rinehart & Winston, 1959, pp. 154–166. We have substituted logical validity for the more usual face validity since the latter appears to be a special case of the former. A distinction is usually drawn between two types of pragmatic validity: concurrent validity and predictive validity.

41. Sheldon and Eleanor Glueck, *Unraveling Juvenile Delinquency*. Cambridge: Harvard University Press, 1950, p. 163.

42. *Ibid.*, p. 167.

43. This explanation was suggested to us by Robert Wenkert.

44. In most cases in which construct validity is at issue, the question is whether the theory or the measures account for a failure to find expected relations. In this case, however, it is clear that the fault does not lie with our theoretical expectations.

45. F. Ivan Nye, *Family Relationships and Delinquent Behavior*. New York: Wiley, 1958, p. 15.

46. See Chapter 7.

# 12

# Reliability

# and

# Scaling

Everything changes, and no two situations are altogether alike. This change and this difference are at the root of the concept of *unreliability*. We distinguish four main sources of unreliability: 1. Two or more observers, each looking at the same phenomenon, will see it differently; 2. two or more samples of the same population will give different results; 3. two or more sets of items from the same pool of items will produce different measures; and 4. the results of two or more studies of the same sample by the same investigator using the same items will be different at two or more points in time.

Unreliability is thus a synonym for error, difference, and instability; and its logical complement, reliability, thus connotes accuracy, similarity, and stability. In using these convenient and all-embracing terms one should keep the four sources of unreliability in mind. Each source has been the focus of attention in a different research tradition; as a consequence each has its own terminology and procedures.

201

It is impossible, however, to assign each type of unreliability to a different field; although the terminology comes mostly from psychology, there are contributions from anthropology, economics, sociology, statistics, and probably other fields. Concern with variation over observers appears in such terms as *inter-judge consensus* and *inter-rater reliability*. Variation over items leads to such measures as *split-half reliability* and *alternate-forms reliability*. Variation over time has produced *test-retest reliability* and *panel turnover*. Finally, the effect of variation over respondents has led to much of the literature of statistical inference and, perhaps because of sociologists' dependence on sampling, is of central concern to them. We shall therefore reserve variation over respondents for special treatment in Chapter 13, and treat the other three sources of variation here.

## Variation Over Observers

A researcher predicts that a group of preadolescent boys will not commit delinquent acts during their adolescence. In a follow-up study of these boys he finds that some have come to the attention of the police. His first reaction is to look at the offenses with which these boys have been charged.[1]

[One of the boys] . . . was brought before the Judge for *alleged* assault and battery against another high school boy with whom he had had a fight during which he *accidentally* stabbed him with a knife. . . .

In the case of the second *non-delinquent*, who was sixteen years old when he appeared in court, he was arrested for stealing a pair of pants in a store, which he *steadfastly denied*, and the incident was *no doubt* due to *misunderstanding*.[2]

As soon as one decides to distinguish between the boys who are really delinquent and those who are not really delinquent, it appears to be perfectly natural to see the crimes of nondelinquents as peccadilloes and the peccadilloes of delinquents as crimes. But if delinquency is defined by the commission of delinquent acts, such a double standard can produce highly unreliable results. This subjective reclassification is most marked in research in which boys are divided into one of two categories, delinquent or nondelinquent, good or bad.

Four boys (all nominated 'good' by their teachers) had become known to the police or juvenile court or both, one time each, during the intervening years. One case involved truancy and was disposed of by the police without referring the boy to the juvenile court. A case involving malicious destruction of property and another involving drunkenness and violation of curfew were *held by the police and turned over to the juvenile court.* The juvenile court, however, in handling these two cases without official disposition, probably considered them rather petty matters. The fourth boy was arrested for *borrowing* a neighbor's automobile in the early morning hours to deliver newspapers (he had done this on several occasions, always returning the car to its parking place before the neighbor arose). *The police turned this boy over to the juvenile court,* which in making an official disposition placed him on probation.[3]

Assault with a deadly weapon and auto theft are serious offenses. But stabbing another boy is no longer assault with a deadly weapon if the stabbing is accidental; and everyone appreciates the difference between stealing and borrowing. However, it is worth wondering aloud whether "delinquent" or "bad" boys would be given the benefit of such doubts.

When the investigators concerned with the four good boys again discuss these same boys two years later, their offenses appear even less serious:

At sixteen years of age . . . four of the 103 insulated ('good') boys in the slums had had one minor complaint for delinquency each. One of these was taken to court and placed on probation, while *three* were settled in the field by a warning from the juvenile bureau.[4]

In seeking to validate their predictions the investigators rewrite history. Auto theft is now minor, and offenses that the police had turned over to the juvenile courts now appear innocuously as having been "settled in the field."

The operation of "biases" such as these has been extensively studied and their effects are well known. Mistakes are almost invariably made in a direction favorable to one's hypothesis—partly, of course, because one's theory colors what one sees. What is important here is not the discovery of a case of observer error, motivated or otherwise. The investigators in this study are surely no more likely to commit such errors than are any other experienced investigators. Their fault consists in not having used one or more of the methods available for preventing or reducing the errors that stem from the choice of one observer rather than another.

*The use of ignorance to prevent error.* A simple and sure way to prevent the observer from seeing only what he wants to see is to remove the clues from his environment, to put him in the dark. This technique of insuring objectivity requires no lengthy discussion here. The teacher who covers his students' names before grading their examinations uses it, as does the clinical investigator who sees to it that neither the physician nor the patients know which patients receive the experimental drug and which get the placebo. That such a control on observation is not routinely used in delinquency research, however, is suggested by the following passage.

Before describing our results, one crucial point should be emphasized. In categorizing the cases under each variable—in deciding, for example, which child had been rejected, which loved, which neglected—*we had no prior knowledge of their criminal records.* We did not first select the delinquents and then look back to see factors which correlated with criminality. . . . Rather, we first made judgments about the various factors in their background and therapy, and only then looked to see how these variables related to crime.

In other words, . . . *we could not have been influenced by knowledge of later delinquency.* This is important to emphasize, for unfortunately some inaccurate conclusions can be drawn from retrospective analyses of the lives of criminals. If an investigator knows which of his subjects are criminal, his judgments about causes may be unconsciously influenced.[5]

*Preventing error through the specification of meaning.* After our discussion of the relations between concepts and indicators in Chapter 11, it should suffice here simply to call attention to the need for precise definitions of terms. Not only delinquency, but such other concepts as honesty, good taste, and adequacy of supervision are potential sources of differences between investigators working on the same problem. Moreover, such subjective concepts are necessary in delinquency research; few investigators would want to avoid the difficulty of defining these concepts precisely by trying to do without them.[6]

*Reduction of inconsistency by eliminating discrepant measures.* All of the methods we have presented thus far in this section have dealt with differences between studies. Often, however, there are several observers within a single study: several teachers may rate a boy as good or bad; one coder's judgments about the classification of occupations may be checked by another.

The Gluecks asked both the boys and their mothers about the boys' companions. Although the Gluecks report relatively high agreement between the boys and their mothers, it was far from complete.

There was, however, not so wide a divergence between the delinquents and non-delinquents in respect to agreement between parents and boys as to the boys' companions (53.8%; 68%) as there was in regard to the other aspects of their use of leisure time.[7]

The Gluecks apparently used additional sources of information (teachers, school principals, social workers) to resolve some of the discrepancies. The primary decision, however, was to treat the discrepancies as evidence of ignorance or motivated misperception by the parents:

By and large, it is the impression of the home visitors that the parents of the delinquent boys were actually unaware of many of their activities. This deficiency is revealed in the lesser agreement between the parents and the delinquents than between the parents and non-delinquents as to where the boys played. . . .[8]

In other words, it appears that when the Gluecks were forced to record whether a boy did or did not have delinquent companions, other data led them to rely on the report of the boy rather than on that of the mother or a combination of the two.[9]

*Reduction of inconsistency by averaging.* When one does not have the kind of auxiliary information that the Gluecks used in judging the quality of their data, it may still be possible to reduce error by taking account of the distribution of the responses of the different observers. Consider, for example, the use of informants to rate the residents of a small community on their social class. If three informants put John Smith into the upper-middle class and a fourth puts him into the upper-lower class, it appears reasonable to discard the aberrant rating altogether.

Often, however, this procedure is impossible or unwise. The distribution of observations may not reveal such an obvious discrepancy. Or it may be difficult to decide whether to treat a particular response as an extreme, but valid response (an "outlier") or as an error. In such cases the choice seems to be between throwing away possibly valid data and including possibly invalid data in the analysis. Tukey has suggested a way to escape between the horns of this dilemma: He would replace an extreme observation by the mean of this observation and the next most extreme.[10]

When the data are numerical and when the distribution of responses suggests the presence of many small errors of observation, response, and processing, rather than one or two large errors that can be dealt with individually, it is possible to reduce the errors significantly by taking the mean of the individual observations. In using this technique it is essential that the observations be made independently; in practice, the observers, judges, raters, or coders should reach their decisions individually, rather than as a result of comparison or group discussion. The increase in accuracy of the mean of even three raters over a single rater is impressive; where it is possible to use large numbers of raters, as in describing the behavior of teachers, military leaders, or physicians through averaging the ratings given to them by their students, followers, or patients, the improvement over the quality of ratings derived from even the best-trained observer is startling.[11]

## Variation Over Items

Investigators of delinquency, like other investigators, spend a great deal of time and effort in combining many items into scales to measure their important concepts. Whether the scales are arbitrarily weighted combinations of items (including the simplest scale of all, the equally weighted "number of favorably answered items") or rational procedures like Guttman scales, the main purpose is the same: to reduce the error of classification of respondents. Two mechanisms account for this reduction of error. As in the combination of the ratings of independent judges, the combination of many independent responses reduces the random error in the score assigned to each individual. Unlike the ratings of the judges, however, the responses of a single individual to many items are not independent; it thus takes many more items to increase the reliability of a scale appreciably, which is why a psychological scale may have as many as a hundred items.

Reduction of random error through the pooling of many items makes sense only if the items come from a single conceptual dimension. If one could sample items from a unidimensional universe of content as one samples people from a social group, then unidimensionality would follow necessarily. But the idea of sampling items is only a metaphor; indeed, a leading psychometrician has argued that treating unreliability as the sampling error of items makes little empirical sense.[12] Since it is impossible to draw a sample of items from a single universe of content, one must instead try to determine whether or not some grouping of the items already at hand can be treated as measuring a single dimension. This is the most important reason for the rational scaling procedures. In a well-selected set each item is a good measure of the general characteristic and a poor measure of many other characteristics; combining many such items into a scale thus results in a composite measure that primarily taps the general variable and has only small amounts of other variables in it.

As with judgments by observers, responses to different items may not agree on whether a boy is intelligent or stupid, delinquent or nondelinquent. Most of the methods for estimating the unreliability that comes from disagreement between items were developed in the area of psychological testing. These methods focus on the factorial simplicity or unidimensionality of a set of items, i.e., on their internal consistency.

Nye reports that his measure of delinquency is a scale "by the Guttman definition of the term." He adds: "Guttman considers this property of a measure to be an indication of reliability."[13] Referring to their five-item theft scale, Dentler and Monroe comment:

As the minimal marginal reproducibility index reveals, we could have done *almost* as good a job of categorizing subjects with a summated rating scale. But we considered the Guttman technique worth the gain, however slight, for the evidence it provided of internal consistency and for individual scoring from the resulting response patterns.

Scalability is an adequate test of reliability in terms of internal test consistency. . . .[14]

In order to make the logic of Guttman scaling clear, it may be helpful to think of the items as observers. Suppose that three observers—a policeman, a teacher, and a mother—were asked to classify a group of ten boys as delinquent or nondelinquent. The policeman, using a liberal definition of delinquency, classifies eight of the boys as delinquents; the teacher classifies four as delinquents; and the mother, using a restrictive definition of delinquency, classifies only two as delinquents. If it can be assumed that the only difference between these classifications is that they rely on successively narrower definitions of delinquency, then the two boys classified as delinquent by one observer should also be classified as delinquent by those using broader definitions, and vice versa for those classified as nondelinquent according to the broadest definition of delinquency. In other words, a perfectly reliable Guttman scale reflects perfect agreement between observers (or items) even though it is manifest that all observers (items) do not assign the same score to the same individuals.

In Chapter 4 we argue against Guttman scaling of delinquent acts on the grounds that in this case considerations of causal order and theoretical clarity are more important than evidence of unidimensionality. Our recommendation does not necessarily apply to such other uses of scaling as the measurement of attitudes, where the dispersion of the items over time is not a problem. Nevertheless, we cannot help wondering whether unidimensionality has become a fetish. Along with tests of significance, which we discuss in Chapter 13, the deft use of Guttman scales has become a mark of up-to-date methodology. As such, its justification tends to become social rather than logical. Investigators should recall that some of the most important theoretical concepts, such as social class and degree of bureaucratization, are multidimensional; this does not seem to have lessened their fruitfulness in empirical research.

One reason for the vogue of Guttman scaling is its simplicity. At least on the cookbook level of introductory treatments, one does not need to know any fancy statistics to master the technique; and now that computer programs for Guttman scaling are widely available, one does not need to know anything about the technique in order to have a scale constructed. This simplicity has apparently led many investigators to go no further in their learning of scaling procedures than the Guttman technique. In a kind of Gresham's Law, the easier technique drives out the more difficult, yet there are many situations where more elaborate techniques, such as factor analysis, are preferable—for example, in sorting a large pool of items into a smaller number of dimensions.

Now that the computer has taken both the mathematics and the drudgery out of complex techniques, their use is bound to increase sharply. On the whole, this is a good thing; there is nothing ennobling or illuminating about punching a desk calculator or tending a counter-sorter. And yet there are grounds for doubting whether empirical social research needs as much scaling or as much factor analysis as it is likely to get. As we have said, these techniques usually are—or should be— confessions of ignorance; one constructs a scale or performs a factor analysis because one does not know which items go together or which are good indicators of some concept. Once the dimensions are sorted out and the good indicators isolated, why go through the whole procedure again and again?

Part of the emphasis on these procedures is, we believe, an unjustified borrowing from the theory of psychometric tests. At first glance the construction of psychological scales seems to have the same rationale as the construction of scales in social research, but the differences are at least as great as the similarities. Much of the work in psychometric testing is intended for situations where some action is to be taken on an individual: He is to compete for admission to college, be screened for parole, or be diagnosed for psychotherapy. In all such situations the number of variables on which information is desired is small; there are standards for evaluating the findings; and, most important of all, the social and individual costs of error in either direction (admission or rejection) are high.[15] These factors combine to produce highly refined instruments with dozens or even hundreds of items that yield a small number of scale scores. The cost of designing, administering, and processing such a long instrument is justified by the expected social and individual benefits.

The situation in social research stands in sharp contrast. Here, information is sought on many variables, some of them ill-defined and of undemonstrated value. There are no standards for evaluating the findings, since no individual action will be taken as a result. Thus, the individual costs of error are zero, and it is not at all clear how one would go about evaluating the social costs of error. For one thing, the consequences of using a single item instead of a scale may simply be to attenuate the correlation between two variables—say, from 0.30 to 0.20. Who can measure the social costs of such an error? Furthermore, if the social researcher were to use a small number of long scales, like the psychometrician, he would have to forego a large number of single items that he might otherwise study, and this might well be more costly than the reduction in reliability. Once again, we want to emphasize that we are not against scales, but rather against the mechanical practice of constructing a scale without first deciding why a scale is better for the particular study than a few well-chosen items.

## Variation Over Time

The notion of test-retest or any other "reliability" measure involving a time sequence is antithetical to social science since it must make the incorrect assumption that human thought and behavior is static and, therefore, that any change in response is a reflection of either instrument error or deception. In fact, such recorded changes are more likely to reflect shifts in attitude or behavior on the part of the respondent.[16]

Deutscher is correct in pointing to the difficulty of interpreting crude differences between two measurements of the same concept on the same people as indicating the unreliability of the instrument[17] rather than real changes in behavior; without making some assumptions about which sources of error are negligible, it is impossible to interpret such simple before-and-after measurements. Nevertheless, there is abundant evidence of inadvertent deception, and a great deal of methodological work has been done in separating the different components of observed changes over time.

Anyone who has analyzed longitudinal (panel) data is familiar with the bandwagon effect, the tendency to alter one's recollection of past behavior to appear in a more favorable light. After any election some small proportion of the people who had actually favored the losing candidate before the election report that they had favored the winning candidate. And even the reporting of factual material tends to become less accurate with time.

In many cases of this kind, it is easy to use other sources of data to estimate the magnitude of the error for the total sample, if not for each individual (were accurate data available for each individual, say from records, there would be little point in asking them to provide the data through the admittedly more fallible instrument of the questionnaire[18]). Where this is impossible, as in dealing with attitude data, more powerful analytic techniques are necessary. Among others, James S. Coleman has provided mathematical models for distinguishing real change from one or another kind of error.[19] Although Coleman's work is too recent to have been included in any of the studies we have surveyed, such methodological devices should find an important place in the delinquency research of the future. It is certainly better to try to estimate the relative magnitudes of real change and error, however imperfect these estimates might be, than to pontificate about truth and error entirely on the basis of *a priori* reasoning.

It is not even necessary to be as mathematical as Coleman in order to advance significantly beyond the armchair in treating variability of responses over time. Patricia Kendall has summarized a considerable body of work on the correlates of variability, including the respondent's mood at the times of the interviews and the extent to which the responses involve him in psychological conflict.[20] Taking such factors into account in the design of the study should make it possible to reduce unwanted variability.

There is no easy answer to the problems of unreliability. Progress has come, and will continue to come, from work on many different fronts. Conceptual clarification of the different meanings and sources of unreliability, such as we have tried to provide here, is a good place to start. At a more abstract level of methodology, mathematical models of change and error provide sharp tests of different theories of unreliability. More powerful designs make it possible to reduce errors, as in the averaging of the responses of independent observers. The methodologically aware investigator will find endless opportunities, both in design and analysis, to increase his understanding of the sources of error and of the ways to combat it.[21] In short, error is everywhere, but so are the means of coping with it.

# Notes

1. In the study from which the following quotations were drawn, the information upon which the predictions were based was obtained from juvenile court records. As in the stylized version in the text, the predictions were reportedly blind, i.e., the researcher (Eleanor Glueck) did not know the delinquency records of any of the boys whose behavior she was predicting or, presumably, what proportion of them were delinquents. The author does not say, however, that he decided which of the fifty boys were really delinquent in ignorance of the predictions and in ignorance of the material upon which the predictions were based. See Richard E. Thompson, "Further validation of the Glueck Social Prediction Table for identifying potential delinquents," *Journal of Criminal Law, Criminology and Police Science*, 48, 1957, pp. 175–184.

2. *Ibid.*, pp. 183, 177. (Authors' italics)

3. Frank R. Scarpitti, Ellen Murray, Simon Dinitz, and Walter C. Reckless, "The 'good' boy in a high delinquency area: four years later," *American Sociological Review*, 25, 1960, pp. 555–558. (Authors' italics)

4. Simon Dinitz, Frank R. Scarpitti, and Walter C. Reckless, "Delinquency vulnerability: a cross group and longitudinal analysis," *American Sociological Review*, 27, 1962, pp. 515–517.

5. William McCord and Joan McCord, *Origins of Crime*. New York: Columbia University Press, 1959, p. 17. (Italics in original)

6. Leslie T. Wilkins, "Juvenile delinquency: a critical review of research and theory," *Educational Research*, 5, 1963, p. 114.

7. Sheldon and Eleanor Glueck, *Unraveling Juvenile Delinquency*. Cambridge: Harvard University Press, 1950, p. 130. The figures cited may be interpreted as follows: 53.8 percent of the delinquents agreed with their parents, as compared with 68 percent of the nondelinquents; the difference of 14 percentage points was smaller than they had found elsewhere.

8. *Ibid.*, p. 130.

9. It is sometimes possible to use inconsistencies within a single questionnaire as a measure of the overall quality of response. See, for example, Hanan C. Selvin, *The Effects of Leadership*. New York: The Free Press, 1960, pp. 187–189. This study also illustrates how much one can learn from careful analysis of poor data; cf. the discussion of Barbara Wootton, *Social Science and Social Pathology* in Chapter 2.

10. John W. Tukey, "The future of data analysis," *Annals of Mathematical Statistics*, 33, 1962, pp. 1–67.

11. Selvin, *op. cit.*, Chapter II and Appendix B.

12. Jane Loevinger, "Person and perception as psychometric concepts," *Psychological Bulletin*, 72, 1965, pp. 143–155.

13. F. Ivan Nye, *Family Relationships and Delinquent Behavior*. New York: Wiley, 1958, pp. 15–17.

14. Robert A. Dentler and Lawrence J. Monroe, "Social correlates of early adolescent theft," *American Sociological Review*, 26, 1961, p. 735.

15. For a profound but difficult analysis of these ideas, see Lee J. Cronbach and Goldine C. Gleser, *Psychological Tests and Personnel Decisions*. (Second ed.) Urbana: University of Illinois Press, 1965.

16. Irwin Deutscher, "Words and deeds: social science and social policy," *Social Problems*, 13, 1966, p. 241.

17. The concept of "unreliability of the instrument" is a deplorable borrowing from the physical sciences. Physical instruments may change their properties independently of the observer or the material measured. It is difficult to see how these ideas make sense when applied to lists of questions.

18. Eugene J. Webb *et al.*, *Unobtrusive Measures*. Chicago: Rand McNally, 1966.

19. James S. Coleman, *Models of Change and Response Uncertainty*. Englewood Cliffs, N.J.: Prentice-Hall, 1964.

20. Patricia L. Kendall, *Conflict and Mood*. New York: The Free Press, 1954.

21. An excellent example of methodological ingenuity and awareness is the Methodological Introduction to Alfred C. Kinsey *et al.*, *Sexual Behavior in the Human Male*. Philadelphia: W. B. Saunders, 1948. See also William G. Cochran *et al.*, *Statistical Problems of the Kinsey Report*. Washington, D.C.: American Statistical Association, 1954.

# 13

# Statistical
# Inference

The past decade has seen a lively debate on the merits of tests of significance in nonexperimental sociological research. On one side are those who argue that these tests are generally inapplicable in nonexperimental research.[1] On the other side are those who claim that tests of significance have a legitimate place in sociological research, that their function is to answer (with a certain probability of error) the question, Is there anything in the data that *needs* explaining?[2] Despite disagreement on the overall value of these tests, there is considerable agreement on the conditions for their correct use and on the kinds of mistakes that are often made. An examination of the literature of delinquency provides many examples of these mistakes (although delinquency research is no worse in this respect than other fields of study). It also allows us to examine more closely the general question of whether or not these tests tell the researcher anything worth knowing.

A test of significance is intended to provide a statement of the probability that a difference or association as large as or larger than some specified difference could have occurred as a result of the operation of random phenomena when the "true" difference is zero. Although the two sides in the controversy differ on the point at which a test of significance should be used in the analysis of data, in neither view is the application of a test of significance, by itself, an adequate analysis of the data; yet only too often this is all that is done in delinquency research.

## *Substantive Meaning and the Consideration of Antecedent Variables*[3]

A frequent practice is to report differences between delinquents and nondelinquents as significant or nonsignificant; many examples were cited in Chapter 5. In experimental research, where the influence of extraneous variables has been taken into account in the design of the experiment, this information may be sufficient. The reader of an experimental report can draw useful conclusions from a test of significance because he knows the causal variables. No experimenter would report that group X differs significantly from group Y without stating how the experimental treatments differed. Yet this is essentially the same as reporting only that differences between delinquents and nondelinquents are significant.

A brief sketch of the logic of experimentation may help make clear the distinction between the meaning of the test of significance in this situation and its meaning in nonexperimental research. A researcher wishes to know if the grass in pasture A is better for cows than the grass in pasture B. He assigns cows to the two pastures in such a manner that all other differences between the two groups are random differences. In other words, the basis of assigning cows to the pastures is unrelated to such things as age, breeding, weight, and temperament. Over a long series of trials, average differences between the two groups on these variables will be zero. Now a test of significance can tell the experimenter the probability of obtaining a difference in milk production as large as or larger than a given amount if there were no difference in the quality of grass. If he states in advance the difference that must be achieved to be significant, and if the obtained difference is at least this large, he can be reasonably certain that it is attributable to differences in the grass and not to accidental differences in age, breeding, weight, and so on. Now suppose that this investigator cannot experiment, that he has to take his cows in fields where the farmer has left them. He finds that the cows in pasture A give significantly more milk than those in pasture B. Can he attribute this relation to differences in the quality of the grass? No. Perhaps the cows in pasture A are a different breed; perhaps they are older or were fed a grain supplement. Because they were not randomly assigned to the two pastures, these uncontrolled antecedent variables related both to milk production and to their presence in a given pasture may account for the relation. Because he has not randomized, the delinquency researcher does not know that in a long series of trials the average relation between antecedent variables and the independent variable would be zero. Therefore, an observed relation between the independent variable and the dependent variable may simply be a result of the antecedent variables associated with the independent variable.

In experimental research the result of a test of significance thus has a clear substantive meaning, but in delinquency research, as in other kinds of nonexperimental research, the substantive meaning of a test of significance is obscure. What, for example, is the meaning of the Gluecks' finding that the difference in the birth order of delinquents and nondelinquents is significant at the 1 percent level?[4] At first glance it seems to mean that middle children are more likely to become delinquent than are first-born, youngest, or only children. As we have shown, however, an uncontrolled antecedent variable (family size) is almost certainly the cause of the difference. The significance of their result may have led the Gluecks to believe that their analysis was finished, when, in reality, it had only begun. This one example should demonstrate the danger of taking a statistically significant result as a signal to stop an analysis.

Although the Gluecks ignored the substantive meaning of their finding, most analysts attempt to account for observed differences by some kind of conjectural elaboration. Most such attempts, however, are speculative, in the sense that the additional relations brought in to support or account for the original observations are themselves unverified. Indeed, by a process whose logic is altogether clear (if faulty), the statistical significance of the original findings may serve as evidence for these ancillary speculations:[5]

By virtue of being the first or only child, the adolescent experiences a somewhat different relationship to parents. . . . In addition, the oldest child often plays a semi-adult role in that he exercises control over, and to some extent is responsible for, younger siblings. Successful performance of this role requires acceptance of adult behavior patterns and also meets some of his needs for recognition. *These differences appear to have some effect since a significant difference by birth order is found.* Oldest and only children show less delinquent behavior than intermediate and youngest.[6]

Because other uncontrolled variables may account for the difference, the assurance provided by the test of significance is misleading. Suppose the following explanation of the observed difference were substituted for Nye's: In a cross-sectional sample of children in certain grades of school, the parents of those who are oldest or only children are, on the whole, younger than parents of middle or youngest children. Younger parents generally have smaller families and are better able to care for the needs of their children.[7] Because the differences being explained (in this case, differences in delinquency by birth order) remain the same regardless of the explanation given, the results of a test of significance also remain the same. The test has no more value in this situation, then, than it has when no attempt is made to account for observed differences. If it increases confidence in one explanation of differences, it also increases confidence in an alternative explanation. In short, if the test of significance is used before all important antecedent variables are controlled, it has only one narrow, statistical meaning. If the researcher jumps to substantive conclusions on the basis of the test of significance, he is likely to be wrong and likely to be convinced that he is right. If he simply reports his findings and the results of significance testing, the reader is likely to reach his own substantive conclusions—with the same consequences.

Those who support tests of significance would probably agree that these analyses involve questions that the tests themselves cannot answer. If one accepts the position that these tests answer the question, Is there anything in the data that needs explaining?, then finding a significant difference is a signal to proceed with the analysis, not to end it.[8]

## Total Populations

Tests of significance were intended to aid the researcher in making statements about the correspondence between a set of observations and some underlying phenomena when the observations are subject to some kind of random disturbance —most commonly, random sampling, randomization, or random errors of response and measurement. The idea of statistical significance is meaningless unless some random phenomenon is involved.[9] In many instances in delinquency research, however, there is no obvious source of randomness. The study is not experimental, so there is no random assignment of subjects to treatments; the data are collected in such a way that errors of response and processing are unlikely;[10] and instead of sampling, data are collected on a total population or on "all units of a sort which exist at one time."[11]

Lander had delinquency rates and census data for 155 of Baltimore's 157 census tracts. The omitted tracts "embrace in their entirety the Maryland Penitentiary, Baltimore City Jail, and the Baltimore Hospitals."[12] In a replication of Lander's study, Bordua had data for 366 of Detroit's 369 census tracts.[13] Wattenberg and Balistrieri studied "all investigations made by Detroit police of boys aged ten to sixteen inclusive for 1948."[14] Lentz used the official records of "all . . . of the boys who were committed to the Wisconsin School for Boys during 1948–49."[15] In each case the data are for a total population, not a sample. It might seem, then, that these researchers would have no reason for concern about sampling error: With no sample, there can be no sampling error. Yet all of the studies cited include tests of significance. This practice raises some questions. How do these researchers justify their use of tests of significance? What meanings do they attribute to the results of the tests? More generally, what basis is there for using tests of significance on total populations?

None of the studies we have examined deals with these questions. Lander and Bordua simply use the tests without any explanation of what purpose they might serve in total populations. Wattenberg and Balistrieri justify their use of chi-square tests with the statement that these tests "establish the degree of statistical reliability with which the null hypothesis could be rejected."[16] And Lentz simply claims that his tests enable him "to determine if there were differences between the two groups of boys."[17] Perhaps it is asking too much of investigators to justify their own procedures, for they may simply be relying on the conventional wisdom.[18] It may be worthwhile then to examine some of the arguments that have been offered for the use of tests of significance in analyzing data based on total populations rather than probability samples.

One way out of this difficulty is to postulate a *hypothetical infinite universe* of which the complete enumeration under study is a sample. This is a difficult concept; an example may help clarify it. Suppose that the researcher who found the cows in pasture A giving more milk than those in pasture B wonders what would happen if he were to repeat the experiment. He assumes that day-to-day fluctuations in the cows and their environment would cause the difference in milk production between his samples to vary in a random manner from trial to trial even if there were no differences in the two populations; the distribution of these variations can then be predicted from the mathematical theory of probability. This theory allows him to make statements about the frequency of extreme results in a long series of independent trials.

One basic problem remains. On what grounds does he assume that the real situation conforms to the theory—that repeated trials would result in a distribution of differences similar to that predicted by the mathematical model? The answer is simple: There is considerable empirical evidence that they would; it is possible to repeat experiments comparable to his, and others have done so. The ultimate justification for applying mathematical models to the real world is that the conclusions derived from them may be checked against the real world. The applicability of the mathematical theory of sampling may be determined by observing what happens in a long series of samples of the same type from a real population.[19]

The idea that a total population may be considered as a sample from an infinite hypothetical universe of possible populations appears to have some intuitive appeal, at least to those who want to use tests of significance. However, unlike the mathematical model of sampling from a real population, which can be tested by properly designed sampling experiments, there is no way to demonstrate that the model of sampling from a hypothetical universe corresponds to reality.[20] The idea that one can study the operation of sampling error when there is no real sample is wishful thinking about a world that never was.

Although none of the researchers discussed thus far has explicitly used the notion of an infinite hypothetical universe to justify his use of tests of significance, other investigators of delinquency have:

Technically, the findings must be regarded as parameter values, i.e., characteristic only of the populations studied. . . . Statisticians point out, however, that any sample may be assumed to be a random sample of some universe. . . . Since our interest transcends the particular cases we are studying, it seems useful to apply tests of statistical significance to our findings. . . . We recognize that the assumptions governing tests of significance are not met by our research design. Generalization beyond these groups must, therefore, be recognized as speculation, but as the sort of healthy speculation calculated to assess more inclusive theoretical significance.[21]

Is there, as Short implies, a statistical technique for inferring valid general statements from a particular sample? Some statisticians would extend the logic of drawing a sample from a finite, existing population to assuming that a sample already drawn has come by a random process from an infinite hypothetical universe.[22] As we have already remarked, there is no way to demonstrate that the sample provides any guide to statements about the population. Instead of trying to warp the demonstrable principles of statistical inference into an undemonstrable canon of inductive inference, it seems better to agree with Karl Popper that there is no such thing as a technique of inductive inference or, what amounts to the same thing, that one can never prove a general proposition.[23]

All that one can do, says Popper, is to try to disprove the proposition. The more stringent the tests that are not failed and the greater their number, the higher one's level of confidence in the truth of the generalization. Sooner or later, every proposition will be disproved. The creative theorist then formulates a new proposition that meets the last test and that, he hopes, will survive many new tests. Popper's argument, in short, is that science moves toward generality by trying to replicate and that the credibility of the general proposition increases in proportion to the stringency of the tests it has passed.

Although the notion of a hypothetical universe does not justify the application of tests of statistical significance to total populations, the idea of measurement error may. If the experimenter were to repeat his experiment using the same group of cows (assuming no changes in the cows), he would find variations stemming from errors in weighing, recording, computation, and so on, which we shall lump together as measurement errors. In research involving many kinds of physical measurements, experience has shown that the distribution of measurement errors justifies application of the theory of probability. If the delinquency researcher has empirical evidence that his measurement errors are random—which he usually does not have (and it is doubtful whether measurement errors in delinquency research are random)—he might justifiably use tests of significance with total populations.[24]

The most extreme consequences of using the idea of a hypothetical infinite universe to justify tests of significance may come when the investigator reports his results as though they were a sample from a real population:

The use of statistical tests of signficance was considered justified as 1952 is a sample of years and San Diego a sample of cities which might have been used.[25]

Finding a significant difference in San Diego in 1952 allows the investigator to conclude (with a known probability of error) that the same relation holds in all cities at all times.

## Nonprobability Samples

Some studies of delinquency use tests of significance for samples that were not drawn on a probability basis. The Gluecks, for example, selected five hundred "really serious offenders" by searching school and court records. Their nondelinquents were chosen from public schools in particular areas after investigation revealed that they had not committed any serious delinquent offense. A nondelinquent from this pool was retained in the sample only if he could be matched with a delinquent on age, neighborhood, ethnic origin, and intelligence quotient. In other words, selection of the sample was purposive, not random.[26] Yet the Gluecks used tests of significance to determine whether "a difference as great or greater than this [the observed difference] could occur by chance or by random sampling."[27] The differences, we can assume, did not occur as a result of random sampling, as the sample was not random. What is the meaning of a test of significance based on such a sample?

Assuming that the Gluecks could have gone on to draw additional samples using the same procedures, it would have been possible for them to say how often a difference of a certain size might occur as a result of sampling error. They did not draw such samples, so the sampling distributions of their statistics are unknown. Computations of sampling error thus become meaningless arithmetical exercises. Even the assumption that such distributions could be known is questionable; while empirical sampling distributions may be obtained for some nonprobability sampling procedures, this entails controls on the data collecting process that cannot be duplicated in cases similar to the Gluecks'.[28]

As a matter of fact, there are few probability samples in delinquency research. Only one of the studies thus far discussed in this chapter is based on such a sample. Nye used a systematic sample of high-school students in "three medium-sized Washington towns . . . who were in school the day the data were collected."[29]

Even with a probability design, the delinquency researcher is likely to end with a nonprobability sample. In dealing with noninstitutionalized populations, for example, nonresponse is a persistent problem. The least accessible persons tend to be delinquents—as the term is defined by the researcher. If a questionnaire is given in school, then delinquents are less likely to be enrolled, less likely to agree to take the questionnaire, less likely to be in attendance the day the questionnaire is given, and less likely to answer all the questions if they do take the questionnaire.[30]

The solution to this problem is not to compute tests of significance as though the sample were random, but, wherever possible, to attempt to determine the effects of the bias by appropriate analysis.

## Ex Post Facto Hypotheses

A sociologist is playing stud poker. Most of the time he plays along like everyone else, making his bets, occasionally winning, occasionally losing. At one point, however, the dealer gets four aces. Because a hand as good as this would occur very rarely if the cards were being dealt properly, the thought crosses the sociologist's mind that the dealer may be cheating. He therefore computes the probability of getting four aces under the null hypothesis that the cards are well shuffled and properly dealt. This probability is extremely small, 1/54,145. The sociologist rejects the null hypothesis, pulls out a gun, and shoots the dealer.

Before condemning the sociologist for statistical naïveté, one should consider how often a parallel situation occurs in empirical research. The investigator examines many tables, finds an extreme result, formulates the null hypothesis, tests it for statistical significance, and concludes that such a result would occur by chance so infrequently as to justify rejecting the null hypothesis.

The poker player and the delinquency researcher have both selected extreme results for testing; in so doing they violate a fundamental requirement of the testing of statistical hypotheses—that hypotheses and the rules for rejecting them be stated in advance of examining the data. Every random collection of objects (whether it be a table of random numbers, a hand of playing cards, or a set of data subject to random error) will contain combinations and sequences that appear to be nonrandom. If these nonrandom combinations are selected for testing, the hypothesis of randomness will usually be rejected. The procedure of significance testing makes sense only if one states the hypothesis and the rules for accepting or rejecting it before examining the data. To do otherwise—to test a hypothesis on the same data that suggested it, or to formulate or change the rules for rejection after the results are examined—is to make the test of significance a magic rite rather than a scientific procedure. We cannot emphasize this point too strongly: To hunt through a pile of tables for one that looks important enough to test, or to publish a handful of statistically significant tables without telling the reader how many unpublished tables were not significant, is to rob the procedure of all meaning. It becomes an empty gesture, a way of pretending to be scientific.[31]

These practices are so pervasive in delinquency research that there is little point in citing examples. In fact, it is easier to cite those few investigators who seem to be aware of the problem. Wattenberg and Balistrieri, for example, report the number of tables they examined and the proportion significant at the 5 percent level, and they go on to consider the significance of the entire set of results.[32] Others have made a start in this direction by reporting the number of relations examined.[33] We are sorry not to have more to say on this problem. Of all of the mistakes made in the use of statistical tests of significance, this one is probably the most common, the most serious in its consequences, and the least often recognized.[34] Aside from reserving a random subsample of the data to use in testing one or two hypotheses dredged from the remainder of the data, a procedure of definite value but limited applicability, there is only one way to test the significance of a result derived from examining the same data: on an independently gathered body of data.

This is almost a truism, and it is of little value in the day-to-day conduct of research. The investigator wants to know now, not a year later, whether or not a particular result might have been produced by random errors. Given the choice between waiting for another study to replicate the relations discovered in the study he is doing now and performing a quick-and-easy test of statistical significance, most investigators will do the test. This includes many who are aware of the controversy over the applicability of the tests to exploratory survey research; they apparently think that the test cannot do any harm and may do some good. This argument appears conservative; nevertheless, it is wrong.[35]

Perhaps the only way to keep investigators from using illegitimate tests is to offer them a legitimate alternative, one they can perform without waiting for a new study. The alternative we foresee is difficult to assess statistically (i.e., its significance level and power function are unascertainable), but it is simple, cheap, and intuitively appealing. Hypotheses will soon be testable on other, independent bodies of data, not data to be gathered in the future but data already in existence.

Even now, large amounts of suitable data are available in the "data libraries" in existence or being developed at many universities. Since these data libraries, data archives, or data banks, as they are variously called, are still unfamiliar to many social scientists, it will be useful to describe them briefly before discussing the ways in which they may be useful in the conduct of survey research generally.

The first and still the best-known data library is the Roper Public Opinion Research Center at Williams College, Williamstown, Massachusetts. Established in 1957 by a gift from Elmo Roper, the Roper Center now has the punched cards of hundreds of different studies conducted by over fifty university and commercial research organizations around the world—for example, there are studies from all of the Gallup affiliates, extending back into the 1930's. Users can work at the Center or get its services by mail—a single table, a set of tables, or a complete deck of cards that the user can analyze for himself. Research organizations at several American universities, notably Columbia (the Bureau of Applied Social Research) and the Survey Research Centers at the University of Michigan (Ann Arbor) and California (Berkeley) have established similar data libraries. There is now an International Association of Social Science Data Archives with its headquarters at the Bureau of Applied Social Research to coordinate the work of these centers and to provide information about their use.

The ways in which social scientists can use these libraries

are limited only by the imagination of the investigator. In sociology the recent work of Seymour Martin Lipset has been especially noteworthy. For example, Lipset has used such data to analyze the sources of support for right-wing political movements.[36] A comparative analysis of five countries cost him less than $100 for duplicate cards; to gather comparable data for any one of the countries he studied would have cost tens of thousands of dollars. And for many kinds of studies that can be done with data libraries, there are no other comparable data. Thus Lipset has compared the sources of support for three right-wing causes in the United States over the past thirty years—Father Charles E. Coughlin in the 1930's, Senator Joseph R. McCarthy in the 1950's, and the John Birch Society in the 1960's.[37] One has only to contrast this kind of historical analysis of public opinion with that of, say, A. V. Dicey's *Law and Opinion in England* to see what a revolutionary tool the data library is. The historian of the future will have resources unavailable to the historians of the past and unknown to many historians of the present.

The scale on which these libraries can be used ranges from the large comparative study to the statistical testing of a single hypothesis. If it is indeed meaningless to hunt through survey data for interesting relations and to test these relations for significance with the same data, then the survey library may provide a useful alternative to the long and slow procedure of conducting an independent study. The important point is that the hypothesis be formulated before examining the data. However, this principle is usually taken to mean that the hypothesis must be formulated before gathering the data. This is not necessary: All that matters is that the investigator not know what is in the data before he examines them.

The survey analyst may well look forward to a hypothesis testing service from these data libraries. For a small fee he would be able to send his hypothesis to a data library, specify the kinds of questions involved and the nature of the populations he desires to include, and receive a detailed account of the replications that were made. Indeed, with telephone links to computers now coming into wide use, such a test of significance may take less time and cost less money than the conventional calculations. The chief problem remaining to be solved is information retrieval—finding studies with the right combinations of questions amid the hundreds of studies in a large data library. The Center for International Studies at the Massachusetts Institute of Technology is now putting the entire Roper collection on magnetic tape as a first step in a computerized information retrieval system.

The use of data libraries for tests of significance will do more than guard against random error. Properly conducted, these replications are vital in the task of inductive inference, the formulation and testing of general propositions from particular sets of data.[38] When replications can be conducted in days instead of years, one may look forward to a revolution in the testing of sociological theory. It will no longer be necessary to conclude an empirical study with a pious plea for further research. Within the limits of the available data—and they are broad indeed—each investigator can conduct many of his own replications.

# Notes

1. Hanan C. Selvin, "A critique of tests of significance in survey research," *American Sociological Review*, 22, 1957, 519–527, and Hanan C. Selvin and Alan Stuart, "Data dredging procedures in survey analysis," *The American Statistician*, 20:3, 1966, pp. 20–23. These two papers contain references to most of the other discussions.

2. Leslie Kish, "Some statistical problems in research design," *American Sociological Review*, 24, 1959, p. 331. (Italics in original) Compare Santo F. Camilleri, "Theory, probability, and induction in social research," *American Sociological Review*, 27, 1963, pp. 170–178.

3. We believe that these tests should not be used until all relevant *antecedent* variables have been controlled. An early statement of this position asserted incorrectly that *all* relevant variables should be controlled before a test of significance is meaningful. See Selvin, *op. cit.* pp. 520–22.

4. See Chapter 5, pp. 78–80.

5. If theory A predicts outcome B and B turns out to be true, the conclusion that A must be true is a logical fallacy. Alternative theories, of course, may also predict B.

6. F. Ivan Nye, *Family Relationships and Delinquent Behavior*. New York: Wiley, 1958, p. 37. (Authors' italics) The reader is invited to compare these findings with those reported by the Gluecks; see Chapter 5. The Gluecks' finding was significant at the .01 level, Nye's at the .001 level.

7. Nye found an inverse relation between size of family and delinquent behavior for boys. *Ibid.* p. 38.

8. Of course, as was shown in Chapter 7, a small or zero difference may need explaining. In this case, the test of significance would give the wrong answer if this position is accepted. In the end, the decision on what needs explaining rests as much on the analyst's theoretical position as on the data.

9. Cf. Camilleri, *op. cit.*

10. Where the randomness is not produced by the investigator, as in random assignment and random sampling, there must be some evidence that the errors behave randomly. It is not enough to assume randomness. See Lancelot Hogben, *Statistical Theory*. New York: Norton, 1958.

11. Margaret J. Hagood and Daniel O. Price, *Statistics for Sociologists*. New York: Holt, Rinehart & Winston, 1952, p. 329. Cf. Camilleri, *op. cit.*, pp. 173–174.

12. Bernard Lander, *Towards an Understanding of Juvenile Delinquency*. New York: Columbia University Press, 1954, p. 19.

13. David J. Bordua, "Juvenile delinquency and 'anomie': an attempt at replication," *Social Problems*, 6, 1958–59, p. 231.

14. William W. Wattenberg and James Balistrieri, "Automobile theft: a 'favored group' delinquency," *American Journal of Sociology*, 57, 1952, p. 576.

15. William P. Lentz, "Rural-urban differentials and juvenile delinquency," *The Journal of Criminal Law, Criminology and Police Science*, 47, 1956, p. 332.

16. *Op. cit.* pp. 576–77.

17. *Op. cit.* p. 333.

18. Few textbooks treat this problem. The most complete discussion we have found is in Hagood and Price, *op. cit.*, pp. 286–294, 419–423. It is worth noting that these authors do not arrive at an unequivocal interpretation of tests of significance applied to total populations.

19. For a detailed account of such experimental studies of sampling theory, see Frederick F. Stephan and Philip J. McCarthy, *Sampling Opinions*. New York: Wiley, 1958, Part II.

20. Camilleri, *op. cit.*, goes considerably beyond our discussion to consider more general problems of inductive inference.

21. James F. Short, Jr., "Differential association and delinquency," *Social Problems*, 4, 1957, p. 237. Unfortunately, it is impossible to determine from Short's discussion of the selection of his sample whether or not he used all of the sixteen- and seventeen-year-old boys and girls in the state training schools or how those used were selected. He had, apparently, either a complete census or what Deming calls a *chunk* (those who happened to be available). See William E. Deming, *Some Theory of Sampling*. New York: Wiley, 1950, pp. 14–15.

22. For an explicit equating of inductive inference and statistical inference see Kenneth R. Hammond and James E. Householder, *Introduction to the Statistical Method*. New York: Alfred A. Knopf, 1962, pp. 235–237, 340–341.

23. Karl Popper, *Conjectures and Refutations*. New York: Basic Books, 1963.

24. See Hogben, *op. cit.*, Part II, "The calculus of error and the calculus of exploration."

25. Kenneth Polk, "Juvenile delinquency and social areas," *Social Problems*, 5, 1957–58, pp. 214–217.

26. This is not meant to suggest that the Gluecks should have used random methods to select their sample. In fact, random samples may be inferior to samples carefully chosen to allow examination of relations between variables. The question here is not sample selection, but tests of significance.

27. Sheldon and Eleanor Glueck, *Unraveling Juvenile Delinquency*. Cambridge, Harvard University Press, 1950, p. 75.

28. "Under certain reasonable assumptions . . . it seems clear that the repeated application of a specified quota sampling procedure will generate an empirical distribution for an estimate and that we can then attempt to estimate the variance of this distribution from one or more samples drawn according to this procedure." Stephan and McCarthy, *op. cit.*, pp. 211–212.

29. Nye, *op. cit.*, p. 17.

30. On the last point, see Arthur L. Stinchcombe, *Rebellion in a High School*. Chicago: Quadrangle Books, 1964, pp. 186–189.

31. Selvin and Stuart, *op. cit.*

32. Wattenberg and Balistrieri, *op. cit.*, p. 577.

33. For example, Nye, *op. cit.*, p. 18, and T. C. N. Gibbens, "Car thieves," *British Journal of Delinquency*, 8, 1958, p. 259.

34. It is obviously unfair to condemn delinquency researchers, as if they were the only ones guilty of this misuse of statistical tests. The problem is general in nonexperimental research, and one can only hope that the statisticians will pay some attention to it. The problem is both simpler and more tractable in experimental research. See, for example, Thomas A. Ryan, "Multiple comparisons in psychological research," *Psychological Bulletin*, 56, 1959, pp. 26–47.

35. See Selvin and Stuart, *op. cit.*, and Selvin, "Survey analysis," in *International Encyclopedia of the Social Sciences*. New York: The Free Press, 1968.

36. Seymour Martin Lipset, *Political Man*. Garden City, N.Y., Doubleday, 1960, Chapter 5.

37. Seymour Martin Lipset, "Three decades of the radical right: Coughlinites, McCarthyites, and Birchers," in Daniel Bell, (ed.), *The Radical Right*. Garden City, N.Y.: Doubleday, 1963, Chapter 14.

38. See the discussion of replications in Selvin, "Durkheim's *Suicide*: further thoughts on a methodological classic," in Robert A. Nisbet, *Emile Durkheim*. Englewood Cliffs, N.J.: Prentice-Hall, 1965.

# Description

# and

# Prediction

Statements such as the following are common in delinquency research: The design of the study did not allow the determination of causal relations. By such statements the investigator affirms that his purpose is merely descriptive, that the criteria for judging a causal analysis do not apply. The decision to treat data as merely descriptive frees the analyst from many problems of presentation and inference. He is no longer bound by rules concerning the proper presentation of independent and dependent variables; he is no longer concerned about investigating causally spurious relations—for example, the finding that middle children are more likely to be delinquent would remain descriptively true even if it could be shown that the relation between birth order and delinquency was causally spurious.

In much the same way, the investigator wishing to predict delinquency is not bound by the rules of causal analysis. He is not required to show that the relations upon which he bases his predictions are nonspurious, and his concern for the how

235

of causal two-variable relations (i.e., for intervening variables) is usually minimal. At the same time, however, prediction requires higher congruence between the sample in which the prediction instrument is devised and the population in which it is to be used (or, at least, more concern for such congruence) than does causal analysis.

Stated in this methodological language, these distinctions may seem both obvious and unimportant. In actual practice, however, the meaning of these distinctions often eludes investigators, and, as we shall show in this chapter, the consequences of confusing causal, descriptive, and predictive modes of presentation may be serious.

Suppose that an investigator uses school records to choose a sample of one thousand delinquents and one thousand nondelinquents. At one point, wanting to study the relation between sex and delinquency, he constructs Table 14-1a. He now has to choose between two different modes of percentaging; he can base the percentages on the column totals, as in Table 14-1b, or on the row totals, as in Table 14-1c. If he chose

### Table 14-1—Delinquency and Sex (hypothetical)

**a. ORIGINAL FREQUENCIES**

| | Girls | Boys | Total |
|---|---|---|---|
| Delinquent | 100 | 900 | 1000 |
| Nondelinquent | 400 | 600 | 1000 |
| Total | 500 | 1500 | 2000 |

**b. PERCENTAGED IN THE CAUSAL DIRECTION**

| | Girls | Boys | Total |
|---|---|---|---|
| Delinquent | 20% | 60% | 50% |
| Nondelinquent | 80% | 40% | 50% |
| Total | 100% | 100% | 100% |
| Number of cases | (500) | (1500) | (2000) |

**c. PERCENTAGED IN THE EFFECTS DIRECTION**

| | Girls | Boys | Total | Number of cases |
|---|---|---|---|---|
| Delinquent | 10% | 90% | 100% | (1000) |
| Nondelinquents | 40% | 60% | 100% | (1000) |
| Total | 25% | 75% | 100% | (2000) |

Table 14-1b, he would say: Among the girls 20 percent are delinquent, as compared with 60 percent among the boys, a difference of 40 percentage points. Or, looking at Table 14-1c, he could say: Among the delinquents 10 percent are girls, as compared with 40 percent among the nondelinquents, a difference of 30 percentage points. The two statements are compatible; both show an association between being male and being delinquent.[1] Which is the better of these two procedures?

Zeisel presents two rules for choosing the direction of percentaging:

    1. Percentage in the causal direction.
    2. Percentage in the representative direction.

Zeisel's first rule[2] leads to the percentages in Table 14-1b, because the causal direction is from sex to delinquency. The application of his second rule is less clear, unless one knows something of how the sample was chosen. Assuming that the delinquents and the nondelinquents in the sample are drawn from the populations of delinquents and nondelinquents in the school records, one would use Zeisel's second rule and get the percentages of Table 14-1c.

These are simple rules. It is hard to believe that violating them could have serious consequences, but following an actual analysis in some detail will illuminate the dangers and make it easier for others to avoid them.

## *Percentaging in the Causal Direction*

In their Boston study the Gluecks found a relation between delinquency and employment of the mother. They also found that delinquency and adequacy of supervision were related. In a later analysis of these data they present a table showing the relations among all three variables (Table 14-2).

### Table 14-2—Unsuitable Supervision and Mother's Employment by Delinquency*

| | DELINQUENTS | | NONDELINQUENTS | | DIFFERENCE | |
| | Number | Percent | Number | Percent | Number | Percent |
|---|---|---|---|---|---|---|
| Total | 314 | 63.5 | 61 | 12.5 | 253 | 51.0 |
| Housewife | 126 | 48.1 | 23 | 7.0 | 103 | 41.1 |
| Regularly employed | 85 | 84.2 | 25 | 28.0 | 60 | 56.2 |
| Occasionally employed | 103 | 78.6 | 13 | 18.6 | 90 | 60.0 |

* The format of this table is that used by the Gluecks. See Sheldon and Eleanor Glueck, "Working mothers and delinquency," *Mental Hygiene*, July, 1957, p. 331. The table shows, for example, that 314 of the delinquents (63.5 percent) are unsuitably supervised by their mothers.

Examining this table leads the Gluecks to the following conclusion:

. . . from the column labeled *Difference*, it is learned that a boy who is carelessly supervised and who has a mother who is of the kind who works occasionally is far more likely to become delinquent than is the poorly supervised son of a mother who does not go out to work.[3]

Our first observation is that the Gluecks' table is hard to understand; at best, it is in a form that is unfamiliar to most readers. However, since it includes all of the necessary data, it can be put into the more familiar form of Table 14-3.[4]

### Table 14-3—Unsuitable Supervision and Mother's Employment by Delinquency

| | Mother's Employment | | | | | |
| | HOUSEWIFE | | REGULARLY EMPLOYED | | OCCASIONALLY EMPLOYED | |
| | Delinquent percent | Nondelinquent percent | Delinquent percent | Nondelinquent percent | Delinquent percent | Nondelinquent percent |
|---|---|---|---|---|---|---|
| Supervision unsuitable | 48.1 (262) | 7.0 (329) | 84.2 (101) | 28.0 (89) | 78.6 (131) | 18.6 (70) |
| Percentage difference | 41.1 | | 56.2 | | 60.0 | |

238

Now consider the elements in the Gluecks' statement, First, there is "a boy who is carelessly [unsuitably] supervised." Then there is "a mother who is of the kind who works occasionally" and "a mother who does not go out to work." Boys with such mothers are in the left third and the right third of the table. The Gluecks' statement thus directs the reader to look at the following figures: 48.1 and 7.0 at the left and 78.6 and 18.6 at the right. Do these figures support the statement quoted from the Gluecks? The answer is that they have nothing to do with the statement: They neither support nor contradict the statement because they refer to something else, i.e., to rates of unsuitable supervision rather than to rates of delinquency. The first figure, 48.1 percent, is the proportion of unsuitably supervised boys among delinquents whose mothers are housewives; the second is the proportion unsuitably supervised among nondelinquents whose mothers are housewives. Comparable statements can be made for the figures of 78.6 and 18.6 at the right. With these figures the Gluecks could have made either of the following statements:

1. A boy who is delinquent and has a mother who is of the kind who works occasionally is far more likely to be unsuitably supervised than is the delinquent son of a mother who does not go out to work. (This compares 48.1 percent with 78.6 percent).[5]
2. A boy who is delinquent and has a mother who is of the kind who works occasionally is far more likely to be unsuitably supervised than is the nondelinquent with the same kind of mother. (This compares 78.6 percent with 18.6 percent).[6]

Because the Gluecks have constructed their table inappropriately, it cannot be used to study the effects of (a) mother's occupation on (b) delinquency within (c) categories of supervision, which is what they wanted to do. It can be used to study the effects of (a) mother's occupation on (c) supervision within categories of (b) delinquency, but they did not want to study this bizarre relation.

The mistake that the Gluecks made here is more than simply percentaging in the wrong direction. What may be nothing worse than awkward phrasing in a two-variable table, where percentaging in either direction will reveal the presence of an association, becomes a serious error in a three-variable table. In examining a three-variable table the analyst asks how the association between two variables is affected by the values of a third variable. There are three different ways to combine the three variables. Each demands a different mode of percentaging; choosing the wrong mode means examining the wrong relation.

The Gluecks' statement can be studied, however, by recomputing the percentages in the right direction (i.e., treating delinquency as the dependent variable in the table, so that it corresponds to their text). This table (Table 14-4) leads to either of two types of statements (we are again paralleling the Gluecks' text):

### Table 14-4—Delinquency and Supervision by Mother's Employment (Second revised form of Table 14-2)*

| | Mother's Employment | | | | | |
| | HOUSEWIFE | | REGULARLY EMPLOYED | | OCCASIONALLY EMPLOYED | |
| Supervision: | Suitable | Unsuit-able | Suitable | Unsuit-able | Suitable | Unsuit-able |
|---|---|---|---|---|---|---|
| Percent delinquent | 31 | 85 | 20 | 77 | 33 | 89 |
| Number of cases | (442) | (149) | (80) | (110) | (85) | (116) |
| Percentage difference | 54 | | 57 | | 56 | |

* This table is adapted from Eleanor E. Maccoby, "Effects upon children of their mothers' outside employment," in Norman W. Bell, and Ezra F. Vogel, A Modern Introduction to the Family. New York: The Free Press, 1960, p. 523. Although Maccoby focuses on the substantive issues raised by the Gluecks' data, she notes that her method of percentaging "permits viewing delinquency as a dependent variable." As now constructed, this table emphasizes the relation between supervision and delinquency within categories of mother's employment. If statements such as (3) are the analyst's primary interest, he should group all of the values of mother's employment within categories of supervision. We have left the table in its present form in order to compare the percentage difference row with the Gluecks' difference column in Table 14-2.

3. A boy who is carelessly supervised and who has a mother who is of the kind who works occasionally is *only very slightly* more likely to become delinquent than is the poorly supervised son of a mother who does not go out to work. (This compares 89 percent with 85 percent, a difference of 4 percentage points.)

4. A boy who is unsuitably supervised and who has a mother who works occasionally is far more likely to be a delinquent than is the suitably supervised son of the same kind of mother. (This compares 89 percent with 33 percent.)

Statement 3 is the relevant finding for the Gluecks. Because it cannot be derived or even approximated from the Gluecks' table, one should not be surprised that it differs markedly from their conclusion.

The Gluecks' method of analyzing Table 14-2 falls into two parts. The first, which we have just considered, is to compute the wrong set of percentages. The second part of their method is to use the *Difference* column in Table 14-2, which appears as the *difference* row in the Tables 14-3 and 14-4.

Consider first the sons of mothers "who are of the kind who work occasionally." The figure of 56 in the difference row has already turned up in our statement 4 (see Table 14-4). It shows a strong relation between supervision and delinquency when the mother is occasionally employed; unsuitably supervised boys in this group are far more likely to be delinquent than are suitably supervised boys. Since the difference figure for the sons of housewives (54) is virtually identical to the figure for the sons of occasionally employed mothers, the same statements apply to them. The Difference thus allows the investigator to compare levels of association in different subgroups of the sample.

Now the Gluecks' original statement does not refer to a difference between suitably and unsuitably supervised boys (which is what each of their "differences" measures) or to a difference between differences (which seems implicit in their claim to have reached their conclusion by examining the *Dif-*

241

*ference* column).[7] So this procedure, too, is defective: It cannot lead to the kind of conclusion the Gluecks report even when it is applied to a correctly percentaged table. Obviously, it has even less to do with their conclusions when applied to an incorrectly percentaged table.

There are several lessons in this example: 1. Poorly constructed tables can mislead the analyst and discourage the reader. 2. Any procedure, even one as elementary as percentaging, can lead to erroneous conclusions if followed mechanically. 3. Even after publication of the original report, a careful reanalysis can clarify findings and rectify mistakes.[8]

## Percentaging in the Representative Direction

Most methodological principles have their exceptions. The example in the preceding section shows what can happen when the analyst fails to percentage in the causal direction, but following this rule mechanically leads to another kind of error in two types of situations: 1. estimating rates of behavior in the population from which the sample was drawn; 2. predicting rates of delinquency in various social categories.

*Estimating rates in populations.* The Gluecks use Table 14-5 to study the effects of church attendance on delinquency in Boston; this effect, however, is clearer in Table 14-6, and

### Table 14-5—Delinquency by Church Attendance*

| Attendance | DELINQUENTS | | NONDELINQUENTS | | DIFFERENCE |
| | Number | Percent | Number | Percent | Percent |
| --- | --- | --- | --- | --- | --- |
| ·Regular | 193 | 39.3 | 334 | 67.1 | −27.8 |
| Occasional | 266 | 54.2 | 143 | 28.7 | 25.5 |
| None | 32 | 6.5 | 21 | 4.2 | 2.3 |
| Total | 491 | 100.0 | 498 | 100.0 | |

* Glueck and Glueck, *Unraveling Juvenile Delinquency.* Cambridge: Harvard University Press, 1950, Table XIII-21, p. 166.

242

this latter mode of percentaging is necessary if there is to be any further analysis of the relation between church attendance and delinquency.

**Table 14-6—Delinquency by Church Attendance**
**(Table 14-5 rearranged and repercentaged)**

| | ATTENDANCE | | |
| | Regular percent | Occasional percent | None percent |
|---|---|---|---|
| Delinquents | 37 | 65 | 60 |
| Nondelinquents | 63 | 35 | 40 |
| | 100 | 100 | 100 |
| | (527) | (409) | (53) |

Suppose, however, that one wants to use these data to estimate some characteristics of·the population the Gluecks studied. For this task the percentages in Table 14-6 are grossly misleading. They show, for example, that 37 percent of the boys who attend church regularly, and 65 percent of those who attend occasionally, are delinquent; Boston surely was never like this! The source of the difficulty is, of course, the way in which the sample was put together. Since it is composed of five hundred delinquents and five hundred nondelinquents, it does not represent the boys of Boston proportionately; delinquents have a much greater chance of being included than do nondelinquents. Although the subsample of delinquents may fairly represent the population of delinquents and the subsample of nondelinquents the corresponding population of nondelinquents, the overweighting of delinquents in the total sample means that the rates of delinquency in the various categories of church attendance in Table 14-6 are too high. This table is the right one to use for studying the effect of church attendance on delinquency, but it is the wrong one to use for describing the population. In other words, when one wants to estimate rates for a population from a table based on a sample, the percentages must be computed in the direction that is representative of that population.

If one can assume that the two subsamples of delinquents and nondelinquents are indeed representative of the corresponding populations, then Table 14-5 is percentaged in the representative direction. The figures in this table are then valid estimates of the population rates; for example, the proportion of delinquents in Boston who attend church regularly should be close to 39.3 percent. Thus each of these tables has a valid interpretation, but neither should be used for the purpose of the other.

*Predicting delinquency.* The direction in which a table should be percentaged depends upon whether the analyst wishes to describe a population or to assess the effects of an independent variable. If, however, the analyst wants to predict whether a boy will become delinquent from knowledge of his attendance at church, it is no longer merely a question of the difference between modes of percentaging. At this point the difference between the proportion of delinquents in the sample and the proportion of delinquents in the population for which predictions are to be made becomes crucial.

In *Unraveling* the Gluecks construct prediction instruments using "factors that clearly differentiate the delinquents and nondelinquents in this research."[9] The technique for constructing these tables is as follows: Because 83.2 percent of those who are unsuitably supervised are delinquents, any boy who is unsuitably supervised is given a "failure score" on this item of 83.2; likewise, since 9.9 percent of those who are suitably supervised are delinquents, suitably supervised boys are given a failure score on supervision of 9.9. This procedure is repeated for each of the items used (the number of items never exceeds five), and each boy receives a total failure score. The percentage of delinquents within each failure-score category is then considered to be the chances of delinquency for boys with the score in question (Table 14-7).

**Table 14-7—Detailed Prediction Table from Five Factors of Social Background***

| Weighted failure | Number of delinquents | Chances of delinquency (per hundred) | Number of nondelinquents | Chances of nondelinquency (per hundred) |
|---|---|---|---|---|
| Under 150 | 5 | 2.9 | 167 | 97.1 |
| 150–199 | 19 | 15.7 | 102 | 84.3 |
| 200–249 | 40 | 37.0 | 68 | 63.0 |
| 250–299 | 122 | 63.5 | 70 | 36.5 |
| 300–349 | 141 | 86.0 | 23 | 14.0 |
| 350–399 | 73 | 90.1 | 8 | 9.9 |
| 400 and over | 51 | 98.1 | 1 | 1.9 |
| | 451 | | 439 | |

* Sheldon and Eleanor Glueck, *Unraveling*, p. 261.

By assigning to each delinquent and non-delinquent, concerning whom information was available on all five factors, his score on each, summating the scores, and distributing the cases into the appropriate score class, we arrive at the detailed prediction table . . . after translating the number of cases in each subclass into a percent of the total number in each score class. These then became the chances out of a hundred of potential delinquency and non-delinquency.[10]

The Gluecks assume that boys with failure scores between, say, 350 and 399 will become delinquents 90.1 percent of the time. In an early review of the Gluecks' book, Reiss argued that "unless this [sampling rate of 50 percent delinquents] is the actual rate in a similar population for which the predictions are made, the tables will yield very poor prediction."[11] Reiss then shows how the predictive power of the instrument would be affected by its use in a population in which only one boy in ten was delinquent.[12]

The first three columns of Table 14-8 are taken from the Gluecks' table. In the fourth column Reiss calculates the

### Table 14-8—Prediction Table for Five Factors of Social Background*

| (1) Weighted failure Score (Gluecks) | (2) Number of delinquents (Gluecks) | (3) Number of nondelinquents (Gluecks) | (4) Number of nondelinquents (Rate delinquency estimated at 10 percent) | (5) Chances of delinquency (Gluecks) | (6) Chances of delinquency (Rate estimated at 10 percent) | (7) Expected errors (Rate estimated at 10 percent)** |
|---|---|---|---|---|---|---|
| Under 150 | 5 | 167 | 1,503 | 2.9 | 0.3 | 5 |
| 150–199 | 19 | 102 | 918 | 15.7 | 2.0 | 19 |
| 200–249 | 40 | 68 | 612 | 37.0 | 6.2 | 40 |
| 250–299 | 122 | 70 | 630 | 63.5 | 16.2 | 122 |
| 300–349 | 141 | 23 | 207 | 86.0 | 40.5 | 141 |
| 350–399 | 73 | 8 | 72 | 90.1 | 50.3 | 72 |
| 400 and over | 51 | 1 | 9 | 98.1 | 85.0 | 9 |
| Missing cases | 49 | 61 | 549 | 44.5 | 8.2 | 49 |
| Total | 500 | 500 | 4,500 | 50.0 | 10.0 | 457 |

* Reiss, op. cit., p. 119. We have added the column numbers.
** The percentage reduction in the error of prediction is 8.6 percent.

number of nondelinquents that would occur in each row if there were 4,500 nondelinquents instead of 500 (thus making the delinquents 10 percent of the population) and if these 4,500 nondelinquents distributed themselves in the same proportions as the 500 nondelinquents in the third column (1,503 is the same proportion of 4,500 as 167 is of 500). Column 6 is derived from columns 2 and 4 in the same way that column 5 was derived from columns 2 and 3: $5/(5 + 167) =$ 2.9 percent; $5/(5 + 1,503) = 0.3$ percent.

The two "Chances of Delinquency" columns, 5 and 6, are the basis for prediction. Whenever the chances are 50 percent or more, the best prediction that can be made is that all of the boys in that category are delinquent. When the chances are less than 50 percent, the best prediction is that all are nondelinquent. Column 7 shows how many errors would be made by following these rules of prediction in the 10 percent delinquent population. In the first row, all 172 cases would be predicted nondelinquent, but 0.3 percent, or 5 cases, would actually be delinquent. The same reasoning applies to all but the last two rows, where all cases would be predicted delinquent by both methods. Finally, Reiss computes an overall measure of the value of the revised prediction: the reduction in the proportion of errors made by taking into account the failure scores, as compared with the best prediction that could be made without them. It is a disappointing 8.6 percent.[13]

Despite the attacks by Reiss and others on the Gluecks' predictive instrument, the issue is not as clear as it may appear at first glance. Thus the Gluecks' reply to their critics:

Reiss and similar critics have not clearly explained just why the adjustment to a supposed actual proportion of 9:1 is necessary; or, why differences in the incidence of delinquents and non-delinquents in any population should and would have a serious distorting influence on the distribution of scores of the predictive factors as presented in our 50–50 table.[14]

However, as further passages from the Gluecks' reply indicate, the Gluecks and their critics sometimes appear to be talking about two different things:

*The use of equal numbers in the samples* originally compared is not only legitimate but important for the accurate determination of the incidence of the factors under comparison. It is, for example, a frequent technique in medical research. . . . Assuming that the sample of delinquents and the sample of nondelinquents are fairly representative of the populations from which the cases were derived, the fact that the total group of nondelinquents in the general population is nine times as numerous as the total group of delinquents can have little to do with the outcome when comparing the two samples; and it should, equally, have little to do with the outcome when applying the table to new populations.[15]

As we have already shown, it is possible to use the Gluecks' tables to describe their delinquent and nondelinquent populations—for example, to predict the proportion of delinquents who attend church regularly. Insofar as such predictions are concerned, the Gluecks are correct: The use of equal numbers of delinquents and nondelinquents is perfectly legitimate.

The critics, however, are not arguing that the incidence of the factors cannot be predicted accurately; they are arguing that delinquency cannot be predicted accurately. And this is a separate question. The difference becomes clearer in still another quotation from Sheldon Glueck's defense:

If one were making a study comparing the incidence of blood pressure [sic], pulse [sic], certain chemicals in the blood and urine, etc. of persons with a malignant disease, with their incidence among healthy persons, would it make any difference whether the *general* incidence of such diseased persons in the particular community amounted to 10 per cent or 50 per cent? And, assuming that in the city in which the original experiment was done the population proportions of the well and the ill were 50–50, would this fact interfere with the predictive capacity of a table of indications and symptoms when applied to a city in which the proportions were 90:10?[16]

Again, two different questions are being asked. The answer to the first one is No, it wouldn't make any difference if one wanted to predict the incidence of (high) blood pressure, (rapid) pulse, certain chemicals in the blood and urine, and so on, from knowledge of the presence or absence of malignant disease. One simply follows the rule of percentaging in the representative direction.

The answer to the second question, however, is clearly Yes, it certainly would.[17] The accuracy of predictions of disease from a set of symptoms depends on the proportion having the disease for the same reason that the efficiency of the Gluecks' predictive instrument depends upon the percentage of delinquents in the population on which it is used.

This argument may be more compelling with an extreme example. Suppose that five hundred persons with stomach cancer are compared with five hundred healthy persons on the variables suggested by the Gluecks and that the following results were obtained.

| | Stomach cancer patients | Healthy persons |
|---|---|---|
| With high blood pressure, rapid pulse, and chemical X in blood and urine | 450 | 50 |
| Without high blood pressure, rapid pulse, or chemical X in blood and urine | 50 | 450 |

Following the Gluecks' logic, there is a 90 percent chance that a person with high blood pressure, rapid pulse, and chemical X in his blood and urine is suffering from stomach cancer. This seems sufficient to justify an exploratory operation. Suppose, however, that the proportion of persons in the population with stomach cancer is only 1 percent. The following table would be obtained from a representative sample of this population (assuming the same proportions as in the table above):

|  | Stomach cancer patients | Healthy persons |
|---|---|---|
| With high blood pressure, rapid pulse, and chemical X in blood and urine | 450 | 4,950 |
| Without high blood pressure, rapid pulse, or chemical X in blood and urine | 50 | 44,550 |

It turns out, then, that the chance that a person with the described symptoms has stomach cancer is only 8.3 percent (450/5,400). (The chance that a person with stomach cancer has the described symptoms is, of course, unchanged.) Let us all hope that this "frequent technique in medical research" is used only to predict symptoms once the presence of the disease is known and that it is not the basis upon which surgeons decide to operate.[18]

The Gluecks' prediction tables thus illustrate an important methodological point: If an investigator wishes to make statements about the population from which his sample was drawn, he must percentage within categories representative of that population.[19] The Gluecks can (perhaps) make accurate statements about the distributions of their independent variables within the delinquent and nondelinquent populations; they cannot make accurate statements about the distributions of delinquency within categories of their independent variables for some larger population.

Sheldon Glueck suggests that this is an empirical question: ". . . one should not dogmatize at the outset that the influence of differences in proportions will seriously affect the outcome; one must await the proof of the pudding."[20] It is, on the contrary, strictly a logical question. The Gluecks' predictions for populations with different distributions of the dependent variable cannot be correct unless the data upon which the original predictive device was based were in error. How, then, is one to account for the many validation studies that purport to show the accuracy of the Gluecks' predictive device?

It should be pointed out that the tables reflecting the experience in these checkups resemble *not* the adjusted tables of Reiss and others, but the original Glueck table.[21]

Most of these studies examine the distribution of delinquency prediction scores within samples of delinquents or nondelinquents.[22] Again, this is not the issue. The prediction device was designed to predict delinquency from individual characteristics, not vice versa.

The New York City Youth Board study, which followed a sample of 301 boys from the time they entered school until they were seventeen, got results much like the original Glueck table.[23] Since only about one boy in seven in this sample was eventually classified as delinquent, it may appear that the rocks in the pudding had no effect on its quality. However, what this study really shows is that purely logical truths are unaffected by empirical investigation.

In the Youth Board study, only 5 of 257 nondelinquents had scores on the prediction scale indicating that they were very likely to become delinquent, while 28 of the 44 delinquents had such scores, for an 85 percent (28/33) success rate. This success rate compares favorably with the 89 percent success rate expected on the basis of the *Unraveling* sample. Now, in order to do almost as well in a sample in which one of seven boys is delinquent as one did in a sample in which one of two boys is delinquent, something has to give: In this case, of course, it is the distribution of scores on the items used to predict delinquency. Only about one-fourth as many nondelinquents are incorrectly predicted delinquent as one would expect by comparing the composition of the *Unraveling* and the Youth Board samples. To compensate, there are only about one-fourth as many nondelinquents with high scores on the predictive instrument as one would expect from their relative distribution in the *Unraveling* sample. There is abundant evidence that vagaries of sampling alone do not account for the unexpected dearth of nondelinquents with high scores:

After cases were initially scored . . . , we agreed that *the number of boys rated potentially delinquent was out of proportion to the total number of delinquents in the population of the areas from which the boys emanated*. We therefore [!] decided to study those boys whose fathers were away from home for the major portion of the boy's life . . .[24]

This "back to the drawing board" or "if at first you don't succeed" approach to validation of a predictive instrument was not counted upon by the critics.[25] They assumed they were giving the Gluecks the benefit of a very serious doubt by simply extending the relation found in *Unraveling* to populations differing in the ratio of delinquents to nondelinquents. They did not suspect that the Gluecks' data-dredging procedures had produced a predictive instrument more strongly related to delinquency in samples other than the one suggesting it. For that matter, how did the Gluecks know that their *Unraveling* data were consistently underestimating the relations between their independent variables and delinquency?

## Causal Analysis in Nonrepresentative Samples

We began this chapter with a brief discussion of the distinctions among causal, descriptive, and predictive uses of data. By discussing two examples at some length, we have tried to show how the validity of the investigator's use of a particular technique depends on whether he is asking causal, descriptive, or predictive questions.

Since by now it may appear that we are opposed to the

Gluecks' percentaging regardless of what it might be, we shall briefly summarize the differences in the two situations we have used as examples. In the first case, the Gluecks are interested in the relative likelihood of delinquency among boys with different combinations of traits within their sample (a causal question). In the second case, they are interested in the absolute likelihood of delinquency among boys with different combinations of traits in the population (a predictive question). The effect of nonrepresentativeness in the second case has already been shown. To conclude this discussion of percentage comparisons, let us see how nonrepresentativeness may affect the first case by reconstructing Table 14-4 using Reiss's assumption that the population ratio of delinquents to nondelinquents is 1:9.

**Table 14-9—Delinquency and Suitability of Supervision by Mother's Employment when the Ratio of Delinquents to Nondelinquents is 1:1 and when It Is 1:9**

| | Mother's Employment | | | | | |
| | HOUSEWIFE | | REGULARLY EMPLOYED | | OCCASIONALLY EMPLOYED | |
| Supervision: | Suitable | Unsuitable | Suitable | Unsuitable | Suitable | Unsuitable |
|---|---|---|---|---|---|---|
| **1:1** | | | | | | |
| Percent delinquent | 32 | 84 | 19 | 77 | 32 | 88 |
| Number cases | (457) | (149) | (82) | (110) | (89) | (116) |
| Difference | 52 | | 58 | | 56 | |
| **1:9** | | | | | | |
| Percent delinquent | 5 | 37 | 3 | 27 | 5 | 45 |
| Number cases | (2945) | (341) | (610) | (310) | (577) | (228) |
| Difference | 32 | | 24 | | 40 | |

Several things can be observed by comparing the two parts of Table 14-9. First, the percentage differences are considerably smaller in the table based on the estimated true proportions of delinquents and nondelinquents. Second, the rank of the partial tables with respect to strength of relation (using the percentage-point difference as a measure) is upset. In the

**253**

original table, suitability of supervision discriminates most strongly among the regularly employed (comparing 19 with 77 percent), in the revised table the corresponding partial relation is the smallest. Finally, as an ironical conclusion to this long examination of the Gluecks' use of percentage comparisons, we should note that their original statement about the effects of mother's occupation and supervision on delinquency, which was not supported by their own table, is partially supported in this representative table.[26]

In contrast to the percentage comparison, Yule's $Q$[27] is not affected by changes in the relative distribution of either the dependent or the independent variable; thus one would get the same value of $Q$ in Table 14-1a if all the frequencies in the first row were reduced to one-tenth of their present values; the percentage differences of Table 14-1b would change markedly. $Q$ for the three relations in the lower part of Table 14-9 is −0.83, −0.86, and −0.88 —a third ordering of the strength of the relations.

# Notes

1. The difference between the two percentage-point differences reflects the asymmetry of percentage comparisons as a measure of association; only when the row totals and the column totals have the same distribution will the two sets of percentages and the two differences be the same.

2. Hans Zeisel, *Say It With Figures.* (Fourth ed.) New York and Evanston: Harper & Row, 1957. Instead of "Percentage in the causal direction," it might be clearer to say "Percentage within categories of the independent variable."

3. Sheldon and Eleanor Glueck, "Working mothers and delinquency," *Mental Hygiene,* July, 1957, p. 332.

4. The reader can easily verify that we have simply reorganized Table 14-2. For example, the figure of 48.1 percent in the first column of Table 14-2 is the proportion unsuitably supervised among the delinquents whose mothers are housewives. The Gluecks report the numerator of this fraction (126); following the usual convention, we report the denominator (262). As the figures in the Total row of Table 14-2 do not play any part in the analysis reported here, we have left them out of Table 14-3. Finally, we would have preferred to round the percentages to the nearest integer, because two-place accuracy is enough for this kind of survey data. However, in order to facilitate comparisons of our table with the Gluecks' table we have left the percentages unchanged.

5. Most analysts would go on to compare this difference with the corresponding difference for nondelinquents (7.0 and 18.6 percent).

6. This statement omits the comparison among the sons of housewives. Cf. preceding note.

7. The Gluecks test each difference and each difference between differences for statistical significance. After testing the difference between the percentage differences for housewives and occasionally employed mothers, they conclude: ". . . the divergences are significant at the .05 level, indicating a special etiologic impact of the already generally criminogenic influence of unsuitable maternal supervision on those youngsters whose mothers were occasional workers as compared with those whose mothers spent their full time at home as housewives." Glueck and Glueck, "Working mothers," p. 332.

8. Maccoby's detailed reanalysis of some of the data presented in the Gluecks' article, "Working mothers and delinquency," is an excellent example of what can be done.

9. Items used in the "Social Factors" prediction table are 1. discipline of boy by father; 2. supervision of boy by mother; 3. affection of father for boy; 4. affection of mother for boy; and 5. cohesiveness of family.

10. Sheldon and Eleanor Glueck, *Unraveling Juvenile Delinquency.* Cambridge: Harvard University Press, 1950, p. 261.

11. Albert J. Reiss, *"Unraveling*

*Juvenile Delinquency,* II. An appraisal of the research methods," *American Journal of Sociology,* 57, 1951, pp. 115–120.

12. This seems to be a reasonable figure for illustrative purposes: ". . . even in the most marked 'delinquency areas' or delinquency subcultures of our cities, not more than a small fraction of the boys (say 10 or 15 percent) become delinquent." Sheldon Glueck, "Ten years of *Unraveling Juvenile Delinquency,*" *Journal of Criminal Law, Criminology and Police Science,* 51, 1960, p. 300.

13. Had nothing been known about the boys, the best prediction would have been that each boy was nondelinquent; this would have resulted in five hundred errors. Using the revised prediction table yields 457 errors, a reduction of 43 errors, or a proportionate reduction of 43/500 (8.6 percent).

14. Sheldon Glueck, "Ten years of *Unraveling Juvenile Delinquency,*" p. 302.

15. *Ibid.,* p. 303.

16. *Ibid.*

17. We are assuming that the medical researchers have samples of equal size of persons with malignant disease and of healthy persons and that they wish to be able to predict disease from an examination of symptoms. That is, we are assuming that the case is analogous to the Gluecks' case.

18. The logic of our example is exactly the same as that used by Reiss and the other critics of the Gluecks' predictive instrument.

19. Unless, of course, population distributions are known; it would then be possible to weight the results appropriately.

20. Sheldon Glueck, "Ten years of *Unraveling Juvenile Delinquency,*" p. 303.

21. *Ibid.,* p. 305.

22. Many of the validation studies are briefly summarized in Sheldon Glueck, *ibid.,* pp. 303–307. See also Sheldon and Eleanor Glueck, *Predicting Delinquency and Crime.* Cambridge: Harvard University Press, 1959, and their *Ventures in Criminology.* Cambridge: Harvard University Press, 1964, Part II.

23. Maude M. Craig and Selma J. Glick, "Ten years' experience with the Glueck Social Prediction Table," *Crime and Delinquency,* 9, 1963, pp. 249–261. See also *A Manual of Procedures for Application of the Glueck Prediction Table.* New York City Youth Board, 1964.

24. Craig and Glick, *op. cit.,* p. 256. (Authors' italics)

25. Alfred J. Kahn ("The case of the premature claims: public policy and delinquency prediction," *Crime and Delinquency,* 11, 1965, pp. 217–228) notes several adjustments that transformed this attempt to validate the Gluecks' prediction device into an exploratory study. The issues raised by the "success" of the Youth Board study are more serious than our discussion of sampling error and the direction of percentaging suggests. See also Kenneth Keniston, "Entangling juvenile delinquency," *Commentary,* June, 1960, pp. 486–491.

26. The percentage-point difference is a poor measure of association for comparing the strength of relations in several different tables because it is sensitive to the relative distribution of the variable treated as the independent variable.

27. In a 2 × 2 table of the following form, $Q = \dfrac{ad - bc}{ad + bc}$:

|  |  | VARIABLE 1 | |
|---|---|---|---|
|  |  | + | − |
| VARIABLE | + | a | b |
| 2 | − | c | d |

# 15

# Individual

# and

# Group

# Variables

$I$n both theory and research, the investigator is interested in the relations among properties of units—individuals, gangs, census tracts, cities, or even nations. He may study properties as diverse as aspirations, height, and television viewing. When these properties may have different values from one unit to another, they are called *variables*.[1]

Theory involves conjectures about relations among variables for a given set of units, usually individuals. Observing relations between the properties of one kind of unit often leads the theorist to conjectures about relations between the properties of other kinds of units. For example, if lower-class areas are known to have higher crime rates than upper-class areas, the theorist may infer that *individuals* with low incomes are more likely to commit crimes than individuals with high incomes.

The theorist also shifts rather freely from one variable to another. Thus, he may assume that a relation between school achievement and delinquency is evidence for a relation between intelligence and delinquency and continue from there to construct an elaborate explanation of the causes of misconduct.

Adequate as such reasoning may be in theorizing, it is not satisfactory in research. To be sure, all research is a mixture of conjecture and fact, of observation and inference, of findings and interpretations. Problems arise when it is not evident which is which. If the investigator shifts illegitimately from one unit to another or from one variable to another, he presents as "fact" what may be at best a poorly supported conjecture. Since many conjectures and "facts" depend on the validity of earlier ones, such shifts may have consequences out of proportion to their apparent seriousness. In fact, some of these shifts are so subtle as to make it hard to see that they are false.

## Shifting the Unit of Analysis

The delinquency researcher frequently finds himself in possession of data on gangs, census tracts, or other units that include many individuals. These data are potentially valuable —they may suggest new insights into the causation of delinquency—but they are also potentially misleading.

*The ecological fallacy.* In 1950 Robinson demonstrated that "an ecological correlation [one in which the values correlated are those of census tracts or other units made up of individuals or smaller units] is almost certainly not equal to its corresponding individual correlation."[2] Taking these two correlations as equal is an example of the ecological fallacy, the illegitimate shift from relations among the properties of groups to relations among the properties of individuals. The delinquency rate and the proportion nonwhite, for example, are properties of groups (often census tracts in delinquency research). It is one thing to say that these properties of census tracts are related; it is something else to infer that the corresponding properties of individuals are related. Thus, on the basis of a positive correlation between the proportion nonwhite and the delinquency rate in census tracts, it may be erroneous to infer that nonwhites are more likely than whites to become delinquents.

Robinson's paper has had several good consequences. Although students of delinquency have continued to draw inferences about the behavior of individuals from ecological correlations, they have usually noted the dangers of this procedure.[3] Goodman and others have shown that it is sometimes possible to derive estimates of the individual relation from group data,[4] and Menzel has pointed out that ecological correlations are often necessary in the study of groups and other aggregates.[5]

The ecological fallacy is pervasive and insidious; problems of ecological reasoning turn up everywhere, as in the discussion generated by Merton's famous paper on anomie.[6] Merton's theory appears to assume a zero-relation between aspirations and social class: All members of the society feel the same pressures to succeed. Hyman's paper on class values questions this assumption. He shows that people in the lower classes are less likely to have high aspirations.[7] Merton's reply notes that ". . . it is not the relative proportions of the several social classes adopting the cultural goal of success that matter, but their absolute numbers."[8]

The real question, it seems to us, is whether those individuals in the lower classes who have "internalized the goal" are more likely to commit deviant acts. If they are, the theory is confirmed. If they are not, the theory is falsified—*regardless* of the ecological correlation between social class and adoption of the cultural goal of success.

*The synecdochic fallacy.*[9] The delinquency researcher typically divides his sample into two or more groups, and compares them on other variables. In Matza's words:

Differentiation is the favored method of positivist explanation. Each school of positive criminology has pursued its own theory of differentiation between conventional and criminal persons.

There can certainly be no objection to this characterization of quantitative delinquency research. It might almost serve as a definition of *analysis*. Note, however, that Matza adds the following statement: *"Each in turn has regularly tended to exaggerate these differences."*[10] Matza is referring to positivistic theory rather than research, but his comments apply to both. To see how this exaggeration arises, consider Table 15-1. This

### Table 15-1—Hostility Toward the Father by Delinquency (hypothetical)

|                            | Delinquent | Nondelinquent |
|----------------------------|:----------:|:-------------:|
| Percent hostile to Father  | 65         | 30            |
| N                          | (100)      | (200)         |

table can be read in several ways: 1. Delinquency and hostility toward the father are positively related; 2. Delinquents are more likely than nondelinquents to express hostility toward their fathers; 3. Delinquents are more hostile toward their fathers than are nondelinquents.

Strictly speaking, the third reading of the table is inaccurate. It ignores variation within each group in suggesting that all delinquents are more hostile to their fathers than all nondelinquents. It thus implies a perfect relation between hostility and delinquency. In short, it exaggerates differences between the two groups.[11]

This mode of table reading is common in delinquency research:

High Theft scorers not only spent more time after supper at community hangouts; they also spent more time at bowling alleys and skating rinks after school than in the school gym or the corner drugstore . . . deviants attended church less frequently than non-deviants.[12]

In Racketville, delinquents aspired within ten years to a median weekly wage of $325; non-delinquents, to $200.[13]

They [insulated boys] liked school and rarely played 'hookey.'[14]

The school attainment of the delinquents was far below that of the non-delinquents, even less than might be expected in the light of their achievement. . . .[15]

Is the exaggeration entailed in this method of table reading justified by the compactness and readability of the formulation? We do not think that it is. In fact, many of the theoretical and logical difficulties in the study of delinquency can be traced to just such exaggerations. A perfectly reasonable expectation of a relation between intelligence and delinquency is bandied about until it eventually becomes: Delinquents are feeble-minded. As evidence mounts that most delinquents are not feeble-minded in any meaningful sense of the term, it suddenly appears that intelligence is not related to delinquency—and present-day researchers are forced to express surprise when they find it is related to delinquency in their samples. When theories are based on an assumed perfect relation between social class and delinquency, it soon becomes necessary to invent special theories to account for the recent upsurge in middle-class delinquency. It is easy to multiply such examples.

*The profile fallacy.* A common device for summarizing a set of findings on delinquency is to describe the typical or average delinquent or nondelinquent. Thus Reckless and his

collaborators, after comparing insulated and potentially delinquent boys on "18 questions involving self-concepts and interpersonal relationships, using the chi-square test of significance," draw this profile of the insulated boys:

They . . . did not ever expect to have to be taken to juvenile court
or jail. They indicated a desire to avoid trouble at all costs and
they rarely engaged in any form of theft, and they had few if any
friends who had been in trouble with the law. They liked school
and rarely played 'hookey.' They conceived of themselves as
obedient sons who did not frequently behave in a manner contrary
to their parents' wishes. They evaluated their families as being as
good or better than most families and the relations in the home
as harmonious and cordial. They felt that their parents were neither
overly strict nor lax and certainly not unnecessarily punitive. . . .[16]

This quotation summarizes at least ten two-variable tables,
which indicate, for example, that a greater proportion of insulated than potentially delinquent boys evaluated their families as superior and that more of them liked school. Although
insulated boys are more likely to possess each trait, it does not
follow that they are more likely to possess both traits, as suggested in this quotation. In fact, the number of insulated boys
with both attitudes cannot be determined by this kind of
analysis.

**Table 15-2—Characteristics of Insulated and Potentially
Delinquent Boys (hypothetical)**

| 1) Evaluation of Family | Insulated boys | Potentially delinquent |
|---|---|---|
| Superior | 60 | 40 |
| Other | 40 | 60 |
| | 100 | 100 |

| 2) Likes school | Insulated boys | Potentially delinquent |
|---|---|---|
| Yes | 60 | 40 |
| No | 40 | 60 |
| | 100 | 100 |

In the first part of Table 15-2 insulated boys are more likely than potential delinquents to evaluate their families as superior; in the second part they are more prone to like school. In order to determine whether insulated boys are more likely to have both traits, it is necessary to construct a three-variable table.

**Table 15-3—Delinquency Potentiality by Evaluation of Family and Attitudes Toward School (hypothetical)**

| | Evaluation of Family | | | |
|---|---|---|---|---|
| | SUPERIOR | | OTHER | |
| Likes school | Insulated boys | Potentially delinquent | Insulated boys | Potentially delinquent |
| Yes | 20 | 30 | 40 | 10 |
| No | 40 | 10 | 0 | 50 |
| | 60 | 40 | 40 | 60 |

Although the two parts of Table 15-2 could be constructed from Table 15-3, the latter cannot be constructed from the former—it contains information that the earlier tables do not contain. We have constructed Table 15-3 so that it does not support the assertion implicit in the profile: that insulated boys are more likely to evaluate their families as superior and to like school. (It shows that they are less likely to possess both traits. Twenty insulated boys and thirty potentially delinquent boys have the traits ascribed to the insulated boys by the profile.) This outcome is reasonable. The sixty insulated boys who evaluate their families as superior are not the same sixty insulated boys who like school (see Table 15-3).[17] The point is that unless the number of boys with both traits is known (that is, unless the two traits are cross-tabulated), assertions about joint distributions are unfounded and may be untrue.[18]

Such short-hand methods of summarizing findings may deceive the reader, if not the researcher. In Chapter 12 we showed a consequence of the discovery that insulated boys can also commit delinquent acts. Obviously, if the fact of variation within the insulated group had been recognized, if the investigators had used variables rather than ostensibly homogeneous types to predict future delinquency, they would not have found the failures in prediction so perplexing.[19]

The requirement of examining joint distributions in some detail before constructing a set of types may appear unreasonable. A nineteen-variable table would undoubtedly contain hundreds of empty cells, even in studies with extremely large samples. Furthermore, there might well be hundreds of distinct types. The investigator wishing to compare on a variety of variables boys nominated by teachers as good boys with boys nominated as potentially delinquent cannot be expected to describe what may be a peculiar combination of traits for each boy.

The solution, in our opinion, is not simply to recognize the limitations of such descriptive devices as profiles and then proceed to use them anyway. It is, rather, to ask the function of such types in the research for which they are isolated. Reckless and his collaborators asked teachers to nominate sets of good boys and bad boys. These boys were then given a questionnaire, containing, among other things, the items previously mentioned in the profile. Four years later, the two sets of boys were again compared on self-concept items as well as a variety of measures of delinquency. As a group, the good boys still had better self-concept scores and had committed considerably fewer delinquent acts. The conclusions from this study are summarized, in part, as follows:

In our quest to discover what insulates a boy against delinquency in a high delinquency area, we believe we have some tangible evidence that a good self concept, undoubtedly a product of favorable socialization, veers slum boys away from delinquency, while a poor self concept, a product of unfavorable socialization, gives the slum boy no resistance to deviancy, delinquent companions, or delinquent sub-culture.[20]

Could the same conclusions have been reached without using the types isolated by teachers? We think that they could —with less inferential distance between them and the data.[21] If self-concept is the primary independent variable, why not relate self-concept directly to delinquency? The items designed to measure self-concept are clearly better as measures of self-concept than are teacher ratings on delinquency vulnerability. The typological procedure, by suggesting that good boys all have equally good self-concepts and that bad boys all have equally bad self-concepts, implies that the types are direct, perfectly valid measures of self-concept. They are not, as the data presented in these studies clearly show.[22]

## Shifting Variables

Perfect relations among sets of variables provide the investigator with a remarkable tool. If A is perfectly related to C, and if B is also perfectly related to C, then A and B must be perfectly related to each other. In other words, the investigator can make logical deductions from examined to unexamined relations.[23] In most cases in delinquency research, however, such deductions from examined to unexamined relations are merely plausible—they thus may or may not be true.

*The syllogistic fallacy.* The apparently perfect relations created by ascribing group means or proportions to all individuals in the group create such an illusion of logical deduction. Because these deductions appear axiomatic or tautological, we refer to this error as the syllogistic fallacy.

. . . the delinquents were much more the victims of the indifference or actual hostility of their fathers and mothers, and were, *in turn*, less attached to their parents. Not only did they derive less affection from their mothers and fathers, but they were also regarded with less warmth by their brothers and sisters.[24]

The implications of this passage are that boys whose parents are indifferent or hostile are, as a result, less attached to them. This seems to be a plausible conclusion, but the Gluecks' data may not support it. Their tables show the relation between each of the independent variables and delinquency; they do not show the relations between the two independent variables. We do not know that the boys whose fathers were hostile or indifferent are the same boys who were less attached to their fathers, or that they, in turn, are the same boys who were regarded with little warmth by their siblings. An accurate picture of the relations among independent variables cannot be derived from relations between independent and dependent variables of the magnitude usually found in delinquency research.[25]

When this kind of inference is used as a rhetorical device in summarizing the results of a study, the consequences may not be serious: A few conjectures appear to have the status of findings, and nothing more. When such an inference affects the design of a study, however, the consequences are serious, as in Fannin and Clinard's study of "differences between lower and lower-middle class white delinquents in conception of self as male, and [of] behavioral correlates of such differences."[26]

In this study, twenty-five middle-class and twenty-five lower-class delinquents were asked to rank sets of fifteen traits according to how well they felt the traits actually described them as males, how they would like to be as males, and so on. Scoring the traits 0–4 (the boys ranked five subsets of three traits at a time) and computing means produced the results in Table 15-4, which is adapted from Fannin and Clinard.

### Table 15-4—Self-concept Trait Means by Social Class

| Trait | ACTUAL SELF | |
|---|---|---|
| | Lower class | Middle class |
| Fearless | 1.89* | 1.52* |
| Loyal | 3.05* | 3.71* |
| Brave | 2.58 | 2.49 |
| Strong | 2.26 | 2.33 |

* Difference between class means significant at .05 level.

Fannin and Clinard comment on the results:

The findings indicate that while the male self-conception is very similar across class lines, there are a few crucial differences which apparently are related to a diverse range of behavior patterns.[27]

They then go on to describe the self-conceptions of the two groups, using the traits whose averages were significantly different, and ignoring many traits with higher average scores that did not differentiate the two groups:

Lower class boys felt themselves to be . . . tougher [1.88], more powerful [2.04], fierce [2.58], fearless [1.89], and dangerous [1.11] than middle class boys. . . . Middle class delinquents, on the other hand, conceived of themselves as being more loyal [3.71], clever [2.95], smart [2.86], smooth [2.72], and bad [1.57].[28]

Although Fannin and Clinard have quantitative evidence that "the male self-conception is very similar across class lines," they find other evidence suggesting that the key elements of the self-conceptions of middle- and lower-class boys are not those they share, but those on which they differ:

These differences were strongly supported and supplemented by the results gained from informal interviewing. While discussing the type of "reputation" desired among their closest male friends, and among females and police, lower class boys stressed their ability and willingness to fight ["Fighter" has a mean of 1.68 among lower-class boys and ranks eleventh in a set of fifteen traits. Its mean does not differ significantly from that of middle-class boys (1.48) and its rank is identical.], their physical power over others, and their fear of nothing. . . . Middle class boys, on the

267

other hand, stressed loyalty to friends above all, their desire to be clever and smooth, and also to be daring.[29]

The differences between the two groups seem to grow progressively larger. At the outset loyalty was ranked highest in both groups. Now it is not sufficiently salient among the lower-class boys to be noted in the informal interviewing, but it retains its pre-eminent position among middle-class boys. The stage is set for an illegitimate logical leap: If self-conceptions differ sufficiently between social classes—that is, if the relation between social class and self-conception is sufficiently strong—then one can test propositions about the relations between self-conceptions and behavior by examining relations between social classes and behavior, and this is what Fannin and Clinard do.[30]

While self conceptions were quite similar, lower class boys did conceive of themselves as being tougher, more fearless, powerful, fierce, and dangerous, while middle class boys felt that they were more clever, smart, smooth, bad, and loyal. Descriptively, these were labeled as "tough guy" [lower class] and "loyal and daring comrade" [middle class] self-conceptions.
These self-conceptions [class differences] were then found to be related to specific types of behavior. The "tough guys" [lower-class boys] significantly more often committed violent offenses, fought more often and with harsher means, carried weapons, had lower occupational aspirations, and stressed toughness and related traits in the reputation they desired and in sexual behavior.[31]

Are self-conceptions related to behavior? As our bracketed comments suggest, no such relation was examined by Fannin and Clinard. Although they had the data to examine this relation, they chose not to do so. Instead, they examined the relation between social class and self-concept and between social class and behavior. This indirect approach is at best a poor substitute for examining the relation in which they were interested. And the weak relation between social class and self-conception makes it altogether unconvincing.[32]

All of the studies discussed in this chapter exaggerate differences between delinquents and nondelinquents, between good and bad boys, between middle- and lower-class boys. As Matza suggests, this potential for exaggeration is present in any mode of explanation based upon differentiation (as every explanation must be). Recognizing the problem and its costs in unfounded and misleading assertions, the researcher should analyze and present his data so as to avoid suggesting that the relations he observes are stronger than they actually are. One way of avoiding such suggestions is to distinguish carefully between properties of individuals and properties of the distribution of individual traits over a group or class.

# Notes

1. The term *concept* is often used to denote a theoretical variable. Unfortunately, concepts are also often constants, e.g., primary group or the concept of property space. Confusion between the two meanings of *concept* is the source of a great deal of misunderstanding in both sociological theory and research. See Chapter 8, *passim*.

2. William S. Robinson, "Ecological correlations and the behavior of individuals," *American Sociological Review*, 15, 1950, p. 357.

3. Jackson Toby, "The differential impact of family disorganization," *American Sociological Review*, 22, 1957, p. 509; Bernard Lander, *Towards an Understanding of Juvenile Delinquency*. New York: Columbia University Press, 1954, p. 43.

4. Leo A. Goodman, "Some alternatives to ecological correlation," *American Journal of Sociology*, 64, 1959, pp. 610–625.

5. Herbert Menzel, "Comment" on Robinson's paper, *American Sociological Review*, 15, 1950, p. 674.

6. Robert K. Merton, *Social Theory and Social Structure*. (Rev. ed.) New York: The Free Press, 1957, Chapter IV.

7. Herbert H. Hyman, "The value systems of different classes: a social psychological contribution to the analysis of stratification," in Reinhard Bendix and Seymour Martin Lipset, *Class, Status and Power*. New York: The Free Press, 1953, pp. 426–442.

8. *Op. cit.*, p. 174.

9. Robert Wenkert, "Reply" to "Some comments on 'Working class authoritarianism'," by Emanuel Schegloff and Carlos Kruythosch, *Berkeley Journal of Sociology*, 6, 1961, pp. 109–112.

10. David Matza, *Delinquency and Drift*. New York: Wiley, 1964, p. 11. (Authors' italics)

11. Percentaged in the correct direction, this exaggeration is less likely to lead the researcher astray, because this mode of percentaging would emphasize the difference between the hostile and the nonhostile rather than the difference between delinquents and nondelinquents. Thus, when the investigator moves on to another independent variable, the previous exaggeration is somewhat canceled by the following one. For example, compare the following statements: 1. Boys of low intelligence, boys hostile to their fathers, and boys from large families are more likely to be delinquent; 2. Delinquents are more likely to have low intelligence, to be hostile to their fathers, and to come from larger families.

12. Robert A. Dentler and Lawrence J. Monroe, "Social correlates of early adolescent theft," *American Sociological Review*, 26, 1961, p. 740.

13. Irving Spergel, *Racketville, Slumtown, Haulburg*. Chicago: Uni-

versity of Chicago Press, 1964, p. 96.

14. Walter C. Reckless, Simon Dinitz, Barbara Kay, "The self-component in potential delinquency and non-delinquency," *American Sociological Review*, 22, 1957, pp. 566–570.

15. Sheldon and Eleanor Glueck, *Unraveling Juvenile Delinquency*. Cambridge: Harvard University Press, 1950, p. 153.

16. Reckless, Dinitz, and Kay, *op. cit.*, pp. 566–570.

17. The sixty boys will be the same only when the association between the two traits is perfect. If the association between all traits used in the profile were perfect, the profile would be an accurate description of individuals. Perfect associations, however, are extremely rare.

18. The internal frequencies in Table 15-1 and 15-2 become the marginal frequencies (totals) in Table 15-3. In this sense, the profile fallacy involves inferences about joint distributions from marginal distributions. For another example of the explicit construction of profiles of individuals from marginal distributions, see Albert J. Reiss, Jr., "Social correlates of psychological types of delinquency," *American Sociological Review*, 17, 1952, p. 716.

19. For a historical account of the profile problem and references to modern methods of measuring typicality, see Hanan C. Selvin, "The computer analysis of observational data," paper read at the International Symposium on Mathematical and Computational Methods in the Social Sciences, Rome, July, 1966. (The *Proceedings* of this symposium, edited by B. Jaulin, are in press.)

20. Simon Dinitz, Frank R. Scarpitti, and Walter C. Reckless, "Delinquency vulnerability: a cross group and longitudinal analysis," *American Sociological Review*, 27, 1962, pp. 515–517.

21. This, of course, does not mean that teacher nominations were not a valuable device for assuring variation in self-concept and delinquency.

22. Half of the bad boys responded favorably to the question, Up to now, do you think things have gone your way? Dinitz, Scarpitti, and Reckless, *op. cit.*, p. 517. Interestingly enough, only twenty-seven of the seventy bad boys had police records during the four-year period of the follow-up. (We should make it clear that we think the treatment of the data in this study worked against the hypothesis and that our criticism is in no way intended to suggest that the conclusions are invalid.)

23. For a detailed discussion of the limits and assumptions of such procedures, see Herbert L. Costner and Robert K. Leik, "Deductions from 'axiomatic theory,'" *American Sociological Review*, 29, 1964, pp. 819–835.

24. Glueck and Glueck, *op. cit.*, p. 133. (Authors' italics)

25. *Ibid.* See our Chapter 6, pp. 93–94 for further discussion of these conjectures.

26. Leon F. Fannin and Marshall B. Clinard, "Differences in the conception of self as a male among lower and middle class delinquents," *Social Problems*, 13, 1965, pp. 205–214.

27. *Ibid.*, p. 210.

28. *Ibid.* The figures in brackets are group averages for the trait in question. The use of comparatives such as "tougher, more powerful" suggests that the two groups were ranking themselves against each other, when actually the standard against which a boy evaluated himself was not specified by the research procedures.

29. *Ibid.*

30. The logical design of this study is identical to that of Reckless and his associates discussed in the section on the profile fallacy. In both cases, two groups differing in average self-concept are compared on other variables to determine the effects of self-concept. In the Reckless study, the two groups are apparently much further apart on self-concept than is true here.

31. Fannin and Clinard, *op. cit.*, pp. 213–214.

32. In a letter to the editor of *Social Problems* (published in Vol. 13, Summer, 1966, pp. 104–105) about Fannin and Clinard's article, H. Taylor Buckner notes the error discussed here: "The second [serious] error is the assumption that because self-concept has been related to social class, and social class has been related to behavior, self-concept has been related to behavior. It has not." After suggesting that "substantive issues are obscured by this endemic preoccupation with the minutiae of methodology," Fannin and Clinard present further evidence that measures of self-concept and social class are by no means interchangeable. In the last analysis, the importance of methodological criticism depends on what it says about the truth of statements produced by research. Surely truth is of substantive as well as of methodological significance.

# A Final Word

It would be pleasant to conclude this book with a list of specific do's and don'ts—perhaps with a chapter entitled "Seventeen Rules for Better Analysis." Unfortunately, there is no such set of rules. As we have remarked, several of the investigators whose work is discussed in this book got into trouble precisely because they were following some such mechanical rule. In our view, better analysis is more likely to come from approaching the data, whether one's own or someone else's, in the right frame of mind. It is this frame of mind, or set of attitudes, that we have tried to nurture. We can perhaps best reinforce it now by emphasizing its three central components: objectivity, vigilance, and sympathy.

*Objectivity.* When a methodologist reads a research report, he tries to find out what the author wanted to do, whether or not he has succeeded, and what other methods, if any, would have done the job better. This attitude applies alike to the methodologist-as-reader and to the methodologist-as-investigator. Dogmatic adherence to a set of preferred methods is just as bad as dogmatic rejection of a set of disliked methods.

*Vigilance.* Someone has said that all measurement is infested with error. This is a good aphorism; it suggests that even a hundred eyes and a thousand arms may not suffice to get rid of error. The vigilant methodologist looks at the likely consequences of error. He will not press a compulsive search for the smallest mistake in coding when he knows that such an error will have little effect on the analysis. Vigilance thus means the constant scrutiny of all parts of a research study and the weighing of the consequences of errors against the cost of getting rid of them. There is no other formula for getting significant results and no other method of being scientific.

*Sympathy.* The only way to avoid making mistakes altogether is not to do any research. The wise methodologist knows enough social psychology to recognize that no author, however universalistic or stoic he may appear, can fail to be hurt by criticism and that no reader, however kind of heart, can fail to take some pleasure at seeing the sins of the mighty exposed to public view. In the end, therefore, the methodologist should be sympathetic enough to recognize that everyone makes mistakes, vigilant enough to guard against taking the occasional error as an indicator of over-all quality, and objective enough to understand that the most visible target is provided by the best research. In return, he can hope that other methodological critics will appraise his work in the same spirit.

# Index